CW01466894

LONDON STUDIES ON SOUTH ASIA

BRITISH POLICY TOWARDS THE INDIAN STATES
1905–1939

CENTRE OF SOUTH ASIAN STUDIES
SCHOOL OF ORIENTAL AND AFRICAN STUDIES
UNIVERSITY OF LONDON

LONDON STUDIES ON SOUTH ASIA

LONDON STUDIES ON SOUTH ASIA NO. 2

BRITISH POLICY TOWARDS THE INDIAN STATES
1905–1939

S. R. ASHTON

CURZON PRESS

HUMANITIES   PRESS

First published 1982

Curzon Press Ltd : London and Dublin
and
Humanities Press Inc : Atlantic Highlands, NJ : USA

© Stephen Richard Ashton 1982

ISBN
UK 0 7007 0146 X
US 0 391 02329 2

ISSN
0142 601X

Sole distributors in India
India Book House : Bombay and branches

Printed in Great Britain by
Biddles Ltd, Guildford, Surrey

CONTENTS

LIST OF MAPS

For Diane and the Children

PREFACE

The subject of this study is the concept of indirect rule in terms of both its application and consequences. In the process of consolidating their empire in India the British had, during the first half of the nineteenth century, deprived the princes of the power to conduct external relations with each other or with foreign powers. Internally the princes were theoretically autonomous but their sovereignty in this respect was in practice restricted by the paramountcy of the imperial power. Many of the princes resented the manner in which the British used this paramountcy to justify intervening in their domestic affairs. During the second half of the nineteenth century the British maintained the princes as an administrative convenience and as a potential, rather than actual, source of military and political support. By the opening of the twentieth century, however, the British had come to regard the princes as indispensable political allies against the growth of nationalism in India. In order that the princes would serve willingly as allies the British adopted a policy of non-interference in their domestic affairs. In practice intervention was reduced to an absolute minimum and would only be contemplated in cases of gross misgovernment. This study offers an explanation for the failure of British policy towards the states. Its central argument is that the non-interference policy actually encouraged princely misgovernment and allowed administrative standards in the states to stagnate or deteriorate. By the late 1930s many of them had become obvious targets for nationalist attack. The British belatedly realized that the non-interference policy had failed to make credible or worthwhile allies of the princes. On the contrary, they had become a serious liability because of it. Some vain attempts were made to reverse the trends of the previous thirty years but the British had basically invalidated their own justifications for maintaining the states and thus in 1947 had no alternative but to leave the princes to negotiate their fate with the politicians of the new Indian Dominion.

The introductory chapter is divided into two sections. The first deals with the political geography of the states and emphasizes not only the diversity of princely India but also the insignificance of the vast majority of the states. The second, which examines the nineteenth-century background, emphasizes the failure of the British to emulate the success achieved by their Mughal predecessors in establishing a political partnership with the princes based upon trust and equality. It begins with a brief discussion of the policies adopted by the Mughal emperors towards the princes of the Rajput states. It proceeds, by way of contrast, to examine the nature of the British subsidiary alliance system and also the manner in which, during the first half of the nineteenth century, the views of the reformers who wished to terminate princely rule in order to confer the blessings of western civilization upon the whole of India, gradually overcame the views of the conservatives who wished to preserve princely rule upon the grounds of security. The impact of the mutiny is then discussed.

The British repudiated territorial expansion but still pursued interventionist policies towards the states in order to ensure that administrative standards were maintained and improved. The mutiny also made the British aware that the princes had potential as political allies but subsequent efforts to mobilize princely support in this respect met with only limited success.

The second and third chapters discuss the nature and consequences of the alliance established between the paramount power and the princes at the beginning of the twentieth century. The second examines the reasons for the non-interference policy and also how, under pressure from an emerging group of westernized princes from the medium-sized states who sought to dismantle the traditional barriers of princely isolation, the British conceded constitutional recognition to the states by the establishment of a Chamber of Princes in 1921. The third assesses the impact of the non-interference policy and emphasizes in particular how, despite repeated criticisms of the policy, abuses and oppression were allowed to accumulate in some of the states until such time as the subjects of the princes concerned were on the verge of, or actually in, rebellion.

The fourth and fifth chapters are concerned with the constitutional position of the states. The fourth discusses the struggle over paramountcy between the Chamber princes and the Political Department of the Government of India which culminated in the report of the Indian States Committee in 1927. The fifth examines, from the point of view of the British and the princes, the constitutional negotiations between 1930 and 1935 concerning the proposal to establish an All-India Federation.

The sixth chapter is again divided into two sections. The first seeks to explain the reasons for the failure of federal negotiations with the princes. Here it is argued that the question of timing was a crucial factor in determining the princely rejection of federation in 1939 and that it was the India Office rather than the Government of India that was responsible for the delay over negotiations with the princes. The second explains the official abandonment of the non-interference policy during the viceroyalty of Lord Linlithgow. It discusses how, when confronted by Congress threats to the states, the British made a belated attempt to return to the interventionist policies of the nineteenth century. Princely resistance and a lack of trained personnel within the Political Department, both direct consequences of the non-interference policy, combined to ensure that the attempt to put the clock back would meet with little success.

The conclusion is combined with an epilogue which briefly examines the fate of the princes immediately before and immediately after the transfer of power in 1947.

It is with particular pleasure that I acknowledge the contribution made by Dr. B.N. Pandey to the publication of this work. I studied for a prolonged period under his guidance at the School of Oriental and African Studies and shall always be grateful for his encouragement, patience and support. I would like to thank Dr. T.G.P. Spear for giving freely of his time and making some invaluable suggestions as to how an earlier version of this study could be improved. Dr. P.G.

Robb meticulously read the manuscript and I am indebted to him for suggesting some final improvements. Among many helpful archivists, Dr. Richard Bingle and Mr. Martin Moir of the India Office Library in London and Mr. Patrick Cadell of the National Library of Scotland in Edinburgh, are remembered with particular gratitude. Grateful acknowledgement is made to Elaine Holley of the Department of Geography at the School of Oriental and African Studies for her meticulous preparation of the maps included in this volume. Sue Dorney-Smith kindly assisted with the typing of several drafts of the manuscript. Finally, I want to thank my parents. They have stood by me through many trials and tribulations.

STEPHEN R. ASHTON

ABBREVIATIONS

AGG	Agent to the Governor-General.
AISPC	All India States' People's Conference.
Chamber of Princes	*Proceedings of the Meetings of the Chamber of Princes (Narendra Mahal).*
Coll	Collection.
Conference of Ruling Princes	*Proceedings of the Conference of Ruling Princes and Chiefs held at Delhi on the 30th October 1916, 5th November 1917, 20th January 1919 and 3rd November 1919.*
FPD	Foreign and Political Department.
GGC	Governor-General in Council.
GOI	Government of India.
ICS	Indian Civil Service.
IOL	India Office Library, London.
Montford Report	*Report on Indian Constitutional Reforms, 1918.* Cmd. 9109, 1918.
PCI	Political Correspondence with India.
PIC	Political (Internal) Collections.
PIF	Political (Internal) Files.
POL	Political.
PP	Parliamentary Papers.
PSCI	Political and Secret Correspondence with India.
PSSF	Political and Secret Subject Files.
PY	Abbreviation used by the Political Department of the India Office, denoting Political (Internal).
S/S	Secretary of State.
telg.	telegram.

British Provinces and Indian States in 1939.

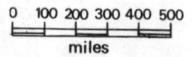

CHAPTER I

INTRODUCTION

The Political Geography of the Indian States

Prior to 1947, two-fifths of the Indian subcontinent was not British territory and two-ninths of its inhabitants were not British subjects. This territory was broken into over 600 individual states which were governed by hereditary princes of varying rank owing allegiance to the British Crown as suzerain. The states displayed an extraordinary diversity in terms of size, population and revenue. Collectively they covered an area of nearly 600,000 square miles with a population of just over 80 million. Individually they ranged from Hyderabad, the principal state, with an area of 82,698 square miles, as large as England and Scotland, and with a population of over 14 million, to the tiny Kathiawar estate of Veja-no-ness with an area of about three-tenths of a square mile and a population of 184.[1] In general, however, statistics indicate the insignificance of the overwhelming majority of the states. There were only 28 with a population of over 500,000 with the first eight of these accounting for half the total population, area and revenue of all 28. Hyderabad alone accounted for one-sixth of these totals.[2]

Equally remarkable was the irregular geographical distribution of the states. In one region, Rajputana for example, the states were few and of comparatively large size, while in others, such as Central and Western India, they were petty and very numerous. The explanation of these irregularities lies partly in the policies pursued by the British at various times and partly in the course of events over which they had no control. In some parts of India a stronger power had made a clean sweep of upstarts and petty ancient dynasties before the British advanced. During the second half of the eighteenth century the ground had been cleared in the south of India by the Nizam of Hyderabad, the Nawab of the Carnatic and Tipu Sultan, the Muslim usurper of Mysore. When therefore the Carnatic fell under British control and Tipu Sultan was finally overthrown in 1799, large united territories had to be disposed of either by annexation or, as in the case of Mysore, by restitution to a former dynasty. Here the work of consolidation had been accomplished by others before the British became involved. The situation was different in Central and Western India. This was Maratha country, a loose confederacy of five military units under the nominal leadership of the Peshwa who controlled Western India from his capital at Poona. The other four units were led by the Gaekwar of Baroda, the Bhonsla Raja of Nagpur, the Maharaja Scindia of Gwalior and the Maharaja Holkar of Indore. The Marathas had risen to prominence in the seventeenth century under Shivaji's leadership as vigorous opponents of the Mughal drive into the Deccan. By the close of the eighteenth century, however, unity of purpose was an alien concept to the five chiefs of the confederacy. They thought only in terms of personal aggrandizement and regarded each other as rivals in an unceasing struggle for supremacy. The result was that territories in Central and Western India were constantly changing hands right up until 1818 when not only the Maratha chiefs, but also the plundering mercenaries known as Pindaris who had once been the auxiliaries of the Maratha military machine, were brought to heel by the British. It then fell to the Governor-General, Lord Hastings, to stabilize these territories by imposing a political settlement. As they contained little arable land capable of yielding taxable crops, they were not for the most part brought under direct military control. The Peshwa's territories were the only major exception. They were annexed to form the core of the Bombay presidency, the Peshwa himself being pensioned off near Kanpur. Elsewhere Hastings acknowledged the *status quo* as it then existed. There was no general inquiry into titles, nor was pause given for the consolidation of states by the will of the strongest: existing acquisitions were recognised once and for all. The consequent plethora of numerous petty states in Central and Western India stood in marked contrast to the situation in Rajputana where, despite Maratha and Pindari intrusions, seventeen proud states with an ancient lineage had preserved their separate political existence. The chief of these were Udaipur (Mewar), Jodhpur (Marwar), Jaipur and Bikaner.[3]

The physical characteristics of the states displayed the same diversity. Much of Rajputana was desert while in the deep south Travancore enjoyed a tropical luxuriance. Hyderabad and Mysore were rich in mineral resources contrasting in their wealth with the poverty of the hill states of the Punjab and the humble resources of the agriculturalists in Kathiawar. Equally diverse were the varieties of population and religion. The primitive and mostly animistic tribes of the Assam states and Manipur on the Burmese frontier contrasted with the wealthy Muslim nobles of Hyderabad and the proud chieftains of Rajputana. In Kashmir the prince was Hindu and the population was largely Muslim; in Hyderabad and Junagadh the reverse was the case.[4]

Many of the states exhibited feudal conditions. The essential features of Mughal administration remained in force in Hyderabad until the state was integrated into the Indian Union in 1948. Land was divided into two categories: *khalsa* and non-*khalsa*. In the *khalsa* areas the land revenue and various administrative departments were centrally administered. The non-*khalsa* areas consisted of numerous estates or *jagirs*, the incumbents of which were known as *jagirdars*, who exercised considerable authority in judicial and police administration. Some thirty-two *jagirs* had their own police forces and enjoyed judicial powers. The most important *jagirdars* were the Paigah Amirs. The Paigah *jagirs* comprised 23 *talukas* or districts covering an area of 41,134 square miles with a population of over one million. They were created by Asaf Jah, the former Mughal *subahdar*, or governor, of the Deccan, who founded the Osmania dynasty in Hyderabad in 1713. After a bitter succession dispute in 1877 the original Paigah *jagirs* were divided between three principal claimants who subsequently enjoyed separate titles and became the most important families in Hyderabad after the ruling dynasty. In Mughal times *jagirdars* had been military commanders. They were not the proprietors of the soil but were assigned the right to collect the state revenues from a specified area in lieu of a salary from the royal treasury. Asaf Jah had constituted the Paigahs in this manner during his struggle with the Marathas. However, the last Nizam of Hyderabad encountered frequent difficulties in getting the *jagirdars* to accept this position. On more than one occasion he had to issue a *firman*, or government mandate, declaring that the *jagirdars* were not entitled to occupancy rights over the lands within their *jagirs*, except in cases where they could prove that by their own initiative they had brought waste land under cultivation and were cultivating it themselves or through their servants.[5]

Feudal concepts were widespread in the states of Central India and Rajputana. In Central India numerous minor Rajput chiefs, known as *thakurs*, existed as feudatories of the great Maratha princes, Scindia at Gwalior and Holkar at Indore. The *thakurs* were often descendants of nobles who ruled the territory before it was conquered by the invading Marathas and their relations with their new overlords - insubordination on the one hand and undue repression on the other - were frequently a bitter source of discontent.[6] A different situation obtained in Rajputana. Here the states were traditionally regarded as the property of a territorial nobility, not the individual prince who was only *primus inter pares*. In certain states the powers of the nobility were considerable. In Udaipur twenty-eight principal nobles commanded the subsidiary allegiance of nearly one-third of the population and their estates comprised just over half of the area of the entire state.[7]

In a few states embryonic representative institutions had emerged during the early years of the twentieth century. In Mysore and Travancore, the two premier states in south India, and also in Baroda in Western India, legislative councils had been established. Their functions were limited to the technical duties of discussing, suggesting amendments to and recommending for the ruler's adoption bills introduced by his government.[8] Mysore and Travancore also possessed representative assemblies, the object of which in Travancore was described as being 'to allow duly elected representatives to bring before the Darbar the needs and requirements of the country'.[9] Elsewhere the prevailing system of government was autocracy modified only by the varying degrees of authority exercised by feudatories and nobles in certain states. Laws were a conglomeration of local customs, enactments based on British Indian models and personal decrees of the princes. They could be modified or withdrawn at the discretion of the prince. There were no independent judicial systems and the princes permitted no appeals to an authority higher than themselves. No security of tenure existed for state officials;   administrators, judges and ministers were appointed and dismissed according to the whim of the prince.

The diverse physical characteristics of the states were more than complemented by the attitude of their rulers towards each other.

Princely unity was a rare commodity. The princes could neither think nor act as members of a common order. No doubt during the nineteenth century the principal reason for this was that the British pursued a deliberate policy of isolating the princes from each other for fear that if they were allowed to combine they might constitute a major threat to imperial control. However, the abandonment of this policy during the first two decades of the twentieth century revealed that these fears had been exaggerated. A century of isolation had done nothing to erode lingering historical feuds based upon racial animosities, religious prejudices and petty jealousies in matters of prestige and status. Indeed, as the princes could no longer vie with each other for supremacy in a military sense they now expended their energies and played out their rivalries in an artificial and pretentious world of protocol and symbolism. The number of guns to their salutes, their precedence at ceremonial gatherings, the manner in which they conducted relations with the imperial power and their capacity to accumulate additional honours and titles were all of vital importance to the princes as they jostled with each other for position and status. The British, as we shall see, were frequently prepared to exploit the psychology of the princes in order both to manipulate them and retain their allegiance. Whenever the princes did co-operate it was almost invariably for the purpose of representing sectional interests. But even on these occasions their efforts were frequently disrupted as they competed with each other for imperial favours. In the long-term these jealousies and rivalries were to have the most damaging consequences for the princes. Lacking the strength that derives from unity they would always be at a disadvantage in the turbulent world of twentieth-century Indian nationalism.

For the purposes of political control and the conduct of their relations with the paramount power, the states were divided at the beginning of the twentieth century into two categories: those that conducted relations through officers of the political section of the Foreign Department of the Government of India, and those that conducted relations in the first instance through the provincial governments of British India. The Foreign Department was responsible for relations with the princely states, India's foreign policy, which was essentially a question of controlling and defending the frontier areas in the north-east and north-west, and relations with the states of the Persian Gulf. It had originated in September 1783 as the Secret and Political Department and became known as the Foreign Department in May 1843. By the early years of the twentieth century the burden of work had become too much for a solitary departmental secretary. Two distinct foreign and political sections were created and in January 1914 it was officially renamed the Foreign and Political Department. A separate Political Secretary was appointed to take charge of relations with princely states while a Foreign Secretary remained responsible for frontier matters and the Gulf states. There was, however, only one pool of officers for both sections of the department. The Indian army provided seventy per cent of recruits and the Indian Civil Service thirty per cent. Indian

Civil Service officers became eligible for transfer after four years of service in the provinces of British India. In the case of military officers, candidates with university commissions or those who displayed evidence of exceptional linguistic ability were favoured.[10]

In 1918 a total of 176 states conducted relations with the Political Department, which is the term we shall use when referring to the period after 1914, of the Government of India. Of these only the premier states of Hyderabad, Mysore, Baroda and Kashmir corresponded directly through four first-class Residents. The remaining states in this category were grouped into three agencies: the Central India agency, consisting of 150 states, the Rajputana agency, consisting of 20 states, and the Baluchistan agency, with only 2 states. In the agencies a duplication of political control existed. Political Agents, who were assigned to individual states or groups of states, corresponded with an Agent to the Governor-General (AGG). The AGG had overall responsibility for a particular agency and corresponded in turn with the Political Department. This pattern was repeated for the second category of states conducting relations through provincial governments. In 1918, Assam conducted relations with 16 states, Bengal with 2, Bihar and Orissa with 26, Bombay with over 350, the Central Provinces with 15, Madras with 5, the Punjab with 34, and the United Provinces with 3. Apart from Bombay, which until 1924 had its own Political Department consisting of some twenty-eight political officers, these states were supervised in the first instance by provincial commissioners and collectors. Each provincial government corresponded on behalf of the states with the Government of India. In the 1920s and 1930s the first category of states was enlarged at the expense of the second. As provincial governments became more autonomous and more responsible to elected provincial legislatures, the British adopted a policy of transferring the responsibility for conducting relations with the states located in the provinces to the Political Department of the Government of India.[11]

The extent to which a prince could consider himself completely independent in the conduct of his internal affairs was in all cases determined by the paramount power. Some thirty-nine states had entered into treaty relations with the East India Company at the beginning of the nineteenth century and of these only twenty had received definite assurances to the effect that they were absolute as regards their subjects and that their administrations would not be interfered with. However, although some of the premier states in terms of size, population and revenue were included in the twenty, the British never considered themselves under an obligation to maintain in perpetuity the absolute authority of the princes concerned. Indeed, in the late 1920s the Political Department of the Government of India was firmly of the opinion that the very inclusion of non-interference assurances in the treaties served as 'a signal demonstration of the inequality of the contracting parties - or, in other words, of the Paramountcy of the British Government, which exists and existed independently of the treaties and was not essentially affected by their conclusion'.[12] The assurances themselves merely indicated that the paramount power regarded the states concerned as separate administrative entities which were 'not to be encroached upon without good reason'.[13]   Many of the princes resented this dismissive interpretation of their treaty rights and their struggle against the views of the Political Department will be examined in detail in subsequent chapters of this study.   The department's   attitude,   however,   requires   some   preliminary explanation.

From the outset the British had persistently maintained that it was impossible to achieve a precise definition of the paramountcy they exercised over the Indian States. They argued that the treaties which had been concluded could never be regarded as definitive simply because no such agreement could survive indefinitely in its original form. For the British paramountcy was not a static function performing well-defined rights and mutually-agreed obligations, but a concept of growth that had developed according to the changing needs and circumstances of the time. Sir William Lee-Warner, a leading authority on paramountcy at the turn of the century, wrote: 'Even if the whole body of Indian treaties, engagements and *sanads* were carefully compiled, with a view to extracting from them a catalogue of the obligations or duties that might be held to be common to all, the list would be incomplete.'[14] In order to accommodate changing needs and circumstances a body of political practice or usage had been steadily built up. There can be little doubt that such usage as existed was employed primarily to promote imperial interests and to supply imperial needs. Whenever a fresh law was introduced into British India which required co-operative action by a state embedded in British territory, some addition had necessarily to be made to the rules of conduct which regulated the relations of that state with the British Government. The legitimacy of this procedure could not be denied if the addition was made only with the state concerned but it was often the case, particularly when laws related to the construction of roads and railways and the development   of   commercial   policy,   that   the   new   principles established in the relations with the one state were subsequently taken to apply to them all. Thus for the British the terms of the original treaties were not the final arbiter, nor even a dependable guide in most cases, to the actual political relationship existing between themselves and the Indian States. Usage, in a constant state of   development   and   interpreted   ultimately   by   the   Political Department which supervised the states, regulated that relationship. In practice, therefore, the operation of paramountcy meant that 'the full extent of British interference in the Home Departments of the states has never been and never can be defined'.[15]

The Mughal Legacy and Paramountcy during the Nineteenth Century

By 1818, having defeated the Marathas and suppressed the Pindaris, the British, in the shape of the East India Company, had emerged as the paramount power in India. Superior military power and the ability to exploit divisions between competing Indian factions had, over the course of the previous fifty years, brought the Company to this position of supremacy. Yet the supremacy gained was not based upon direct rule over the whole of India. This had never been attempted nor was it ever the intention. The basic concern of the Court of Directors, the governing body of the Company in London, had been to create the necessary conditions in which trade could flourish and administrative costs could be kept to a minimum. Direct rule was thus limited to those economically viable and politically strategic areas based upon Bengal and the presidencies of Bombay and Madras. Elsewhere British control and influence were indirectly exercised through a system of subsidiary alliances and treaties which had been concluded with indigenous rulers who had been either defeated in war by Company forces or in need of Company protection against more powerful neighbours. For these rulers the essence of the subsidiary system was security at the price of dependence upon the British. In return for guarantees of support against either external aggression or domestic revolt they had all forfeited the right to conduct an independent foreign policy and many had agreed to pay for the upkeep of a body of Company troops which would be stationed within their states under the control of a British Resident. For the British the subsidiary system had been devised primarily to provide a cheap means of pacifying and subordinating regions not under their own direct control.

Given the evolutionary nature of paramountcy, the settlement imposed by Lord Hastings in 1818 could never be regarded as permanent. The new rulers of India were thus immediately confronted by a problem. Having established their initial supremacy, the British had to decide how best to utilize the princes in a manner which would strengthen the imperial position and at the same time reconcile the princes to their subordination. The problem proved to be intractable. At no time in the nineteenth century did the British really create a climate which would have enabled these requirements to be fulfilled. This failure upon the part of the British stands in marked contrast to the success achieved by their Mughal predecessors. One of the most significant Mughal achievements, and one which contributed to the consolidation of their Indian empire, was the manner in which, for a period extending over one hundred years, they were able to establish an effective political partnership with the princes based upon equality and trust. This contrast between the British and the Mughals can be attributed in part to the fact that while both were acutely aware of their alien status, the British sought to maintain a distinct and separate identity, whereas the Mughals attempted to integrate themselves with the hierarchies of those over whom they ruled. In the case of the British, their own religious and social *mores* precluded them from any form of partnership with the indigenous community. Moreover, in seeking to maintain their aloofness, they baulked at the idea of partnership because of the attendant risks. Suspicion and distrust became the order of the day as the British adopted a policy of keeping the princes at arm's length from the government and isolated from each other. Yet this policy had the most debilitating consequences for the princes. Under the British system of tutelage they had no hope of achieving either fame or distinction. Confined to their own territories and with no prospect of advancement, they began even to lose the compulsion to maintain decent and orderly standards of administration. Instead they became increasingly dependent upon British guarantees to protect them against either external aggression or internal revolt. It was only towards the turn of the century, and then with very limited success, that the British attempted to rejuvenate the princes by enlisting their participation in the defence of the empire. The purpose of the remainder of this chapter is to examine the main currents of British policy during the nineteenth century. Three themes are investigated. First, for the purpose of later comparison, there is a brief review of Mughal policy towards the Rajput states. This is followed by a review of the period between 1818 and the mutiny of 1857 when, in an effort to impose western standards of civilization throughout India, British policy became expansionist and threatened the princes with total extinction. Finally there is a review of the period between the mutiny and the turn of the century when, having abandoned their expansionist policies, the British maintained the right to intervene in the states to improve administrative standards but manifestly failed to find a more meaningful role for their princes.

Mughal Policy towards the Rajput States

Mughal policy towards the states was founded upon the Rajput alliance, the framework of which had been devised by the Emperor Akbar, the greatest of the Mughals, who ruled between 1556 and 1605.[16] As an imperialist, Akbar's aim was to establish his own personal hegemony over the widest area possible. His ambition could not be realized without the submission of the Rajput chieftans whose territories were concentrated to the east of the Mughal establishments at Delhi and Agra. The Rajputs were renowned for their chivalry and heroism but their fierce pride and clan loyalty inhibited collective action. In his opening campaigns against them, Akbar was able to take full advantage of their chronic dissensions. An appeal for help by Jaipur, the nearest state to Delhi, against the premier Rajput state of Mewar (Udaipur), led to the conquest of the latter's two great fortresses - Chitor, which fell in 1568, and Ranthambor, ruled by the Raja of Bundi, a vassal of the Rana of Mewar, which fell in 1569. By the end of 1570 virtually the whole of Rajasthan recognized the suzerainty of Akbar. The only significant exception was Mewar, whose subsequent opposition to the Mughals served as an irritant rather than a threat.[17]

The submission of the Rajput chiefs was not accompanied by their humiliation. Their own personal sovereignty was admittedly diminished. They had to pay tribute, acknowledge the right of the Mughal emperor to recognize and regulate successions to their thrones, and they had to adhere to the principles of Mughal foreign policy. They were, however, more than compensated for these impositions. Akbar in fact elevated the Rajputs to a position whereby they became equal partners in the administration of the empire. There were shrewd political motives for this policy. Akbar's Muslim aristocracy consisted principally of foreign mercenaries, some of whom were frequently quarrelsome and often disloyal. There were thus obvious advantages to be gained by using the Rajputs as a counterpoise against the foreign nobility, particularly the Turanis (Central Asians), the Iranis (Persians) and the Afghans.[18] Moreover, as Muslims, the position of the Mughals in India was that of an alien ruling minority. Akbar realized that no empire could either be secure or endure which did not attempt to reconcile the Hindu population. To this end the active support and co-operation of the Rajput chiefs would be invaluable. As prestige and status meant everything to the Rajputs, Akbar's first step in the cultivation of closer relations came in 1562 when he married the daughter of Bhar Mal, the ruler of Jaipur.[19] He later married into the ruling families of Bikaner and Jaisalmer. Although intermarriage was frowned upon by some Rajput chiefs, most notably the Rana of Mewar, others welcomed it because it raised their status and gave them influence at the Mughal court. Akbar further flattered their dignity by allowing them to beat their drums (a sign of royalty) in the capital and to enter the Hall of Public Audience fully armed. Above all, however, under Akbar the Rajputs were fully integrated into the imperial service. Whereas previous Muslim dynasties in India had used Hindus in their administrations and armies only in a subordinate capacity, Akbar treated the Rajputs as partners. Some, like Bhagwan Das, the adopted son of Bhar Mal, and the latter's grandson, Man Singh, were high among his confidential adivsers. As governors of provinces or military commanders the Rajputs became part of the *mansabdari* or office-holding system upon which Mughal administration was based. The system was one of patronage in which *mansabdars*, employed in either a civil or military capacity, were graded decimally and given a *zat* rank, indicating their personal salary which was dependent upon their position within the official heirarchy, and usually a *swar* rank, indicating the number of cavalrymen and horses they were required to maintain. The form of payment was either a cash salary direct from the royal treasury or the assignment of a tract of land, a *jagir*, from which the *mansabdars* were allowed to collect the land revenue on their own behalf. In the main *mansabdars* were drawn from the foreign nobility, but under Akbar Rajputs such as Bhagwan Das and Man Singh were ranked amongst the upper echelons of the official hierarchy.

Akbar's Rajput policy was maintained by his successors, Jehangir (1605-27) and Shah Jahan (1628-58). It was continued during the early years of Aurangzeb's reign between 1658 and 1707 although by the latter stages it had come under a severe strain. Aurangzeb had come to the throne after killing his brothers Dara and Murad and imprisoning Shah Jahan, his own father. Jaswant Singh of Marwar (Jodhpur) had sided with Dara against Aurangzeb during the war of succession. Yet despite Jaswant's crushing defeat at the battle of Dharmat in 1658, Aurangzeb promoted him to a premier position within the *mansabdari* system and twice entrusted him with the governorship of Gujarat (1659-61 and 1670-72). In 1665 Jai Singh of

Jaipur was made Viceroy of the Deccan, one of the most important charges within the empire, which was normally only entrusted to Mughal princes. In this capacity Jai Singh was responsible for bringing Shivaji to Aurangzeb's court at Agra in 1666 after the Maratha leader had sacked the Mughal port at Surat in 1664.[20]

However, the circumstances of Aurangzeb's accession also help to explain why, during the second half of his reign, Rajput fortunes began to decline. The emperor had to prove himself in order to justify the deaths of his brothers and the imprisonment of his father. In 1659 he embarked on a massive programme of military expansion designed to demonstrate his ability and to rally support from the Muslim nobility behind his throne. Territorial expansion had always been an essential element of Mughal statecraft in that it provided fresh fields for the assignment of *jagirs* which could be used to satisfy the urge for promotions amongst the *mansabdars*. However, many of the emperor's campaigns met with setbacks and by the 1670s it had become clear that no rapid expansion could be expected. Consequently, Aurangzeb began to consider reducing the number of Rajputs employed in order to provide for the needs and ambitions of his foreign nobility. He served notice of his intentions in 1679 upon the death of Jaswant Singh of Jodhpur. By supporting a rival claimant to the throne in preference to Ajit Singh, who had been acclaimed as Jaswant's successor, Aurangzeb provoked a rebellion by the Rathors and Sisodias, the respective clans of Marwar and Mewar, between 1680 and 1681. The ease with which the rebellion was crushed could not conceal the damage which had been inflicted upon relations between the Mughals and the Rajputs. The bonds of trust and friendship had been broken. Moreover, once Aurangzeb became obsessed with the conquest of the whole of the Deccan towards the end of his reign, they could never be fully repaired. The campaigns against the sultanates of Bijapur and Golkunda and the unceasing war of attrition against the Marathas, imposed an enormous strain upon the *mansabdari* system. An essential part of Aurangzeb's strategy had been to subvert the opposition by offering *mansabs* and *jagirs* to enemy officers. However, the resources of the south had been devastated by famine and war to such an extent that the military and diplomatic requirements of the emperor could be met only by assigning *jagirs* in northern India to nobles from the Deccan. The constant stream of newcomers inevitably meant that the recruitment and promotion of the older groups within the nobility would suffer. None suffered more than the Rajputs who, at a time when Aurangzeb was establishing a new justification for his reign by emphasizing the Islamic character of the empire, could easily be penalized because of their different religion. The days when the Rajputs could achieve distinction and status within the imperial service were clearly over.[21]

The failure to maintain the Rajput alliance in the spirit of Akbar, deprived the Mughal empire of one of the main pillars upon which it had been erected and thus contributed to its eventual decline. Nevertheless, Aurangzeb's policies during the latter stages of his reign should not be allowed to obscure the very solid Mughal achievement over the previous one hundred years. Accepted as partners and treated as equals, the Rajputs had, for the most part, become staunch supporters of the Mughal dynasty and a most effective instrument for the consolidation of Mughal rule throughout the country.

British Policy 1818-1857

During the first half of the nineteenth century, the Mughal experience of relations with the Rajput states had little relevance for the new British rulers of India. The British had not achieved their supremacy with the aid of foreign mercenaries whose loyalty could not always be depended upon. Moreover, as a result of reforms introduced by Lord Cornwallis, Governor-General between 1786 and 1793, the British had resolved to rule as a class apart, reserving senior administrative positions within the Company's service exclusively for Europeans. They were conscious of their position as an alien ruling minority but this did not necessarily lead them to draw the same conclusions with regard to the princes as their Mughal predecessors. Indeed in this respect, British opinion during the first half of the nineteenth century was far from unanimous. In an ongoing debate concerning the relative merits of British and Indian rule the outstanding question that had to be decided was whether the princes and their states were to be maintained at all or absorbed by further territorial expansion. Supporters of the latter view believed that the operation of the subsidiary system left them with no other alternative. Although they recognized the financial and strategic advantages of the system they also held it responsible for the wretched condition of many of the princely administrations that they encountered. They not only considered that the burden of maintaining subsidiary troops had brought many of the states to the verge of financial ruin but also that the nature of the system itself encouraged corrupt and oppressive government. In the past, princes guilty of such vices could be overthrown either by foreign conquest or domestic rebellion. Now, under British protection, they were not only secure from every foreign or domestic enemy but also free to govern in an arbitrary manner, defying the wishes of their subjects with impunity. One of the most forthright critics of the subsidiary system was Sir Thomas Munro who became Governor of Madras between 1820 and 1827. Munro was essentially a conservative in the sense that he respected indigenous customs and institutions and wanted to preserve them in order to conciliate all sections of Indian society. Britain's role in India, he believed, should be confined to the provision of sound and efficient government. It was in this respect that he condemned the subsidiary system. In 1817 he expressed his views to the Governor-General, Lord Hastings:

> There are many weighty objections to the employment of a subsidiary force. It has a natural tendency to render the government of every country in which it exists weak and oppressive; to extinguish all honourable spirit among the higher

classes of society and to degrade and impoverish the whole people. The usual remedy of a bad government in India is a quiet revolution in the palace, or a violent one by rebellion or foreign conquests. But the presence of a British force cuts off every chance of remedy by supporting the prince on the throne against every foreign and domestic enemy. It renders him indolent, by teaching him to trust to strangers for his security; cruel and avaricious, by showing him that he has nothing to fear from the hatred of his subjects. Wherever the subsidiary force is introduced, unless the reigning prince be a man of great abilities, the country will soon bear the marks of it in decaying villages and decreasing population.[22]

Munro's reflections led him to conclude that 'the subsidiary system must everywhere run its full course, and destroy every government which it undertakes to protect'.[23] Once this stage had been reached the British would have to take over the states and begin the arduous task of rehabilitation.

Similar sentiments were expressed fifteen years later by Henry Russell, who had spent nine years as Resident at Hyderabad between 1811 and 1820. In his evidence before a House of Commons Committee in 1832, Russell remarked that the princes could choose 'between a violent and a lingering death'. If, like the Peshwa, they attempted to reassert their independence, they only precipitated their own destruction; if they submitted, like the Nizam and the Maharaja of Mysore, their states declined from one stage of weakness to another until they expired from exhaustion. In a similarly pessimistic vein, Russell contemplated the ultimate outcome of the subsidiary system:

> The evil of which our subsidiary system has thus been productive is the more to be lamented, that it is manifestly irremediable ... It is now too late for us to recede ... It is vain to think of ... reviving among the native states that vigour which has been extinguished; their decline is not to be arrested; they must proceed and complete their course. In spite of everything that we can do to prevent it, they must fall successively into our possession, and partake at last of our downfall, of which, whether it be slow or sudden, the period will probably be hastened by every increase of our territory and subjects.[24]

The misgivings of Munro and Russell were shared by the liberal reformers of the early Victorian era. The reformers, however, were not prepared to wait until the subsidiary system had run its course and destroyed the governments of every state it was supposed to protect. Convinced that western civilization was superior and inspired by the belief that Britain had a moral obligation to reform Indian society, the reformers were appalled to learn that British policy encouraged princely misgovernment. Despite their anti-imperialist sentiments, they thus advocated the termination of princely rule and became committed to a policy of annexing the states. James Stuart Mill, the apostle of early nineteenth century liberalism who served the Company as an Assistant Examiner of India Correspondence, was adamant that the people of the states would continue to suffer while princely governments remained responsible for the administration of justice and the collection of revenue. In concluding his evidence before the Committee of the Commons in 1832, Mill declared: 'In my opinion the best thing for the happiness of the people is, that our government should be nominally, as well as really, extended over those territories: that our own modes of governing should be adopted, and our own people put in charge of the government.'[25]

The views of the annexationists, however, were by no means universally endorsed. Mountstuart Elphinstone and Sir John Malcolm were prominent amongst those who disagreed with the criticisms of the subsidiary system and who strenuously opposed the idea of bringing princely rule to an end. Like Munro, Elphinstone and Malcolm were essentially conservatives but their own experiences in India led them to draw completely different conclusions about the princes and their states. Elphinstone, with experience as Resident at Poona and as Governor of Bombay, believed that such decay and stagnation as existed in the states was due, not to the subsidiary system, but to what he described as the 'ephemeral character of Asiatic governments':

> Scarcely any State that has sprung up in India since the fall of the Mughal Empire has retained its vigour after the death of its founder, and not one has failed to sink into complete decay by the third generation ... the states with which we have formed alliances would have lost even their political energy, as they have done, if the English had never landed in India.[26]

Elphinstone also saw fit to warn any would-be annexationists that the stability of Britain's existing possessions in India was to a large extent dependent upon the maintenance of princely territories which afforded 'a refuge to all those whose habits of war, intrigue, or depradation make them incapable of keeping quiet in ours'.[27] In this respect he was supported by Malcolm, one of the Company's greatest servants who had been responsible for the settlement of Central India after the defeat of the Marathas and who had succeeded Elphinstone as Governor of Bombay. In 1832 Malcolm declared himself to be 'decidedly of the opinion that the tranquillity, not to say the security of our vast Oriental possessions is involved in the preservation of the native principalities which are dependent upon us for protection ... their co-existence with our rule is of itself a source of political strength the value of which will never be known until it is lost'.[28] Malcolm recognized that territorial expansion and the introduction of western reforms were perhaps inevitable but warned of serious repercussions if they were not accompanied by restraint. Although Indians were divided by their separation into caste and tribe, there were still 'some general sympathies associated with their prejudices and religion' which gave them 'a disposition to unite'. Moreover, what

Malcolm described as the 'more instructed part' of Indian society knew how to take full advantage of such feelings:

> The Mahomedan priests, the Brahmins and other civil classes, have for ages been the nominal servants but real masters of the turbulent and bold, but ignorant and superstitious, military races of their countrymen. Their knowledge how to use this dangerous influence has been rendered complete by frequent exercise; and when we consider what they have lost by the introduction and extension of our dominion, it would be folly to expect exemption from their efforts to subvert it: their success wil depend on the means we place within their reach.[29]

Like Elphinstone, therefore, Malcolm firmly opposed the views of those who wanted to leave the states to die of their own accord simply to bring them 'soonest to the point at which we can assume the country and give it the benefits of our immediate rule'. Yet despite their concern to preserve the states, neither Elphinstone nor Malcolm could envisage a more positive role for their rulers. Although they recognized that the princes possessed a certain legitimacy in the eyes of their subjects which the British as aliens could never claim, they were not prepared to advocate the policy of the Mughals which had enabled them to assume administrative responsibilities beyond their states and military commands in the army. For the conservatives who wanted to maintain the states, therefore, the princes would remain on the periphery of the imperial structure serving only as safety valves in order to provide for the security of British rule.

Any examination of the quarter century that preceded the outbreak of the Indian mutiny in 1857 reveals that little heed was taken of the warnings of Elphinstone and Malcolm. In an age when liberal values were being translated into practice in British India with the introduction of far-reaching measures of educational, land and social reform, the Indian States were increasingly regarded as antiquated relics of an effete and frequently barbarous eastern civilization. This is not to say that in the period before 1848 the British were fully committed to a policy of annexing the states. The Board of Control and the Court of Directors in London were basically opposed to any further territorial expansion other than that dictated by political or military necessity. Successive Governors-General were likewise opposed to expansion at the beginning of the administrations but local circumstances, together with the inevitable urge to check abuses as and when they occurred, frequently led them to abandon their earlier views. Lord Bentinck, for instance, Governor-General between 1828 and 1834, was at first a non-interventionist as far as the states were concerned. He believed that there was already far too much 'petty interference', particularly in the private and personal lives of the princes, and even advocated the removal of political officers from all states except those in which subsidiary troops were stationed.[30] However, Bentinck soon found himself threatening the errant ruler of Oudh that he would have to forfeit his throne unless he mended his ways.[31] Furthermore, he placed Mysore under British administration following a rebellion in 1831, and annexed the state of Coorg in 1834 on the grounds of misgovernment.[32] Upon assuming office as Governor-General in 1842, Lord Ellenborough not only disavowed territorial expansion but also instructed political officers to refrain from interference in either the private or public affairs of the princes. Yet within a year he had presided over the annexation of the state of Sind and was duly recalled by the authorities in London in 1844. In this instance, the problem of slow communications between England and India together with the personal ambition of Sir Charles Napier, the British army commander in Sind, had combined not so much to force Ellenborough's hand, as to leave him powerless to influence events.[33]

It was not, however, until the time of Lord Dalhousie, Governor-General between 1848 and 1856, that annexation became a salient feature of British policy. Utterly convinced of the superiority of British rule and the degeneracy of the Indian States, Dalhousie made his views clear at the outset of his administration in August 1848:

> I cannot conceive it possible for anyone to dispute the policy of taking advantage of every just opportunity which presents itself for consolidating the territories which already belong to us, by taking possession of States that may lapse in the midst of them; for thus getting rid of those petty intervening principalities, which may be made a means of annoyance, but which can never, I venture to think, be a source of strength, for adding to the resources of the public treasury, and for extending the uniform application of our system of government to those whose best interests, we sincerely believe, will be promoted thereby.[34]

The doctrine of lapse and persistent misgovernment were the pretexts used by Dalhousie to deprive seven princes of their kingdoms. As paramount power, Britain possessed the right to regulate successions in the states. According to Hindu law princes without direct heirs could adopt successors. By refusing to sanction such adoptions Dalhousie enforced the doctrine of lapse to gain possession of three Maratha states, Satara, Nagpur and Jhansi, together with Bhagat and Jambalpur. As a corollary to the doctrine of lapse, Dalhousie's administration also abolished the pensions and titles of ex-ruling families. Even Bahadur Shah II, the last of the Mughal emperors, was informed that the imperial title would lapse upon his death. The climax of the expansionist phase came in 1856 with the annexation of Oudh upon the grounds of misrule. There can be little doubt that the state of Oudh, which had been part of the subsidiary system since 1801, was in drastic need of reform. Successive Nawabs had been more interested in their own amusement than in promoting the welfare of their subjects. In October 1849 the Resident, W.H. Sleeman, informed Dalhousie that effective government no longer existed in Oudh. The only orders given by the Nawab were through his 'eunuchs and singers'. Beyond the capital at Lucknow the army had been rendered useless for want of pay, and authority had been usurped by the large landowners.[35] However, Sleeman, like his predecessor Colonel Low, did not believe that Oudh should be annexed outright. As conservatives, the Residents were more in sympathy with the views of Elphinstone and Malcolm than with those of Dalhousie. Indeed Sleeman had already warned the Governor-General of the possible consequences of annexing the states: 'If we succeed in sweeping them all away or absorbing them, we shall be at the mercy of our native army, and they shall see it, and accidents may possibly occur to unite them, or a great proportion of them, in some desperate act ... the best provision against it seems to be to be the maintenance of native rulers, whose confidence and affection can be engaged, and administration improved under judicious management.'[36] The recollections of Bishop Heber, who journeyed through Oudh in 1824, seemed to confirm Sleeman's warning. The Bishop was informed of the response of some of the Nawab's troops when it had been suggested to them that the remedy for their grievances might be annexation by the British: ' "Miserable as we are of all miseries keep us from that!" "Why so . . . are not our people far better governed?" "Yes," was the answer, "but the name of Oudh and the honour of our nation would be at an end." '[37] Sleeman was obviously aware of local feeling. In 1852 he proposed that Britain should administer Oudh in perpetuity but allow the Nawabs to retain titular sovereignty. As the Nawabs had been loyal to the British cause for over half a century, even Dalhousie was prepared to support this arrangement.   However, the Governor-General's Council and the government in London feared that civil war might ensue in Oudh if the then Nawab, Wajid Ali Shah, refused to agree.[38]   The subsequent annexation of the state in February 1856 coincided with the end of Dalhousie's administration. Within a little over a year India was engulfed by mutiny.

British Policy 1857-1905

There can be little doubt that the policy of annexing the states was but one of many accumulating Indian grievances that led to the outbreak of the mutiny. The mutiny itself was essentially a last desperate protest by traditional India against the remorseless penetration of the west and in this respect it is perhaps not surprising that it was the princes dispossesed by Dalhousie who provided the rebel cause with its leadership. Nana Saheb, the adopted son of the ex-Peshwa, had lost both his title and pension in 1853.   For generations after the mutiny he was identified in the British mind as the perpetrator of the massacre at Kanpur. In Central India, the Rani or Queen of Jhansi, who had been deprived of her kingdom in 1853, joined forces with the rebels of Gwalior led by Tantia Topi until she fell in battle in June 1858. Similarly, Begum Hazrat Mahal, Queen Regent of Oudh, led the rebel cause in Oudh until she was forced across the border into neighbouring Nepal at the end of 1858. However, the vast majority of reigning princes remained loyal to the British cause and some provided essential military support at critical junctures. In the Punjab, prompt action by the Sikh princes of

Patiala, Jind, and Nabha enabled the line of communication to be kept open between Lahore and the beleaguered British forces at Delhi. In Central India the Maharajas Scindia at Gwalior and Holkar at Indore both remained loyal despite the fact that they lost control over their own troops. Indeed by affecting to take the mutineers from Gwalior back into his service, Scindia prevented them marching on Delhi at a time when British fortunes were at their lowest ebb.[39]

The experience of the mutiny had thus vindicated the views of those conservatives who had earlier warned of the dangers of annexing the states. Moreover, the loyalty of the reigning princes had clearly demonstrated the potential of the Indian States as a political force in support of British rule. Lord Stanley, who became the first Secretary of State for India in September 1858, urged Dalhousie's successor, Lord Canning, to spare no effort in rewarding the princes who had rendered active assistance. The latter needed no prompting and remarked in a dispatch to Sir Charles Wood, who had succeeded Stanley at the India Office in June 1859, that the 'safety of our rule is increased not diminished by the maintenance of Native Chiefs well affected to us'. During the revolt, 'patches of native government' like Gwalior, Hyderabad, Patiala, Rampur and Rewa had, according to Canning, 'served as breakwaters to the storm which would otherwise have swept over us'. He believed that 'should the day come when India shall be threatened by an external enemy, or when the interests of England elsewhere may require that her Eastern Empire shall incur more than ordinary risks, one of our best mainstays will be found in these Native States'.[40]

By implication therefore the policy of annexation could no longer be continued. For the first time under British rule the princes were to be accorded a permanent position as part of the British empire. The Queen's Proclamation declared that the British had no desire to extend their existing territorial possessions and would 'respect the rights, dignity and honour of the native princes as our own'. In order to perpetuate the dynasties of the princes, Canning dispensed with the doctrine of lapse and bestowed 'Adoption *Sanads*' upon all rulers above the rank of *jagirdar* who guaranteed to abide by the sentiments of loyalty and fidelity expressed in their treaties.[41] These *sanads* recognized the prerogative of the princes to adopt successors according to the family custom on the failure of natural heirs to their thrones. Lavish territorial and monetary rewards were also bestowed upon those princes who had proved their loyalty. The Maharaja Scindia of Gwalior received land worth an annual income of three *lakhs* of rupees, Rampur, land worth one *lakh*, while Patiala and Jind received *jagirs* worth over two *lakhs* each. In 1861 a special order of knighthood was instituted, known as the Star of India, and the rulers of Baroda, Bhopal, Gwalior, Indore, Patiala and Rampur all became its honoured recipients.[42]

The change of policy, however, did not mean that the princes would be treated as equals or taken into partnership. Having recognized the right of the princes to adopt heirs to their thrones, Canning proceeded to establish a yet further principle which was to assume an even greater significance for the future relationship between the British and the states. In explaining the adoption procedure in his dispatch to Wood, Canning declared: 'The proposed measure will not debar the Government of India from stepping in to set right such serious abuses in a native Government as may threaten any part of the country with anarchy or disturbance, nor from assuming temporary change of a Native State when there shall be sufficient reason to do so.'[43] This statement significantly qualified the lengths to which the British were prepared to go in order to conciliate their new princely allies. They appreciated that they had been misguided in annexing so many states but remained convinced that their reasons for so doing, particularly in the case of Oudh, could still be justified. Indeed Canning was of the opinion that the recognition of the right of adoption placed the government under an even greater moral obligation to remain vigilant in order to ensure that abuses and misgovernment in the states did not go unchecked. Clearly therefore, although the princes were now secure against annexation, they could not expect complete exemption from British interference in their domestic affairs.[44]

At first British remonstrances with erring princes were extremely mild.   Petty interference would be irritating to a prince and therefore where possible it was considered better 'to guide and influence and lead him when necessary, and not to drive him'.[45] However, this tolerance did not survive long. Viceroys began to assume a more dictatorial tone and lecture the princes on the ideals of efficient government and the meaning of their relationships with the paramount power. Lord Mayo, Viceroy between 1869 and 1872, told them:

> If you wish to be a great man at my Court, govern well at home. Be just and merciful to your people. We do not ask whether you come with full hands, but whether you come with clean hands. No presents that you may bring can buy the British favour; no display which you may make will raise your dignity in our eyes; no cringing or flattery will gain my friendship. We estimate you, not by the splendour of your offerings to us, nor by the pomp of your retinue, but by your conduct to your people at home . . . If we support you in your power we expect in return good government.[46]

Moreover, in place of the annexation of a state the punishment for misgovernment was now deposition of the ruler. The most striking case was that of the Gaekwar of Baroda in 1875. A commission was appointed to investigate complaints brought against the Baroda administration and to suggest reforms. The Gaekwar protested that such a procedure was unwarranted by the treaty relations subsisting between the British Government and the Baroda state. In reply he was informed that the government never had any intention of interfering in his state and that he was responsible for the administration and the welfare of his subjects. If, however, he should fail in his responsibilities:

... if gross misgovernment be permitted, if substantial justice be not done to the subjects of the Baroda state, if life and property be not protected, or if the general welfare of the country and people be persistently neglected, the British Government will assuredly intervene in the manner which in its judgement may be best calculated to remove these evils and secure good government.[47]

A state which was deprived of its ruler was said to be under 'minority' administration. The Government of India either appointed a Council of Regency to administer the state or placed it under the direct charge of a British official. A similar situation obtained if, on the premature death of a ruler, his lineal or adopted successor was too young to assume the full reins of government. Minority periods were the signal for a marked increase in British influence within the state concerned and were used increasingly during the second half of the nineteenth century as 'a matter of deliberate policy, to level up the administration of states in their own "interests", no doubt, but without particular regard for their "traditions", and sometimes perhaps with not enough regard for what might strictly be held to be their rights'.[48]

In 1879, when Lord Lytton was Viceroy, the Government of India had the task of arranging the transfer of Mysore from British back to princely rule. The transfer had been under consideration since 1861 when, with the departure of Sir Mark Gubbon, who had been Commissioner of Mysore since 1834, Krishnaraj Wadir, the former Maharaja deposed in 1831 upon grounds of misgovernment, petitioned Canning for the restoration of his powers. Under Gubbon's tutelage Mysore had become something of a model province and Canning was loath to relinquish British control. He thus rejected the petition, informing the Maharaja in the process that the removal of British officials would probably have 'disastrous' consequences.[49] A further appeal by the Maharaja to Lord Lawrence, Viceroy between 1864 and 1869, drew a similar response: 'Pardon me for saying that, if in the flower of your manhood, after experience of some 20 years' rule, Your Highness failed to govern your country wisely and well, what hope can there now be that you could do so?'[50] Lawrence and the Secretary of State, Sir Charles Wood, were in fact playing for time in the hope that Mysore could be fully incorporated into British India upon the Maharaja's death. However, in 1865 the Maharaja placed them in a quandary by adopting an heir. The British were under no obligation to recognize the adoption, for Mysore had not been under princely rule when Canning bestowed adoption *sanads* upon the princes. Both Viceroy and Secretary of State were prepared to withhold recognition but Wood retired from office in February 1866, and the Liberal government of which he had been a member was defeated at the election held in the summer of that year. In February 1867, Lord Cranbourne, the Conservative Secretary of State, whose respect for princely rule was a frequent source of irritation to Lawrence, pledged that Mysore would be restored to princely rule.[51] From here there could be no retreat by officials in

India. In 1879, however, when considering how best to effect the transfer to the Maharaja's successor, Chama Rajendra Wadiar, the Lytton administration maintained that the only way to avoid a repetition of misgovernment in Mysore was to adopt a general policy whereby at the end of minority periods 'some reasonable limitations' would be placed 'upon the personal power of the ruler, or of the Minister, to whom the administration may be entrusted'.[52] In preparing a draft Instrument of Transfer, the Government of India therefore included detailed restrictions upon the powers of the adopted prince and expressed the wish that they might serve as a precedent to be adopted towards all states emerging from minority periods. The new Maharaja of Mysore would be required to conform to the advice of the Governor-General and his Council on such matters as the management of his finances, the settlement and collection of his revenues, the imposition of taxes, the administration of justice, the extension of commerce, the encouragement of trade, agriculture and industry, and any other matters concerned with the welfare of his subjects and his relations with the British Government. These restrictions came into force in Mysore in 1881 upon the investiture of Chama Rajendra Wadiar,[53] but a more general application of them was disallowed by Lord Cranbrook, the Secretary of State, who considered that they would be interpreted as an unwarranted revision of the treaties with the states. However, Cranbrook did not wish to discourage the Viceroy from using 'such legitimate opportunities as may occur for organizing the administration of particular Native States according to the principles you have laid down' and felt that the only protection for the princes against intervention lay in 'the general and judicious extension . . . of the general system of Government which is applied in British India'.[54]

Lord Lytton was Viceroy for four years between 1876 and 1880. The case of Mysore was only one aspect of his dealings with the Indian States. With the exception of Lord Curzon, he was the only Viceroy during the second half of the nineteenth century to devote any serious consideration to the nature of the problems surrounding the relationship between the princes and the paramount power. Within a mere month of assuming office he was complaining about 'our fitful policy' towards the princes, which had conspicuously failed to secure 'their effectual co-operation' or to associate 'their personal interest and authority with the Imperial Administration'.[55] He was particularly concerned to discover that beyond some vague generalizations, very little was actually known about the 'administrative or fiscal' details of the states. Equally, he considered that the financial and military support Britain derived from the princes was 'ludicrously small' when compared to the benefits they derived from the British connection. In addition to the protection they received against either external attack or internal rebellion, they also benefited, free of cost, from the introduction of railways, roads, telegraphs and commerce.[56] Lytton was perhaps the first Viceroy with what may be described as a *babu* complex, a term disparagingly used by the British to refer to English educated middle-class Bengalis who were to provide the nucleus for the later nationalist movement and who were just beginning to make their presence felt with their demands for political representation and recruitment to the Indian Civil Service. Lytton dismissed them as a 'social anomaly' and had little sympathy for their aspirations. The real people were the peasants whom he described collectively as 'an inert mass'.[57] When they did stir themselves they moved in obedience, not to their British benefactors, but to their 'native chiefs and princes, however tyrannical they may be'. Lytton drew a parallel between the British position in India and the Austrian position in Italy which had been abruptly terminated between 1859 and 1866. The Austrian provinces of Lombardy and Venetia had been the most efficiently governed regions in Italy but the Hapsburgs had made the mistake of snubbing the native aristocracy with the result that the latter had turned against them. The analysis was superficial but for Lytton the moral was clear. As he informed Lord Salisbury, Secretary of State between 1874 and 1878: 'To secure completely, and efficiently utilize, the Indian aristocracy is, I am convinced, the most important problem now before us.'[58]

An imaginative and romantic imperialist, Lytton was almost to the nineteenth century what Akbar had been to the sixteenth. In some ways the comparison is rather unfortunate for in reality the Viceroy's reasoning was based upon an outlook which would have been more appropriate to the sixteenth century than to his own. He believed that the allegiance of the princes could be most effectively procured by exploiting their evident susceptibility to the influence of symbolism. In April 1876 he wrote to Disraeli:

> Nothing has struck me more in my intercourse thus far with the Indian Rajahs and Maharajas than the importance they attach to their family pedigrees and ancestral records . . . (I)n all of them I find evidence that small favours and marks of honour bestowed from time to time by the British Government on the head of the family (such as an additional gun to his salute, the right to a return visit from the Viceroy, or a more honourable place in Durbar, etc.) are quite as highly prized and appreciated as the more substantial benefits (of augmented territory or revenue) conferred in earlier times upon the family by an Aurungzebe or an Akbar. I believe that at the present moment an Indian Maharaja would do anything, or pay anything, to obtain an additional gun to his salute.[59]

It was this reasoning which prompted Lytton to organize the Delhi Durbar of 1877, an uninhibited display of medieval pageantry at which Queen Victoria was proclaimed Empress of India, and banners, titles and additional guns to salutes were bestowed upon those princes fortunate enough to have been invited to attend.

However, theatrical displays of pomp and ceremony were only part of Lytton's overall policy. He wanted to institute a full-scale inquiry into relations with the states in order to elicit more detailed information about their administrations and to devise a code of conduct for the guidance of political officers. He considered that the treaties which had been concluded with the states were out of date, and favoured revising them in order to give the princes 'a certain autonomy' in return for greater financial and military contributions. In this latter respect, the armies of the princes were a source of concern to Lytton. He described them as a 'formidable mass which may some day give us more anxiety than assistance'. In order to neutralize them, he advocated that certain princes should be given military commands 'with definite military duties and services attached thereto'. He mentioned Scindia, the Maharaja of Gwalior, and the Maharaja of Kashmir who, by virtue of the frontier location of his state, could be given the title 'Warden of the Marches'.[60] His most ambitious proposal was for the establishment of an Imperial Privy Council 'to be composed exclusively of only the greatest and most important princes' which would function in an advisory and consultative capacity.[61]   However, only one of these schemes materialized. The proposed inquiry and treaty revision were blocked by members of his own Council who felt that it would be unwise to risk alienating the princes at a time when Britain faced the prospect of war with Russia as a result of renewed friction between Russia and Turkey in the Balkans.[62]   The Secretary of State, Lord Salisbury, expressed a willingness to consider a Privy Council but he was quite unable to overcome the official opposition to the proposal in London. In November 1876 Salisbury frankly admitted that most members of his Council at the India Office were 'liberals' who found Lytton's ostentatious displays somewhat repugnant.   Moreover, his legal advisers were of the opinion that the proposed Privy Council would require parliamentary legislation.   This had been sufficient to dissuade most members of Disraeli's Cabinet who were still licking their wounds following the mauling they had received at the hands of Gladstone's opposition during the earlier Commons debate on the Royal Titles Bill.[63]   The Viceroy was therefore left to confer the rather empty title of 'Councillor of the Empress' on eight states.

The one scheme which did materialize emerged some five years after Lytton's recall by Gladstone following the Liberal victory at the election of April 1880. In March 1885 Britain's vulnerability on the north-west frontier was again emphasized by Russia's defeat of an Afghan army at Pendjah. For a time war between Russia and Britain seemed likely. The crisis soon passed but in the same year the Viceroy, Lord Dufferin (1884-1888), responded by agreeing to the formation of new military units which became known as Imperial Service Troops. These units were recruited entirely from within the states and they were paid for by the governments of the princes. They were trained and inspected regularly by British officers and were made available to the paramount power in times of emergency.[64] Hyderabad and Mysore, together with many of the states in Rajputana, contributed Imperial Service Troops which subsequently distinguished themselves during the Boer War and at the time of the Boxer rebellion in China. The Imperial Service scheme represented a significant step forward in British military thinking and indeed in British policy towards the states. The princes had still not been entrusted with permanent military commands but Lytton would have been gratified to learn that the authorities in India were now prepared to utilize their armies for the purpose of defending imperial interests.

At the turn of the century relations with the Indian States were managed by another great imperialist, Lord Curzon, who was Viceroy between 1899 and 1905. There was an essential similarity between Curzon and Lytton in that both sought to utilize the princes and to exploit their susceptibility to the influence of symbolism. Curzon was responsible for a second spectacular Durbar held at Delhi in 1903 to announce Edward VII's coronation. However, Curzon believed that there were limits to the process of allowing the princes to indulge themselves in ceremonial splendours. Indeed, for the new Viceroy, the process had already gone too far. He took serious exception to the use of a royal crown on the emblems of the rulers of Cooch Behar, Kapurthala and Nabha. Equally, he objected to the playing of the national anthem for the Maharaja of Patiala and the Maharaja of Pudokkottai and to the use of phrases such as 'royal family' and 'throne' by the rulers of Baroda, Cutch, Rampur and Travancore. The Viceroy's attitude in this respect was explained in an official summary of his administration printed in 1908:

> Lord Curzon's view was that though these questions might appear to be trifling, and interference might even be thought to be vexatious, they were really of no small importance. The Chiefs were not in any sense royal and in His Excellency's opinion ought not to wear royal badges. The older and better class of Chiefs did not, as a rule, assume insignia that did not appertain to them, and it was almost always the modernized and, not uncommonly, petty Chief who affected the regal pose.[65]

Clearly, therefore, Curzon's use of symbolism was not intended to encourage the princes to adopt royal insignia denoting equality of status with the British Crown.

Curzon in fact had very little respect for the princes. He found them so lacking in 'intelligence' and 'devotion to duty' that they made on the whole 'a disappointing study'.[66] Many of them exasperated the Viceroy and although in public he always claimed them as his colleagues and partners, in private his references to them were frequently caustic and critical. Nothing could infuriate Curzon in quite the same way as an Indian prince who spent more of his time travelling abroad than in his state. The Gaekwar of Baroda and the Maharaja of Pudokkottai frequently incurred his wrath in this respect, particularly the latter who by 1900 had contrived to spend a mere two years in his state since his accession in 1894. Curzon never objected if a prince wanted to visit Britain to pay 'homage to the King-Emperor' or to broaden his education.[67] What he thought unreasonable, however, was that some princes, of whom the Maharaja of Pudokkottai was a prime example, repeatedly requested permission to travel simply to indulge themselves in extravagant spending sprees at the expense of their states. Curzon objected to the frequency of foreign tours for another reason. Nothing could nauseate him more than the spectacle of what he once described as 'English ladies . . . of the highest rank' curtseying before the most insignificant princes and treating them as if they were royalty.[68] The Viceroy was driven not only to issue a circular outlining the conditions upon which a prince would be allowed to travel abroad but also to beg the question of the princes in general: 'For what are they, for the most part, but a set of unruly and ignorant and rather indisciplined schoolboys?'[69]

Under Curzon, British intervention in the internal affairs of the states reached its zenith. The Viceroy launched what was almost a personal crusade to cajole the states into adopting administrative standards which could be compared favourably with those operating in British India. Few princes gained his admiration. One who did was Maharaja Madho Rao Scindia of Gwalior, whom he described as 'much the most remarkable and promising of the native chiefs'. The reason for this esteem was that in Scindia, Curzon detected a resemblance to himself. As he remarked to Lord George Hamilton, the Secretary of State: 'In his (Scindia's) remorseless propensity for looking into everything and probing it to the bottom, he rather reminds me of your humble servant.'[70]

Curzon's policy towards the princes was based upon the following contention: 'Their duty is one, not of passive acceptance of an established place in the Imperial system, but of active and vigorous co-operation in the discharge of its onerous responsibilities.'[71] He was remorseless in his efforts to translate this principle into practice. Each year political officers were required to submit voluminous administration reports on the states under their control. These reports included discussions on the character and capacity of the princes and their advisers and their attitudes towards the government. Curzon's ultimate intention was that the Foreign Department should prepare a 'Native States Year Book' which would provide 'an index by which the normality or abnormality of any particular State in any detail of its administration might at once be tested'.[72] The proposal was never implemented but the axe still fell heavily on those who showed no signs of responding to Curzon's shock therapy. In all some fifteen princes were either forced to abdicate or temporarily deprived of their powers during his viceroyalty.[73] In this respect Curzon was concerned to bring as many states as possible under the control of the Government of India. He considered that provincial governments were frequently too distant and remote to exercise adequate control and supervision within the states for which they were responsible. The Viceroy made a personal study of the twenty states under the governments of Bengal, Madras, the North West Frontier Province and the Punjab and came to the conclusion that no less than eleven 'have been or are the subject of the gravest suspicion'. He was of the opinion that the situation was particularly serious in the Punjab. The premier Sikh prince, Maharaja Rajindra Singh of Patiala, had been allowed to drift into 'the society of stablemen, jockeys and panders of every description'. In Faridkot, the Raja had become renowned as an alcoholic and a sadist while in Malerkotla, the Nawab had been deprived of his powers only ten years after his accession on the grounds of insanity. These were extreme cases but Curzon was nevertheless convinced that 'the British administration cannot escape responsibility . . . (B)y a lack of persistence, continuity and definite principles in methods we have brought about results which we all deplore'.[74]

Unable to envisage any self-improvement in the forseeable future, Curzon believed that the British had to act to improve the calibre of the princes. He thus devised schemes intended to make them realize that there was more to life than the luxuries of the palace or extravagant sojourns in the European capitals. In July 1905 he suggested that a Council of Princes should be established. It would consist of twenty-five members selected by the Viceroy from princes who contributed Imperial Service Troops. Each member would be appointed in the first instance for three years. The Council would operate in an advisory capacity and its discussions would be strictly limited to matters connected with the Imperial Service scheme.[75] The proposal was still under consideration when Curzon resigned in November 1905. However, one of his earlier ideas did materialize before he left India. At the time of the Boer War he had suggested a cadet scheme to enable selected princes to become eligible for commissions in the Indian army. In May 1905 the Maharaja of Bhavnagar and the heir to the Maharaja of Jaipur were granted commissions having served a three year probationary period as cadets. For Curzon the primary objective of the cadet scheme was to give the princes 'an occupation in fact which will save them from the bejewelled and frivolous idleness in which they may otherwise be tempted to surrender their lives'.[76] Yet as he himself realized it would take many years to educate the princes in their responsibilities. In perhaps his most profound utterance on the states the Viceroy declared:

> There is not a day in my life in which I do not say to myself 'What is going to happen in this country 20 years, or 50 years hence?' And I say with the proudest conviction that any Viceroy or any Government that adopted the attitude of letting all these Princes and Chiefs run to their own ruin, would be heaping up immeasurable disaster in the future.[77]

By the turn of the century the British had failed to emulate the success of their Mughal predecessors in the task of integrating the Indian States within the framework of empire. In the aftermath of the mutiny, Canning's 'breakwater' thesis confirmed that the princes had potential as imperial allies but only Lytton and Curzon of subsequent Viceroys had been prepared to consider how to mobilize princely support in a positive sense. Yet even in these two distinguished cases, viceregal proposals were somewhat limited. Lytton, for all his solicitations, had been mainly concerned to buy princely support and to neutralize the armies of the states which he regarded as a security risk. Curzon had positively frowned upon any hint of equality and did not believe that the majority of princes could be entrusted with any degree of political responsibility beyond their own states. In retrospect, however, it is clear that this inveterate distrust of the princely order was not the only reason for the British failure. With their own supremacy unchallenged since the days of the mutiny, the British had not been under any pressure to contemplate a political partnership with the princes. The 'breakwater' thesis had yet to be put to the test. The alliance with the princes, if such it can be described, had thus come to be regarded more as one of administrative convenience than political necessity. In this respect the mutiny had taught the British not only that it was dangerous to interfere with indigenous religious and social customs but also that they could never aspire to replace the bonds of personal loyalty between a prince and his subjects. Sir Richard Temple, who was the Resident at Hyderabad in 1867, declared:

> The veneration felt for the person and office of the Nizam seems boundless. Though no Native Sovereigns in India can be more secluded, uninformed and even bigotted, than the successive Nizams have been; yet even these Princes must have about them some kingly qualities, some tincture of statecraft, in order to inspire awe and maintain personal prestige as they have done. The British Government can hardly hope to command sentiments of this kind.[78]

The legitimacy of the princes thus enabled them to relieve the Government of India of the responsibility of governing two-fifths of the country , and a population which was now in excess of seventy million. The Foreign Department during Curzon's viceroyalty described this relief as 'great and overwhelming' and expected that it would become 'more and more realized as time passes and the strain on the centre grows'.[79]   At the same time, however, the British remained aware that they had created a system which made it possible for the princes to be neglectful of their administrative responsiblities.[80]   The princes had therefore to be kept under surveillance to ensure that they continued to justify the guarantees and pledges which they had received from Canning in the aftermath of the mutiny. The nature and extent of the surveillance were always something of a problem. The British were frequently inconsistent, as Lord Mayo explained to a friend in England: 'To begin what must be the work of many, many years, an entire change of policy must be adopted.   The present mixture of *laissez-faire* and niggling interference must be abandoned, and the chiefs must be told what they will be allowed to do, and what they will not be allowed to do. But to commence all this, a *man* is needed.'[81] At the turn of the century, Lord Curzon evidently considered that he was the man Mayo was looking for. Curzon certainly appreciated the utility of the princes. In correspondence with Queen Victoria in September 1900 he declared himself to be 'one of those who consider that the maintenance of the Native States and of the Chiefs is essential to the durability of British rule in this country'.[82] Yet at the same time he expressed his conviction that the princes themselves were 'killing the system' and that the time would come, 'unless some higher standard is introduced, when their subjects will turn round, and implore to be relieved from the extravagance and oppression of their rulers'.[83] Thus for Curzon, unless the British maintained constant pressure to ensure that higher standards of administration were adopted in the states, the princes would cease to have any utility at all. However, the Viceroy's subsequent reflections on the effect that the adoption of these standards would have upon the status of the princes was just one of the reasons why they were never enforced.

NOTES TO CHAPTER I

[1] Descriptive note on the Indian States, 1931, PIC, 1931-50, Coll.11, File 4, No. 4.

[2] See Appendix.

[3] For an account of British relations with the Indian States at the beginning of the nineteenth century, see Edward Thompson, *The Making of the Indian Princes*, London, 1943.

[4] Descriptive note on the Indian States, 1931.

[5] Settlement operations in *Jagir* Areas in the Hyderabad State, GOI, FPD, No. 58 - Political (Secret) 1944, Nos. 1-7, Enclosure to No. 6.

[6] For an account of the conflict between Maratha overlords and Rajput feudatories in Central India, see Sir Michael O'Dwyer, *India As I knew it : 1885-1925*, London, 1925, pp. 151-155.

[7] Wilkinson to Holland, 18 May 1921, GOI, FPD, Secret-Internal, May 1922, Nos. 1-35, Enclosure to No. 3.

[8] Representative institutions of government in Indian States, PIC, 1931-50, Coll.13, File 14, part 1, No. 8182/1929.

[9] ibid.

[10] For details about the organization of the Foreign and Political Department, see Sir Harcourt Butler's note, 'Reorganisation of the Foreign Office and Political Department', 15 November 1910, Minto Collection, No. 12638; Sir Arthur Lothian's 'Note on the Foreign and Political Department of the Government of India', 1962, Lothian Collection, No. 15; and T.C. Coen, *The Indian Political Service : A Study in Indirect Rule*, London, 1971, esp. chapter eight.

[11] The reasons for the transfers are explained in more detail in chapter three, The Policy of Non-Interference, 1920-1934.

[12] Note on the Treaties with the Indian States, GOI, FPD, No. 1 - Special (Secret), 1930, Nos. 1-2, Annexure IV. The twenty states with the dates of their basic treaties were as follows: States with direct relations - Hyderabad 1800, Gwalior 1803, Kashmir 1846; Central India - Indore 1818, Bhopal 1818, Dewas Senior and Dewas Junior 1818; Rajputana - Alwar 1803, Bharatpur 1803, Dholpur 1806, Karauli 1817, Kotah 1817, Udaipur 1818, Jaipur 1818, Kishengarh 1818, Jodhpur 1818, Bundi 1818, Bikaner 1818; Bombay - Sawantwadi 1819; Punjab - Bhawalapur 1833.

[13] ibid.

[14] Sir William Lee-Warner, *The Native States of India*, revised second edition, London, 1910, p.201.

[15] ibid.

[16] The account of Mughal policy towards the Rajputs in this section is based upon A.L. Srivastava, *A Short History of Akbar the Great*, Agra, 1957, and M. Athar Ali, *The Mughal Nobility under Aurangzeb*, London, 1966.

[17] Srivastava, op. cit., pp. 24-26.

[18] ibid., pp. 44-47.

[19] ibid., p.22.

[20] Athar Ali, op. cit., pp. 22-26.

[21] ibid., pp. 95-101.

[22] Extract from Munro's letter to Lord Hastings, 12 August 1817. PP 1831-32, Vol. XIV, p. 242.

[23] ibid.

[24] Russell's evidence to the Select Committee, 21 February 1832, ibid., pp. 167-168. Russell has been a figure of some controversy. Together with other members of his family and some senior British officials, including Lord Hastings, the Governor-General, he was associated with the activities of a banking firm, William Palmer and Company, whose terms for making loans and methods of recovering them only served to increase the financial difficulties of Hyderabad. For a recent account of British relations with Hyderabad during Russell's time, see Zubaida Yazdani, *Hyderabad during the Residency of Henry Russell 1811-1820 : A Case Study of the Subsidiary Alliance System*, Oxford, 1976.

[25] Mill's evidence to the Select Committee, 16 February 1832, PP 1831-32, Vol. XIV, pp. 7-8. For an assessment of liberal attitudes towards India in general and the Indian States in particular, see Thomas R. Metcalf, *The Aftermath of Revolt : India, 1857-1870*, Princeton, New Jersey, 1965, pp. 7-15 and 30-36.

[26] Elphinstone to T.H. Villiers, 5 August 1832, PP 1831-32, Vol. XIV, p.155. Zubaida Yazdani's work on Hyderabad has tended to confirm Elphinstone's theory if not his explanation. She attributes the decline of the Nizam's state, not to the ephemeral character of an Asian government, but to the nature of the revenue system during the late Mughal empire. In her conclusion she writes '... the financial instability of Hyderabad was pre-British ... the revenue system of the State was already disorganized and the malaise produced by the disintegration of the revenue system, namely the Naiks and the Pindaris, were already raising havoc with the dilapidated economy'. Yazdani, op. cit., p.130. The Naiks were *zamindars* or landholders from Berar who had turned rebel to escape unreasonable revenue exactions.

[27] Elphinstone to T.H. Villiers, 5 August 1832, PP 1831-32, Vol. XIV, p.156.

[28] Malcolm to T.H. Villiers, 26 March 1832, ibid., pp. 136-137.

[29] ibid., p.139.

[30] Minute by Lord William Bentinck on Oude, 30 July 1831, ibid., p.405.

[31] ibid., p.404.

[32] Metcalf, op. cit., p.31.

[33] For an analysis of the annexation of Sind, see R.A. Huttenback, *British Relations with Sind 1799-1843 : An Anatomy of Imperialism*, Berkeley, 1962.

[34] Dalhousie's minute, 30 August 1848, PP 1849, Vol. XXXIX, p.83.

[35] Sleeman to Dalhousie, 24 October 1849, PP 1856, Vol. XLV, p.160.

[36] Sleeman to Dalhousie, 1848, cited in Coen, op.cit., pp. 17-18.

[37] Bishop Heber, *The Narratives of a Journey through the Upper Provinces of India from Calcutta to Bombay 1824-1825 and of a Journey to Madras and the Southern Provinces*, abridged and edited by Anthony X. Soares under the title, *India a Hundred Years Ago*, Bombay, 1944, p.63.

[38] Metcalf, op. cit., p.36.

[39] ibid., pp. 219-222.

[40] GOI, Foreign Department, Despatch No. 43A to S/S, 30 April 1860, PCI, 1792-1874, Vol. 85.

[41] The terms of the Adoption *Sanad* granted to the Gaekwar of Baroda can be found in C.H. Philips (ed.), *The Evolution of India and Pakistan 1858-1947 : Select Documents*, London, 1962, p.416.

[42] Metcalf, op. cit., pp. 222-223.

[43] GOI, Foreign Department, Despatch No. 43A to S/S, 30 April 1860.

[44] For an analysis of Canning's policy towards the princes, see B. Qanungo, 'A Study of British Relations with the Native States of India, 1858-1862', *Journal of Asian Studies*, 26 (February 1967) pp. 251-265.

[45] Lawrence to Northcote, 3 December 1867, cited in Philips (ed.), op. cit., p.417.

[46] W.W. Hunter, *A Life of the Earl of Mayo*, Vol.1, London, 1876, pp. 213-214.

[47] Cited in *Report of the Indian States Committee, 1928-1929*, Cmd.3302, 1929, para. 25. For an analysis of the Baroda case, see I.F.S. Copland, 'The Baroda Crisis of 1873-1877 : A Study of Governmental Rivalry', *Modern Asian Studies*, 2 (April 1968) pp. 97-123.

[48] Undated note by Sir Arthur Hirtzel, Assistant Under Secretary of State at the India Office, PSSF, 1902-31, File 2811/1917, No. 23228/1916.

[49] Canning to Maharaja of Mysore, 11 March 1862, PP 1866, Vol.LII, pp. 4-7.

[50] Lawrence to Maharaja of Mysore, 5 May 1865, ibid., pp.69-70.

[51] In a speech to the House of Commons in 1867 Cranbourne declared that princely rule expressed the desires and served the needs of the Indian people much better than any alternative system of government. Lawrence took serious exception to this remark. He was convinced that 'the masses of the people are incontestably more prosperous and far more happy in British territory than they are under native rulers', and submitted reports from officers serving in both the states and the provinces of British India in order to substantiate his claim. Metcalf, op. cit., pp. 234-235. Opinions expressed in the reports can be found in *Correspondence regarding the Comparative Merits of British and Native Administration in India*, Calcutta, 1867, IOL, Political and Secret Department Library, L/P & S/20/H44.

[52] GOI, FPD, Secret Letter No. 124 to S/S, 22 May 1879, PSCI, 1875-1911, Vol. 22.

[53] 'Instrument of Transfer', PP 1881, Vol. LXX, pp. 581-583.

[54] Political Dispatch No. 102 to GGC, 25 September 1879, PSCI, 1875-1911, Vol. 324.

[55] Lytton's note, 27 May 1876, GOI, Foreign Department, Secret - I, Nos. 74-76, June 1888.

[56] ibid. Lytton estimated that the states paid collectively £800,000 a year into the exchequer. He considered that this was insignificant when compared to the cost of maintaining agencies in the states and the pensions of conquered deposed families which had been reintroduced after the mutiny.

[57] Lytton to Salisbury, 11 May 1876, Lytton Collection, No. 3/1.

[58] ibid.

[59] Lytton to Disraeli, 30 April 1876, ibid.

[60] Lytton's note, 27 May 1876, loc. cit.

[61] Lytton to the Queen, 12 August 1876, Lytton Collection, No. 3/1.

[62] Note by Sir Alexander Arbuthnot, 11 July 1876, GOI, Foreign Department, Secret - I, Nos. 74-76, June 1888.

[63] Salisbury to Lytton, 10 November 1876, Lytton Collection, No. 516/1B. The Royal Titles Bill of 1876 referred to Victoria's installation as Empress of India.

[64] The idea of the Imperial Service scheme originated with Lord Randolph Churchill who was Secretary of State for India between June 1885 and February 1886. In the autumn of 1885 he suggested to Dufferin that the Government of India should pursue towards the states a military policy analogous to that of Prussia towards the South German states between 1866 and 1870. Each state would be required to maintain a stipulated force which would be frequently inspected, brigaded with British troops when on manoeuvres and armed with the latest weapons. According to Churchill this would reduce military costs, increase internal security and provide an outlet for the military aspirations of the princes which he felt had been unduly repressed since the mutiny. Briton Martin Jr. *New India, 1885 : British Official Policy and the Emergence of the Indian National Congress*, Berkeley, 1969, p.176.

[65] *Summary of the Proceedings of the Government of India in the Foreign Department during the Viceroyalty of Lord Curzon, January 1899 - November 1905 : Native States*, Calcutta : Superintendent of Government Printing, 1908, p.7, Minto Collection, No. 12589.

[66] ibid., p.50.

[67] ibid., p.9.

[68] Curzon's minute, 29 February 1904, PSCI, 1875-1911, Vol. 163, No. 694/1904.

[69] Curzon to Hamilton, 29 August 1900, Curzon Collection, No. 159.

[70] Curzon to Hamilton, 26 November 1899, Curzon Collection, No. 158.

[71] Lovat Fraser, *India Under Curzon and After*, London, 1911, p.212.

[72] *Summary of Curzon's administration*, Calcutta, 1908, pp. 39-41.

[73] ibid., p.34. The princes in question were those of Banganapalle, Banswara, Bharatpur, Bilaspur, Chamba, Indore, Jaso, Jetpur, Jodhpur, Malerkotla, Nayod, Panna, Raghugarh, Sanjeli and Tonk.

[74] ibid., pp. 48-50.

[75] ibid., p.17.

[76] Memorandum by His Excellency the Viceroy upon Commissions for Native Officers, 4 June 1900, Curzon Collection, No. 253.

[77] Curzon to Hamilton, 29 August 1900, Curzon Collection, No. 159.

[78] Temple to Wylie, 16 August 1867, Temple Collection, No. 79.

[79] Foreign Office Note on Sir William Lee-Warner's chapter on Native States for the new Imperial Gazetteer of India, PSCI, 1875-1911, Vol. 163, No. 694/1904.

[80] In 1879, when considering the restitution of Mysore to princely rule, the Lytton administration had declared: 'It is certain that this freedom from fear of the consequences of lax and injurious administration has been to some perceptible extent detrimental in its effects upon the Chiefs, upon their counsellors and officials and upon all those who are influential in the government of the states.' GOI, FPD, Secret Letter No. 124 to S/S, 22 May 1879, PSCI, 1875-1911, Vol. 22.

[81] Hunter, op. cit., Vol. 1, p.212.

[82] Curzon to the Queen, 12 September 1900, Curzon Collection, No. 135.

[83] ibid.

CHAPTER II

REMOVING THE ISOLATION: 1904-1921

The Reaction against Curzon in Britain

The first decade of the twentieth century is a landmark in the relationship between the paramount power and the Indian States. It witnessed the emergence of various factors which began gradually to reduce the subservience of the states and assign to them a much more modern and politically-orientated role within the context of the Indian Empire.

Curzon's ideas were in large part responsible for the new direction in policy towards the states. In 1902 Sir William Lee-Warner had been appointed to the India Council in London. In view of the fact that he was an expert on paramountcy with practical experience of the states[1] he became a member of the Secretary of State's Political Committee. In February 1903, Lee-Warner wrote a draft chapter for inclusion in the Imperial Gazetteer in which he made frequent use of the terms 'sovereign' and 'sovereignty' when describing the states.[2] Curzon objected because he considered that both these expressions belonged to a by-gone age. In a minute written in February 1904 the Viceroy recorded his opinion

> that of the total attributes or functions of sovereignty not only the great majority, but also many of the most vital are no longer enjoyed by the Native States and that to speak of them as sovereignties, or of their rulers as sovereigns, without any qualification, is therefore to employ language in excess of that which is justified by the fact.[3]

One of Lee-Warner's colleagues on the Political Committee, Sir Denis Fitzpatrick, had to admit that terms like sovereign, when used out of context, could give rise to some misunderstanding.[4] Sir Arthur Godley, the Under Secretary of State, agreed and revised the draft in order to give less prominence to the expression and its derivations.[5]

However, the matter did not rest there. Curzon had taken the opportunity in his minute to express his ideas on how future developments would affect the status of the princes. According to the Viceroy, the present trend of British policy would eventually lead to the extinction of the princes in their existing form. His views caused such consternation in the India Office that they merit extensive quotation here:

> For many years, therefore, it has been the practice of the Government of India to desist from the use of phrases implying a recognition of the sovereignty or sovereign rights of the Indian chiefs. In so acting the Government has not only been urging desistence from a practice that is now historically obsolete and

inapplicable, but it has been, perhaps not always with full consciousness, lending its ratification to a change of status that has been proceeding silently but uninterruptedly throughout the past half century, and which, in my judgement, will some day insensibly transform the Indian Ruling Chiefs into an aristocracy of rank and prestige, differing only from the hereditary nobility of ancient countries in the West, in the superiority of its prerogatives, dignities and wealth. If the Indian Chiefs are to be maintained as sovereigns, I doubt their capacity for permanent survival; for the exercise of the rights commonly associated with sovereignty will be found, as time passes, to be increasingly incompatible with the future development of the Indian Empire. If, on the other hand, they are preserved as Ruling Chiefs, secure in their privileges and rights, and gradually more and more associated with the Government of the Empire, they will lose nothing in public estimation or in personal prestige, while adding to the stability of the Imperial fabric. No change or departure of policy is required. It is merely essential that we should continue to go forward not back.[6]

Curzon had not completely abandoned the reasons for maintaining the states. It was not a question of abolishing them, nor was it a question of substituting British rule for Indian. The states would still be governed by hereditary rulers enjoying loyalty and respect from their subjects and they would still relieve the British of some of the burden of administration. However, Curzon's conception of the 'future development of the Indian Empire' was one in which Britain would hold India perpetually in trust. He saw his principal task as maintaining the 'rule of justice, bringing peace and order and good government'.[7] He expected those who ruled the states to do the same but his experience as Viceroy had convinced him that the majority of the princes were quite unfitted for the task. He therefore considered that unless the princes were deprived of their absolute or sovereign status, they would be incapable either of commanding the loyalty of their subjects or of assisting in the government of the country in the desired manner.

This reasoning did not appeal to Fitzpatrick in London. He thought Curzon's sentiments 'so revolutionary and so fraught with dangerous consequences' that it would be 'quite impossible for the Secretary of State to pass them over without remark'.[8] He envisaged some 'gradual and insensible process' whereby the princes would actually become 'British subjects in the proper sense'. He recognized that the extension of railways, telegraphs, canals and commerce had encroached upon the autonomy of the princes and also that the government was under a moral obligation, if it guaranteed the existence of a state, to protect the subjects of that state from gross abuses of power by its prince. He also appreciated that as 'Civilization and enlightenment extend over the whole country' the government felt more obliged to promote the administration of the states, not only by giving advice to princes but also, when a minority occurred, 'by doing our best to train the young Chief and get things in better order for him by the time he attains his majority'. However, according to Fitzpatrick this was as far as it could go: '... we have in the course of the last forty years pretty nearly reached the limit to which, if Native rule is to be maintained at all, our interference can be properly pushed'.[9] Fitzpatrick predicted dire consequences if Curzon's ideas were allowed to stand. What, he asked, would happen if there was only one sovereign in India in the form of the British Crown and the princes were reduced to nobles or aristocrats exercising some sort of hereditary office under the government:

> ... where would our responsibility for all they might do end. We should be inundated with applications to interfere in the administration of the States; we should constantly find that the Chief was doing something which, though it might not call for our interference if it was done by a ruler acting in the exercise of his own sovereign rights, could not be tolerated in a functionary acting in the name of and under the authority of His Majesty; and the ultimate result would be that we should have to put in a minister of our own choosing who would conduct the administration under the control of our political officer, the Native Chief being, for all practical purposes, placed on the shelf.[10]

Instead of easing the burden of administration, Fitzpatrick therefore believed that Curzon's ideas would witness an enormous increase in the government's own responsibilities. He suggested that the government should accept the inevitability, and indeed take advantage of the fact that 'an administration conducted by hereditary rulers of the class here in question must in most cases fall very far short in various respects of our ideas and standards'.

Of even more concern to Fitzpatrick was his prediction of the likely political impact of Curzon's ideas. He considered that it was not a question of maintaining the loyalty of the subjects of the states to their princes but rather a question of maintaining the loyalty of the princes to the British. He could hardly agree with Curzon that no policy change would be involved and believed that it would be impossible to disguise the change from the princes: 'The Chiefs and their advisers are quick to scent anything of the kind, and, even if they were not, there are persons by no means friendly to us who would be only too eager to draw their attention to it.'[11] In this respect Fitzpatrick paralleled the likely implications of Curzon's ideas with the actual consequences of those put into effect by Dalhousie. The contrast was poignant. Curzon justified his views on the grounds that it was essential to go forward not back, yet for Fitzpatrick these same views might put the clock back fifty years and result in another revolt.

Fitzpatrick's views were endorsed by the Political Committee but never officially communicated to Curzon.[12] In the past the India Office had endured many painful confrontations with the formidable incumbent of Government House and Sir Arthur Godley informed St. John Brodrick, the Secretary of State, that it 'might cause some unnecessary friction, and it is a good general principle not to send to India the comments of individuals upon papers on their way through this office, unless for some special reason'.[13] In view of the gravity of the situation expressed by Fitzpatrick it would be difficult to imagine a more special reason but no doubt the India Office consoled itself with the thought that Curzon would not be around long enough to implement his ideas. It was only when Sir Louis Dane, the Foreign Secretary to the Government of India, assumed that Curzon's minute had been approved[14] that Godley replied to the effect that the India Office did not look favourably on a policy of 'reducing the Native Princes to the status of glorified Noblemen'.[15] Clearly the India Office was now in favour of less rather than more interference in the affairs of the states. With the resignation of Curzon in November 1905 certain other factors in India meant that a beginning could be made in this direction.

The Reaction against Curzon in India

One of the most significant factors was the manner in which many British officials in India were also beginning to react against Curzon's policies towards the princes. In October 1906 the Governor of Bombay, Lord Lamington, urged the new Viceroy, Lord Minto, to 'initiate a policy of relieving them (the princes) from so much Government supervision and interference'.[16] Sir George Clarke, who succeeded Lamington in 1907, had every sympathy for the princes and singled out Sayaji Rao III, the Gaekwar of Baroda, for more favourable treatment. With the obvious exceptions of those princes who had either been forced to abdicate or deprived of their powers, Sayaji Rao had perhaps suffered more than most at the hands of the Curzon regime. A recent study of his early relationship with the Government of India has indicated that between 1881, the year of his accession, and 1904, Baroda had become one of the most progressive of the Indian States. Primary education had been made compulsory and free; local self-government had been introduced; industries had been set up with government assistance; and credit facilities in rural areas had been made available by the establishment of new banks and cooperative societies.[17] Yet despite these improvements, Sayaji Rao did not find favour with Curzon. The latter not only fulminated against the Gaekwar's frequent foreign tours but also suspected him of harbouring undue sympathy for the nationalist movement in British India. Sayaji Rao could hardly make a move in either the conduct of his personal affairs or the organization of his administration without first requiring permission from the Government of India. Clarke considered that intervention of this nature was totally unwarranted and informed Minto that if he had been in the Gaekwar's place he would have soon become 'a sturdy malcontent'.[18]

Clarke elaborated on this theme when he explained the Gaekwar's situation to John Morley who had assumed office as Secretary of State in December 1905:

I am convinced that with a man of this type, the tightened rein is unnecessary. Let him and Chiefs like him bear the full responsibility of administering their States. Our theories of the methods of handling such men are hopelessly out of date. We have educated them. They are cleverer than most of us, and they understand the natives much better than we can. Our Political Agents are as a rule intellectually far inferior to men like the Gaekwar, and one can easily fancy how the lives of the latter can be made a burden to them if the Agents are not models of tact.[19]

In pleading the Gaekwar's case, Clarke admittedly had an ulterior motive. He hoped to regain the Bombay Government's political supervision over Baroda which had been lost when one of Sayaji Rao's predecessors had been deposed in 1875.[20] However, this was by no means his only motive. He considered that the treatment of the Gaekwar was symptomatic of a more general malaise which was affecting the manner in which many British officials and civilians in India conducted themselves. Racial prejudice and arrogance appeared to be on the increase. Clarke attributed these characteristics to a fundamental sense of insecurity; to the need for the dominant race, being dependent on force and in a hopeless numerical minority, to assert itself. Totally out of sympathy with this mentality, Clarke was of the opinion that the British would feel more secure only when they began treating Indians with greater respect: '... if we could insure that no civilian, or soldier, or globetrotter should ever come to India without having the duty of courteous treatment of natives driven into his skull, some of our difficulties would, in time, disappear'.[21]

Minto fully endorsed the views expressed by Clarke. The new Viceroy utterly despised everything that his predecessor stood for. His early correspondence with Morley is littered with references to how 'intensely Curzon's egotism (I can call it nothing else) and ambitions have shed their influence over public life in India', and how much 'bitter native feeling' he had aroused.[22] In August 1906 he remarked that there had been 'far too much petty interference with the personal affairs and administrations of Native Chiefs'.[23] A year later he considered that something more serious had been involved. As if to emphasize the point made by Fitzpatrick in 1904 he wrote:

If a true history of Curzon's role is ever written, it will make the world wonder. Few people at home know the legacy of bitter discontent he left for his successor. It is only this morning that I heard of a recent conversation with Scindia in which the latter got very excited, and said that the tyranny of Curzon's rule towards the Native Chiefs had been so unbearable that nothing would have induced them to put up with it, and that they would have united together without regard to religion or caste to throw it off. And yet Curzon always posed as the greatest friend of the Native Chiefs.[24]

Allowance must be made for an element of exaggeration in Scindia's remarks. It would be difficult to imagine the princes uniting under any circumstances. Nevertheless, in view of the fact that Scindia was one of Curzon's favourites, his views are an interesting comment on the attitude of the princes towards the former Viceroy. As far as Minto was concerned, a change of policy was clearly required if the loyalty of the princes was to be maintained.

The reaction against Curzon's policies even extended to the Foreign Department which had the responsibility of supervising the states. This would have surprised Morley who believed that political officers on active service in the states were as much to blame as Curzon for the grievances of the princes. In November 1906 he asked Minto to consider addressing 'an energetic trouncing to those meddlesome gentry in your Foreign Department'. The Secretary of State was of the opinion that 'without an energetic and stern allocation of this species ... the vexatious and humiliating system, which you and I hate, will go on for ever'.[25] Sir George Clarke shared these views and considered that, with one or two exceptions, political officers were either incompetent or completely unsuitable for the delicate task of conducting relations with the princes.[26] One of the most notable exceptions was Sir David Barr, an experienced political officer who had entered the political service in 1869 and who had since served as Resident at Gwalior, Hyderabad and Kashmir. In December 1905 Barr expressed the view that during Curzon's viceroyalty, government interference in the states had been 'converted from paternal to grandmotherly action' and as such had caused a great deal of bitterness and exasperation amongst the princes.[27] Barr's views, however, were certainly exceptional; most political officers fully reflected Curzon's aggressive and dictatorial tone. What the majority were reacting against, therefore, was not so much the ideas behind Curzon's policies but his methods of implementing them, which had reduced their status and curtailed their privileges. Curzon had frequently toured the states in order to bring the princes into closer contact with the central government. Political officers had resented this because it weakened their own influence within the states. Moreover, having resolved that the princes had ceased to exercise sovereign powers, Curzon had also decided that political officers could no longer regard themselves as plenipotentiaries 'invested with ambassadorial functions or dignity'. Officers were thus no longer entitled to take advantage of easements such as housing, servants, carriages and horses which had hitherto been provided for their use by the princes at the expense of the states. When regulations to this effect were issued in July 1905 they caused widespread consternation and resentment within the political service.[28]

The reaction against Curzon's administration, however, was most evident amongst those officials who were directly responsible for the work of the Foreign Department. The Foreign Secretary, Sir Louis Dane, believed that his department was both over-worked and under-staffed. Dane attributed the increase in work to the attempts being made to improve the administrations of the states, and to what he described as the 'nearer advance of Foreign powers' which necessitated much greater care and vigilance in the conduct of India's foreign policy.[29] He produced statistical evidence to support his claims. In 1887 an official Foreign Department staff of 7, and a clerical staff of 57, had dealt with 19,704 receipts and 20,849 issues. In 1905 an official staff of 8, and a clerical staff of 90, had dealt with 36,981 receipts and 40,989 issues.[30] According to Dane, Foreign Department officials, who laboured each day for thirteen or fourteen hours, worked very much harder than their counterparts in the other departments of the Government of India. In order to relieve some of the burden he suggested that the foreign and political branches of the department should be separated and a new Foreign Member appointed to the Viceroy's Executive Council. Although he had reservations about how the princes would react, Dane also recommended transferring more states to provincial control. This was the exact opposite of what Curzon had suggested but Dane considered that the number of cases which reached his staff from the agencies and residencies, had practically turned the Foreign Department 'into a Local Government for one-third of the whole of India'.[31]

Dane was not only concerned at the demands being made of the staff within his department. He also resented the allegations that the Foreign Department was responsible for so much trifling interference in the affairs of the princes. In this respect he received support from Sir David Barr who believed that the principal responsibility lay with the Finance Department of the Government of India. The princes particularly resented interference in matters relating to expenditure within their states which were always referred to the Finance Department. Barr was of the opinion that finance officials were causing unnecessary offence by not only rejecting many of the princes' requests but also by dispatching their orders in a 'stringent and peremptory form'. The villain of the piece was Edward N. Baker, the Finance Member of the Viceroy's executive: 'According to his ideas every State should be rolled and flattened out until it resembles in every particular a district in Lower Bengal'.[32] Minto was inclined to agree with Barr, and confided to Morley that interference in the financial affairs of the princes had become 'a sort of hobby of Baker's'.[33] The Viceroy reported two cases that he had come across. In the first, the government of Patiala had proposed to reward an old European retainer for many years of loyal service by increasing his wage and providing him with a free house. The proposal had been rejected by the Finance Department on the grounds that the retainer was already receiving a British pension for army service. In the second, the Begum of Bhopal had made a request to employ an Indian official in her revenue department. The Finance Department rejected the request despite the fact that it had been supported by the Resident at Bhopal, the AGG for Central India and the Lieutenant-Governor of Bengal.[34] Minto overruled both these decisions and had little difficulty in explaining to Morley why they had been made: 'It is the result of a system for which, I believe, Curzon was largely answerable. Putting myself in the position of a Native Chief I should consider it unbearable.'[35]

Curzon himself once remarked that he would be 'very surprised' if his policy towards the states was received with 'anything but approbation'.[36]   Nothing could have been further from the truth. Many of his policies were doubtless well-intentioned but they had been pursued with complete absence of tact and diplomacy which was so characteristic of the former Viceroy. His methods created such widespread revulsion that a change of policy had become inevitable. The extent of the change and indeed the timing of the new policy were to be determined by developments in British India.

A New Policy and a Political Role Defined

The five years of Minto's viceroyalty were dominated by the growth of militant nationalism in Bengal and Western India. Curzon had done much to inflame this movement by partitioning Bengal in 1905. In an atmosphere heavily charged by bombings and assassinations the British, for the first time since the mutiny, found themselves under serious challenge. The growth of extremism, however, was not only a threat to the British; it was also a challenge to the essentially moderate policies of the early Indian National Congress.   Morley recognized the quandary of the position of the moderates in the Congress and urged the need to conciliate them in order 'to draw the teeth of the extremists'.[37] Minto appreciated the need but did not share Morley's confidence that the Congress could become 'a power for good'.[38] Accordingly he sought more loyal allies and found the princes to be one of the likely possibilities. As early as May 1906 the Viceroy was contemplating 'a possible counterpoise to Congress aims'. He suggested a 'Council of Princes, or an elaboration of that idea; a Privy Council not only of Native Rulers, but of a few other big men to meet say once a year for a week or a fortnight'.[39] It was during the five years of Minto's viceroyalty, especially after January 1908 when Harcourt Butler became Foreign Secretary to the Government of India, that some British officials began seriously to consider the princes as counterweights to the forces of Indian nationalism. As Butler himself remarked: 'We are only, I take it, at the beginning of an anti-British movement which is a permanent factor now in Indian politics. Surely it is beyond measure important to strengthen the position of the chiefs and attach them to our side.'[40] Henry Vere Cobb, who became Resident at Baroda in 1909 at a time when the British were once again expressing doubts as to where the Gaekwar's true loyalties lay, was even more explicit: 'The ruling chiefs exist by our sufferance: and any attack upon us is an attack upon them. If we go under they will go under with us.'[41] Many princes did in fact identify themselves strongly with the imperial cause during the troubles associated with the partition of Bengal. The Government of India and the Bombay government co-operated with the Maharaja of Kolhapur in attempting to replace Brahmins, whom the British equated with extremism, by Marathas and other non-Brahmins in the administration of his state.[42] Such efforts led in August 1909 to an exchange of letters between Minto and some leading princes on methods of suppressing sedition.[43]

Yet despite the advice and support rendered by the princes, it would take time before old traditions could be dissipated. This was clearly illustrated by the discussions which took place on Minto's ideas of a council of princes or notables. A reforms committee appointed by the Viceroy in August 1906 recommended either a council consisting mainly of princes with a few selected magnates from British India, or alternatively a council consisting of more magnates than princes, the object of which would be to bring the government into closer touch 'with native opinion of the best sort'.[44] When he received the report Minto began to express reservations about the political utility of a council of this nature. It would either suffer from lack of material for discussion or grow into a 'political force' likely to hamper the work of the imperial and provincial legislative councils.[45] Most members of the Viceroy's executive were inclined to agree with him.   Only Lord Kitchener, the Commander-in-Chief, favoured a Council of Princes on the grounds that the collective influence of the princes in support of the government would 'carry great weight and give confidence to large numbers of the loyal population who now probably only see the one-sided statements of agitators in the local native press'.[46] Kitchener's views contrasted sharply with those of Sir Denzil Ibbetson, the Lieutenant-Governor of the Punjab, who believed that it would be dangerous to allow the princes to confer because it might encourage them to unite against the government.[47] Morley shared this concern: 'What would the Council discuss?   What power of directing or influencing the executive?   How far could they be allowed to look into the secrets of government?   Would they not try to find them out?   In your Foreign Department, they would be sure to try for a finger in the pie?'[48]

However, at a time when reforms under consideration for British India contemplated extending the composition and powers of the existing legislatures, the authorities in India were convinced that a gesture had to be made in recognition of the loyalty of the aristocracy.   Accordingly, in March 1907 the Government of India recommended the establishment of a Council of Nobles consisting of between forty and fifty members of whom about ten or twelve would be leading princes.   The Council would not have legislative powers, nor would its proceedings be published.   It would function as an advisory and consultative body on a variety of matters including Imperial Service Troops, commissions in the army for the aristocracy, the development of education, social questions such as the reform of infant marriage and the position of widows, boundary disputes and disputed successions in the states.[49]   But again objections were raised.   The princes of the more important states, particularly Hyderabad, Mysore and Baroda, refused to contemplate sitting with lesser princes or magnates whom they considered inferior in status.[50] Moreover, many political officers could not see the point of giving the princes a voice in the administration of the country and argued that they could themselves provide the necessary information just as well as a Council of Nobles.[51] Running out of options, Minto, in the summer of 1908, reverted to his original proposal of a Council of Princes 'small in number to begin with, to deal with questions affecting Native States and their relations with British India, for the express purpose of recognizing the loyalty of Ruling Chiefs and enlisting their interest in imperial affairs'.[52]

Morley's intervention in October 1908 finally resolved the argument. The Secretary of State now considered that the practical difficulties of accommodation and precedence, together with the expense that would be involved, stood in the way of instituting a Council of Princes. He did not reject the idea outright and was prepared to allow it a trial if, after consultation with the leading princes, the Government of India was able to devise an acceptable and workable scheme. Minto was only too ready to accept this decision. In wrestling with the complexities of the reforms for British India, he admitted that a Council of Princes would 'want more organisation than I can find time for'.[53] Moreover, the Viceroy also revealed that 'in the early days' he had thought the proposal 'faddy' and had only supported it in deference to the wishes of a handful of the princes in favour of a council, and led by Scindia, whose name had previously been mentioned in connection with the question of an Indian member for the Viceroy's executive.[54] This in itself was not without significance. The contrast between Scindia's attitude and that of the rulers of the other great states of Hyderabad, Mysore and Baroda, demonstrates how concern for prestige and status could make it difficult for the princes to exert collective pressure on the government.

Yet in one respect the princes did make a substantial, though not immediate, gain from Minto's viceroyalty. A trend began to emerge which subsequently assumed enormous significance, not only for the princes and their states, but also for the future relationship between the states and the Government of India. With the appointment of Harcourt Butler to succeed Dane at the Foreign Department in January 1908, Curzon's ideas were officially discarded and replaced by an entirely new policy of non-interference.

Butler's appointment was surrounded by controversy. The new Foreign Secretary had entered the Indian Civil Service in 1888 and had reached the position of Deputy Commissioner at Lucknow in the United Provinces before being called upon to take charge of the Foreign Department. He could not therefore qualify for the position upon the basis of his seniority. Moreover, he had no previous experience of either the states or frontier matters. His appointment took many senior political officers on active service in the states completely by surprise and they greeted it with displays of open hostility. Letters of complaint and protest flooded into the office of James Dunlop Smith, Minto's private secretary. Claude Hill, the Resident at Udaipur, described the appointment as 'a slur on us all',[55] while the AGG in Rajputana, Elliott Colvin, felt that it would 'deal a blow to the Department from which it would take long to recover'.[56] Hill and Colvin frankly admitted that they resented the manner in which an outsider of inferior status had been promoted to a position which they themselves coveted. Hill wrote to Dunlop Smith: 'I had hoped that I might, one day, be selected'.[57] He was so offended that he even requested a transfer back to service in the provinces. He had joined the Foreign Department from Bombay in 1897 and he could now see no future in a career as a political officer.[58] Similarly, Colvin complained that he was being ignored and overlooked. His career in the Foreign Department spanned eighteen years during which time he had served at Mysore, Kashmir and Baluchistan in addition to his present position in Rajputana.[59] Commenting on these reactions, Sir George Clarke wrote to Morley in Feburary 1908: 'The appointment of Butler raised rather a storm among the Olympians, the idea that certain personages have prescriptive rights to certain posts being unfortunately rampant in India'.[60] Indeed it was this that so annoyed Minto. He described a letter from Sir Arthur McMahon, the AGG in Baluchistan, which asserted that the appointment should have been made from within the political service,[61] as 'a downright piece of impertinence'.[62] As far as the Viceroy was concerned, the field of selection was not confined to any particular department and thus he could choose his Foreign Secretary from anywhere within the civil service.[63]

Minto had his own reasons for appointing Butler. He described him as 'undoubtedly the best coming man in India'.[64] Butler had risen to prominence in 1906 as a result of a pamphlet he had written entitled *Oudh Policy: The Policy of Sympathy*. Here he had echoed Lytton by expressing the view that 'the masses of the people are neither political nor capable of politics: they require a mediator between their rulers and themselves; and this mediator they find in the landed aristocracy'.[65] Butler now had the opportunity of applying his earlier experience with the *talukdars* or landlords of the United Provinces to the princes at national level. He was convinced that it was essential to 'throw the weight of the Chiefs upon the conservative side' in the struggle against the nationalists in British India.[66] Moreover, he rapidly came to the conclusion that the British could learn a great deal from the princes and that there was much to be said in favour of their systems of government and administration:

> The indigenous system of Government is a loose despotic system tempered by corruption, which does not press hard on the daily lives of the people and relies for its sanctions on occasional severe punishments of erring or offending individuals. Our system is a scientific system which presses steadily on the people in their daily lives, controls them, regulates their actions, attempts to be preventive and through its hordes of subordinates makes itself everywhere felt ... he would be a bold man who said that our system was always the better. And my own belief is that we shall see some reaction of ideas. A system which would maintain the simpler executive form of Government and adopt independent judicial courts would suit most States very well.[67]

With such obvious sympathies for the Indian aristocracy, Butler was eminently suited for the task of revising Curzon's policies.

The new Foreign Secretary began his work with an administrative reorganization of his department. As Dane had suggested, he separated the foreign and political branches and proceeded to appoint two deputy secretaries to take charge of these sub-divisions.[68] In order to reduce the amount of work Minto had already discontinued the practice of requiring political officers to submit detailed administration reports on the states and personal reports on the princes and their advisers. Butler took this principle a significant step further. He strongly believed that much depended on political officers being able to establish harmonious personal relationships with the princes. He was therefore of the opinion that the most important princes should always be consulted when political appointments in the states were under consideration. To justify this he declared: 'If the Political Officer is acceptable to the Chief, the ideal of political work can be realized, viz., *that we do not want to settle questions we want questions not to arise.*'[69] Butler's ideal became the kernel of the new policy of non-interference which was to be adopted towards the princes and their states. Minto unveiled the new policy in a speech at Udaipur in November 1909 during the course of which he declared:

> The Governor-General in Council is opposed to anything like pressure on Durbars to introduce British methods of administration. He prefers that reforms should emanate from the Durbar, and grow up in harmony with the traditions of the State. Administrative efficiency is at no time the only or indeed the chief object to be kept in view. This should be specially borne in mind by officers charged temporarily with the administration of a State during a minority, whether they are in sole charge, or associated with a State Council. They occupy a position of peculiar trust, and should never forget that their primary duty is the *conservation* of the customs of the State.[70]

Minto's speech was based upon the contents of a new Political Department Manual which had been prepared for the guidance of political officers by Butler and his colleagues in the Foreign Department.[71] The manual contained instructions which stood in marked contrast to Curzon's ideas. Basically they consisted of a series of do's and don'ts in which the latter heavily outweighed the former. Political officers were not to interfere between the princes and their subjects, they were not to encourage petitions from the latter against the former, and they were not to inspect the administrations of the states except at the wishes of the princes. Ideally, political officers 'should leave well alone; the best work of a Political Officer is very often what he has left undone'.[72] Interference could only be contemplated in cases of gross misrule, and

> It may be stated generally that unless misrule reaches a pitch which violates the elementary laws of civilization, the Imperial Government will usually prefer to take no overt measures for enforcing reform: and in any case the attempt to reform should, as long as is possible, be confined to personal sausion.[73]

Butler's ideas of non-interference also led him to support the principle of direct relations between the states and the Government of India. His reasoning, however, differed significantly from that of Curzon in that it was based upon the theory of reducing rather than increasing government influence in the states. In this respect Butler further proposed that the size of the political establishments which were maintained in those states already in direct relations with the Government of India should be cut. He considered that there were too many political officers serving in the great states of Hyderabad and Mysore and that economies could be effected in the agencies of Central India and Rajputana. The success of his new policy appeared to be dependent upon these reductions: 'If offices are left top-heavy, the policy of non-interference will never be completely carried out.' Butler envisaged that ultimately it would be possible to operate upon the basis of one senior political officer for every state or grouping of states with only one personal assistant.[74]

Various motives had led to the adoption of a policy of non-interference. It had been deemed necessary to reduce the demands being made of the Foreign Department and to relieve the princes of so much vexatious supervision in the conduct of their domestic affairs. Above all, however, the policy had been designed to ensure that the princes would serve as loyal and willing allies in the struggle against nationalism in British India. Despite their reluctance to grant constitutional recognition by establishing a Council of Princes, the British had finally entered into a political partnership with the princes. Yet the adoption of the new policy did not mean that it would become immediately applicable. Both Minto and Butler realized that most political officers were still imbued with the Curzonian spirit. The Viceroy in fact suspected that their opposition to the idea of a Council of Nobles had been influenced by the fear that their direct authority over the princes would be minimized.[75] In a memorandum written for his successor when he resigned to become Education Member of the Viceroy's executive at the end of 1910, Butler admitted that the new policy had already offended the feelings of 'some sensitive officers', but he also expressed the hope that they would be able to adjust and thereby 'gain more by personal influence than they have lost in merely official authority'.[76] In private, however, Butler was anticipating something rather different. As he confided to his mother: 'We are slowly introducing a new spirit, but the real change will come with a change of generation. The leopard cannot change its spots.'[77] Only time would tell, therefore, whether or not the new policy would enable the princes to fulfil the expectations that the British had of them.

Princely Representations and British Responses

The reappraisal of government policy towards the states during Minto's viceroyalty was accompanied by an equally significant development among the princes. A new type of prince, increasingly anglicized in outlook and social habits, began to emerge. Curzon's administration had done much to stimulate this development. In attempting to foster a new sense of responsibility among the princes, Curzon was largely responsible for dismantling the traditional barriers of isolation which had prevented a prince from having an outlook wider than the narrow confines of his own state. He considered that the colleges which had been established in the 1870s and 1880s to educate the sons of the princes had failed not only to produce the desired results but also to inspire confidence in the princes themselves. He assembled two educational conferences, in January 1902 and March 1904, in order that the colleges could be constituted 'not to prepare for examinations, but to prepare for life'.[78] Curzon's influence certainly stimulated a revival of interest. Enrolment at the Mayo College, Ajmer, rose from 60 in 1902 to 143 in 1906. Between 1905 and 1906 there was an increase from 33 to 50 at the Daly College, Indore, and an increase from 64 to 83 at the Aitchison College, Lahore.[79] The system did produce some capable princes like Ganga Singh, the Maharaja of Bikaner, who was a product of the Mayo College. However, the Viceroy's ambitions did not materialize exactly as he would have liked. Of Ganga Singh he remarked: 'The young ruler has charming manners, and I believe an excellent disposition, but he is thoroughly Anglicized in taste and habits, - almost too much so for my conception of what a Native Chief should be.'[80]

The development of these new princes reveals one of the greatest ironies of Curzon's administration. If Ganga Singh did not represent his conception of what a prince should be, who did? Scindia stood highest in his esteem, but as we have seen his regard for this prince was based upon conceit. Moreover, it is unlikely that Curzon could have tolerated too many replicas of himself. In fact Maharaja Madho Singh, who ruled Jaipur from 1880 to 1922 came closest to his definition of an Indian prince:

> He is one of the old-fashioned class of Princes whom I do everything in my power to encourage - conservative, reluctant to move away from their own States, liberal in the distribution of their funds, intensely loyal to the Queen and the British connection, adverse to being too much bothered or fussed, but capable, if skilfully and sympathetically handled, of being guided where we will.[81]

Basically, therefore, Curzon's conception of a prince was one who would remain in his state - 'his real work, his princely duty, lies among his own people' - and one who would, above all, bend before a superior British will.

Many of Curzon's policies, however, produced the exact opposite. No doubt the Viceroy intended that the younger element among the princes would be able to combine careers as army officers with the necessary administrative duties in their states. Yet all too often they did neither, preferring to idle their time in their capitals while accumulating purely honorary military distinctions. Moreover, a number of princes who had been educated at the colleges emerged from adolescence with an increasing awareness of the arbitrary manner in which they were treated. As far as Ganga Singh was concerned it soon became apparent that he would never prove amenable to 'being guided where we will'. Early in his career his autocracy matched the efficiency of Scindia's but as he grew older he became more concerned that the guarantees of his treaty rights and privileges should be fully maintained and respected.

In addition to Ganga Singh, the leading members of this new breed of prince were Jey Singh, the Maharaja of Alwar, Bhupinder Singh, the Maharaja of Patiala, and Ranjit Sinhji, the Jam Sahib of Nawanagar. Until 1921, Scindia could be counted amongst their number. They were an odd assortment and presented many contrasts: Bikaner, dignified and sophisticated; Patiala, petulant and temperamental; Alwar, a brillant intellectual, but devious and sly; Nawanager, a sportsman who made a name for himself as a Test cricketer; finally, Scindia, one of the first to voice the grievances of the princes and to represent their interests. Although he was one of only four princes entitled to a salute of twenty-one guns, Scindia felt awkward and ill at ease in the company of these newcomers. As a Maratha of humble origin, he cowered before Alwar and Bikaner, two blue-blooded princes from Rajputana. When out riding he kept a respectful two lengths behind Alwar, even though as Butler remarked, the size and wealth of his state meant that he could 'buy him out many times over'.[82] For all their differences, however, what these princes shared in common was a greater consciousness of their rights and privileges, an ability to converse with senior British officials and the opportunity to do so: their states were all within relatively easy travelling distance of New Delhi, the capital of British India since 1912.

The forceful and energetic Ganga Singh of Bikaner soon emerged as the principal spokesman and greatest celebrity of this group. He had suffered badly at the hands of the Foreign Department during his early years. Upon his investiture in 1898, he had been given to understand that restrictions on his ruling powers would remain in force for two years only. However, it was not until May 1907 that these restrictions were finally removed.[83] Moreover, Bikaner's first experience of a political officer left a profound impression upon him. From 1888 to 1897 he was confronted with the formidable Sir Charles Stuart Bayley who had a habit of demanding reports on selected petitions from state subjects. When Bikaner protested Bayley informed him:

> You must remember that though I have the pleasure of being your personal friend, I am also your Political Agent and as such have duties to perform, of which I and my superior officers are the only judges, and which cannot be neglected even though they unfortunately clash with your notions of what a Political Officer should do.[84]

Bikaner subsequently spent the best part of his political career attempting to ensure that such a situation would not be repeated elsewhere. This, however, was not his only concern. During the

viceroyalty of Lord Hardinge, who succeeded Minto in November
1910, Bikaner expressed his concern that the proposal for a Council
of Princes should have been rejected while an instalment of British
Indian reform had been introduced by the Indian Councils Act of
1909. He believed that these reforms had unleashed an 'unskilled
democracy' and felt that there was 'more than a possibility of its
eventually becoming intolerant and unsympathetic with those who
have a real stake in the land and in the good government of the
country as has happened elsewhere throughout the world'. To have
excluded the states from the government of the Empire was,
according to Bikaner, fraught with danger for Britain's allies: 'We do
not wish to become mere puppets and share the fate of some of the
European aristocracies.' Moreover, without the states 'the whole
Government of India might sink to a drab dead level of democracy
without any of the interest or distinction that is suited to the
instincts and imagination of the people'. Bikaner did not advocate the
immediate establishment of a Council of Princes. Indeed in view of
the possible British Indian reaction he considered that this would be
'both impolitic and undesirable'. Instead he recommended that before
the Imperial Legislative Council reached a decision on any matter
'even remotely affecting the states', the princes should assemble in
order that their views be known first.[85]

Hardinge thought Bikaner's fears exaggerated and that his note
contained 'a good deal of rubbish'.[86] John Wood, the first Political
Secretary to be appointed when the Foreign Department became the
Foreign and Political Department in January 1914, echoed these
sentiments and could not envisage the time when the princes would
be able to take part in the 'regular machinery of Government'.[87] The
Viceroy, however, could see no harm in the princes discussing some
'anodyne' question affecting themselves and their interests only and
cited the example of the management of states during minorities.[88]
The minorities issue subsequently became the most significant part of
Hardinge's viceroyalty as far as the states were concerned.

In December 1915, Scindia informed the Viceroy that although
political officers had used minority periods to remove long-standing
abuses and improve the finances of the states, their methods had
'shaken the adherence of the people to their traditional customs and
ways'. He considered that minorities had therefore worked to alter
the ties of personal loyalty and obedience between the subjects and
their prince when the latter entered upon his inheritance.[89] Hardinge
felt these complaints were not entirely groundless and considered
that a clear and detailed study of British policy was required in order,
not only to allay the suspicion which existed in the minds of some of
the princes, but also to lay down principles for the future guidance of
the government.[90] To undertake this task, he appointed a committee
consisting of the Maharajas of Bikaner and Gwalior, the Begum of
Bhopal, Wood and two other political officers. The committee sat at
Delhi in February 1916 and recorded their recommendations in a
memorandum which was subsequently communicated to the more
important princes in Central India and Rajputana. The most
significant recommendation was that which declared that any

measure introduced during a minority 'will be liable to revocation by the minor Ruler at any time after he obtains his full powers'.[91] The contents of the memorandum were obviously welcomed by those princes to whom it was communicated but, as we shall see, this was not the case with certain members of the Secretary of State's India Council.

In April 1916 Lord Chelmsford replaced Hardinge as Viceroy. The change was accompanied by a further reappraisal of the Government of India's policy towards the states. The issue this time concerned an assemblage of princes. In May 1916, in sharp contrast to his earlier opinion, Wood recommended that a Council of Princes should be established. He was impressed by the possibilities of gatherings such as the committee which had discussed the minorities issue. They were not only welcomed by the princes, but were also of the greatest value to the Viceroy and the Political Department in that they served as a 'safety valve through which minor grievances find a harmless vent, and tend to prevent subterranean communications behind the backs of Political Officers which are a source of danger to our administration'. Above all, however, the response and contribution made by the princes to the allied war effort during the struggle with Germany had firmly entrenched them in the imperial camp.[92] Wood was anxious that nothing should happen to dislodge them:

> ... it is recognized on all hands that the collective goodwill and support of the Ruling Chiefs is an Imperial asset of incalculable value. If the growing demand for collective discussion is disregarded, we run the risk of alienating the sympathies of those whose support is most worth having.

The constitution, functions and procedures of Wood's Council were not to be embodied in a formal document; the Council would be of a purely advisory character with no statutory powers. Its main purpose would be to strengthen the hands of the Viceroy by enlisting the collective support of the princes in any measure which the paramount power wished to take in connection with the affairs of the states.[93]

When placed before Chelmsford's Executive Council, Wood's proposal received only qualified approval. The reservations expressed ten years earlier by Ibbetson and Morley had by now disappeared but Minto's still remained: it was felt that a Council dealing only with the states would suffer from lack of material for discussion. To compensate for this it was suggested that a Council of Princes should be more closely co-ordinated with other constitutional and political developments then under consideration for British India.[94] Yet it was for this very reason that a Council could not be immediately contemplated. Chelmsford, it has been shown, claimed to have decided in 1915 that British rule in India was 'aimless' and characterized by a 'hand-to-mouth policy of giving reforms piecemeal in response to agitation'. At the first meeting of his executive in May 1916, the Viceroy therefore posed the following two questions:

(1) What is the ultimate goal of British rule in India?
(2) What are the first steps on the road to that goal?[95]

Until answers could be found to these two questions it would not be possible to institute a Council of Princes.

In recognition of the princes' war services, however, a less ambitious scheme of association did receive official endorsement. At Delhi on 30 October 1916, Chelmsford presided over the first session of a Conference of Ruling Princes and Chiefs. Present were nine representatives from the Bombay states, six from the Punjab, eleven from Central India, ten from Rajputana, and the Maharajas of Kashmir, Cochin, Cooch-Behar and Benares. The rulers of the important states of Hyderabad, Mysore and Udaipur abstained, although on this occasion the Gaekwar of Baroda decided to attend. The most important discussion related to the minorities issue and the conference unanimously endorsed the recent memorandum on the subject.[96]

This aspect of the conference, however, disturbed certain members of the India Council in London. It emerged that when the Government of India had circulated the minorities memorandum in 1916, it had not sought approval from the Secretary of State, Austen Chamberlain.[97] Moreover, the Government of India had, according to one member of Council, committed a grave error in drawing up such a document. This was none other than Sir Charles Stuart Bayley, Bikaner's former political agent.[98] Bayley argued that in the past the government had avoided tying its own hands by refusing to define the principles of its policy towards the states. The doctrine of paramountcy was subject to change and growth and thus the principles involved in any one policy had always been kept as elastic as possible. He was quick to point out that both Bikaner and Gwalior had 'axes of their own to grind', and took particular exception to the idea that a prince could rescind a minority measure on assuming his full powers. Revenue settlements, where none previously existed, were invariably the first reforms undertaken during minorities, and to Bayley it was ridiculous that the Government of India would now allow these measures to be rescinded.[99]

The Under Secretary of State, Sir Thomas Holderness, while appreciative of Bayley's views, was also more sympathetic towards the Government of India. He considered that the loyalty of the princes during the war might not have been so effectively secured had a stiff attitude been adopted as regards the prerogatives of the paramount power during minorities. Moreover, he believed there was another side to the argument that relations with the states were subject to change and growth. The altered outlook and education of the princes and their greater knowledge of the power of concerted action made it desirable for the paramount power to absolve itself of something of the claim that its agents should be free to act untrammelled by rules:

> Intelligent men who can cite particular instances in which the occasion of a minority has been utilized by an energetic political to reform the State, and who ask that definite rules should be laid down, expect more than a bare assurance that the Paramount Power will always seek the well-being of its feudatories.[100]

Yet it was precisely the arguments of his Under Secretary that disturbed Chamberlain. Princes like Bikaner and Scindia now seemed to be emphasizing their claims to complete internal independence at the expense of the prerogatives of the paramount power. This tendency caused Chamberlain to make the following important statement on the relations subsisting between Britain and the states:

> In the scrupulous maintenance of our treaty obligations nothing less than the honour of the Sovereign is involved, and no Government could ever seek to belittle them. The relations of the Government with the Chiefs are, however, necessarily subject to variation, and the literal fulfilment of an obligation may become impossible, either through change in essential circumstances, or by the mere passage of time. Again, many of the treaties were concluded before the Crown stood forth in Lord Canning's phrase - the unquestioned Ruler and Paramount Power in all India; and since that event considerations of the general good of the Indian body politic have necessarily become a new factor in their interpretation. While they remain unrepealed in the letter and binding in the spirit, a constant development of constitutional doctrine is in process ... But of that process the superintendence, direction and control must remain in the hands of the Paramount Power.[101]

The Government of India was subsequently obliged to revise the minorities memorandum and omit that section which enabled a prince to rescind a minority measure.[102] It was also advised to furnish the India Office with copies of the agenda for any future conferences. Controversial or objectionable subjects would henceforth be censored.

The minorities issue, however, had more far-reaching implications. Much to Bayley's disappointment, Chamberlain's statement did not mean that the Government of India would have to abandon its non-interference policy. What it did mean was that the Secretary of State considered it impossible to define paramountcy in accordance with the principles of this policy. Yet for princes like Bikaner, Alwar, Patiala and the Jam Sahib, this was the most objectionable feature of their relationship with the Raj. They persistently argued that paramountcy required definition and that this should accord with the principles of non-interference. Moreover, they justified their argument by referring, not to Butler's policy - history had taught them to be wary of the durability of British policies - but to what they considered were everlasting guarantees in their treaties and *sanads*. The ensuing struggle between these princes and the Government of India becomes intelligible only when these two conflicting viewpoints are recognized.

Constitutional Recognition:
The Establishment of a Chamber of Princes

In 1917 many princes viewed the prospect of a further instalment of

British Indian reform with similar apprehensions to those expressed by Bikaner three years earlier. Bikaner himself, however, responded to the situation in a very different way during the first few months of 1917. In order not only to gain sympathy for princely aspirations but also to prove that the states were not obstacles to the political progress of their neighbours, he now openly advocated an adequate measure of British Indian reform. In April 1917, when in London as a participant of the Imperial War Cabinet and Conference, he presented Chamberlain with a note outlining the basic reforms which should be granted to British India. In addition to the 'desirability of greater autonomy being granted to the Government of India as well as to the Provincial Governments . . .', he stressed the 'extreme importance' of an authoritative declaration that 'self-government within the British Empire is the object and goal of British rule in India'.[103]

Bikaner's activities in this respect disturbed Chelmsford. In February 1917 the Viceroy had written to Chamberlain asking him to warn Bikaner against 'holding out encouragement to the political extremists'.[104] In May 1917 the Secretary of State had a long interview with Bikaner and pointed out that just as the states resented any interference by the Government of India in their internal affairs, so the states must reciprocate by refraining from any interference in the affairs of British India. He also warned Bikaner that if the type of reforms he advocated became effective, the Government of India would become more interfering as it became more popular and claim a right of control over the states far in excess of that at present exercised.[105]

The interview left a profound impression upon Bikaner. As early as January 1914 he had envisaged that in the future a 'Federal Chamber representative of the states - and if necessary through the Governors and the Lieutenant-Governors, who could sit with the Ruling Chiefs, the Provinces of British India as well - would gradually grow up with at first advisory functions only'.[106] Henceforth he would only contemplate such an arrangement if the princes received constitutional guarantees that they would remain free from Government of India interference.

In July 1917, fresh impetus was given to the reform movement by a change of personnel at the India Office. Criticism of the Government of India's handling of the Mesopotamian campaign during the war caused Chamberlain to resign. On 20 August 1917 his successor, Edwin Montagu, issued a statement to the effect that 'the progressive realization of responsible government in India as an integral part of the British Empire', was the declared aim of British policy in India.[107]

The reference to 'India' was pertinent, although at the time a mistake. It was inconceivable that responsible government was to be the declared aim for the Indian States. This was meant to apply only to British India, although by implication, the wording of the declaration did indicate that for the first time the problem of the states was to be identified with the political progress of the rest of the country.[108] The significance of this aspect of the declaration was not lost upon the participants of the Conference of Ruling

Princes and Chiefs, a second session of which was held at Delhi in November 1917. Bikaner declared that 'No scheme for the progress of India can be regarded as satisfactory or complete which does not take into consideration questions relating to those important territories outside British India.' Heeding Chamberlain's warning, he disavowed any intention of encroaching upon the affairs of British India and asked only that the states by consulted on matters of 'Imperial or common concern'. To enable the states to keep pace with British India he suggested the early establishment of a 'constitutional Chamber which may safeguard the interests and rights of ourselves and our States'.[109] In reply, Chelmsford said that it might be possible to arrange for an informal discussion with the princes towards the end of Montagu's forthcoming visit to India and suggested in the meantime that they frame the outlines of a scheme on the subject of their political future.[110]

Had it not been for Montagu, Chelmsford would have been at a loss on how to proceed with the princes. In February 1917, Bikaner had requested of the Viceroy that the princes be given land grants in India or in conquered German territory abroad, as rewards for their war services as had been done in appreciation of princely support during the mutiny. In forwarding the request to Chamberlain the Viceroy admitted: 'The position today may be as important as that at the close of the mutiny, but it differs *in toto*, inasmuch as while at that time we had land to give away, today we have none. The truth is we are in a great quandary so far as the chiefs are concerned.'[111] Montagu, however, had previous experience of the princes and their aspirations. He had toured India as Under Secretary of State during the cold weather of 1912-13. The frequent visits he made to the states left him with two impressions. First, he considered the westernized type of prince to be amongst the most distinguished personalities in India and counted Jey Singh of Alwar as his favourite.[112] Secondly, he utterly despised the pompous and overbearing manner of many political officers and held them primarily responsible for the princes' complaints.[113] He found nothing to alter these impressions during his second tour of India from November 1917 to April 1918. Moreover, although he subsequently recognized that democratic and nationalistic 'hopes and aspirations may overleap frontier lines like sparks across a street',[114] the Secretary of State appeared indifferent to the fact that most states were years behind British India in the quality of their administrative systems. His sole concern was to avoid any possibility of estranging the princes: 'Our business ... is to refrain from interference and to protect the States from it.'[115]

The outline of a scheme on the political future of the states that Chelmsford had requested was produced by a committee of princes consisting of Bikaner, Alwar, Patiala and the Jam Sahib of Nawanagar. These four began by asserting that the 'Treaty rights, position as Sovereign Princes and Allies, and the dignity and honour and privileges and prerogatives of the Ruling Princes shall be maintained intact and strictly safeguarded'. To achieve this they recommended the establishment of a 'Chamber of Ruling Princes', and advocated that all states should be placed in direct relations with the Government of India. In addition, an 'Advisory Board' of four princes would be created to advise the Political Department on all matters concerning the states. 'Judicial Tribunals' would be appointed to determine inter-state disputes or disputes between a state and the Government of India and the case for depriving a prince of his ruling powers was to be investigated by a 'Commission of Enquiry'. Finally, there was to be a 'Committee of Reference for matters of Joint Interest' composed of representatives nominated by the Chamber of Princes and an equal number selected by the Government of India from the appropriate legislature. The committee envisaged that when the provincial governments had reached the same level of internal autonomy as the states, the only satisfactory solution to the problem of common interests would 'probably' be a 'confederation' of provinces and states.[116]

The sum total of these proposals indicates that the major concern of the four princes was to gain protection from the arbitrary use of paramountcy. Closely allied to this was the recognition that if they could consolidate their rights against the existing bureaucratic machinery of the Government of India, then they would be in a stronger position to resist any future challenge to these rights should the government become more popular. Furthermore, although they wanted an effective voice in matters of common concern, the princes remained mindful of Bikaner's interview with Chamberlain. Thus they would enter a merger with British India only if their internal autonomy was respected.

At Delhi in February 1918, Montagu and Chelmsford convened a meeting with the princes and received the report of the committee. Besides the four responsible for the report, the meeting was attended by the Maharajas of Gwalior, Jaipur, Jodhpur and Kolhapur, the Maharao of Cutch and the Begum of Bhopal. In discussion the princes complained that there had been a tendency to disregard treaty rights and although they were unable to cite any specific instances offhand, Bikaner made it clear that they were apprehensive about their future and wanted to make sure that 'the fulfilment of the Treaties should not depend on the personal goodwill of high officers'.[117] In order to see how far such claims were justified the Government of India invited the princes to indicate the occasions when they considered the government had failed to fulfil its treaty pledges. In their subsequent report, Montagu and Chelmsford recognized the anxiety of the princes and sought to assure them 'that no constitutional changes which may take place will impair the rights, dignities and privileges secured to them by treaties, *sanads* and engagements or by established practice'.[118] As a positive gesture they suggested that, with the consent of those concerned, the situation could be reviewed 'not necessarily with a view to any change of policy but in order to simplify, standardize and codify existing political practice for the future'.[119] The remainder of the report was largely a reproduction of the scheme presented by the four-man committee and concluded with a vision of the future embracing the 'external semblance of some form of federation'. The provinces would become autonomous units held together by a central government which would deal with matters common to them all, as they would be to the states. The gradual concentration of the Government of India upon such matters would make it easier for the states, while retaining their internal autonomy, to enter a closer association with the central government if they wished to do so.[120]

The two most significant recommendations of the report were those relating to the codification of political practice and the establishment of a Chamber of Princes. Moreover, the significance of these was not merely attributable to the issues at stake. Over both proposals the princes emerged, not as a united and coherent body but as a series of groups and factions urging a variety of demands designed to promote a number of particularist ambitions. Implicit in this disunity was a growing resentment among a large number of states at the manner in which the small activist group of princes, representative of the medium-sized states, had assumed a monopoly interest in all the reform proceedings relating to the states.

At the princes' conference of January 1919, Chelmsford suggested that the proposed Chamber of Princes should consist of three classes of states: those with a salute of eleven guns or over, those which had a nine-gun salute and possessed practically full internal powers, and finally such other states with a nine-gun salute that the government considered fit for the grant of full, or practically full, internal powers. The Viceroy also suggested that a 'reasonable and proportional representation of the lesser states' should be secured to enable them to have a voice in matters affecting their interests. While the conference agreed to the first three categories, many princes of medium-sized states objected to the second suggestion, particularly as the Viceroy had also hinted that some states which were the feudatories of others could be eligible for membership.[121] The matter was referred to the Political Department which, in August 1920, recommended that representatives of states not included in Chelmsford's first two categories, and exclusive of non-jurisdictionary *Thakurs*, Estates and mere feudatories, should form an integral part of the Chamber and be styled 'Representative Members'.[122] This recommendation was accepted: 12 minor princes were to be elected to represent 127 states in this manner. Of the twelve, four came from the Bombay Presidency, three from Bihar and Orissa, two from the Punjab, two from the Central Provinces and one from Central India.

The Chamber of Princes, which was inaugurated by Royal Proclamation on 8 February 1921, was thus to consist of 108 princes who were to be members in their own right, plus 12 representative members. However, inclusive in the former category were the princes of the larger states for whom the very idea of a Chamber was anathema. Their aversion to a princely organization had remained unchanged since Minto's day and they subsequently refused to participate. According to the Nizam of Hyderabad:

I should not like any questions affecting my State being

determined on the advice of other Ruling Princes, or of their representatives, Hindus or Muhammadens ..., it would contravene the essential principle that each Prince is a Sovereign who is entitled to conduct his business direct with the British Government, without the intervention of other Indian States, or of any Legislative Assemblies of British India.[123]

A similar position was adopted by the states of Baroda, Indore, Mysore, Jaipur and Udaipur.

In the absence of the larger states the Chamber was destined to be dominated by a league of princes from the medium-sized states of Rajputana, Western India and the Punjab. They would contemplate no erosion of their position. During the first session of the Chamber a claim was made on behalf of the smaller states that the qualification rules be modified in order to accommodate more of their number. Bikaner replied: 'As regards the Representative Members, there has also been the apprehension expressed, not only of the levelling down process, but of the danger of our being flooded and out-voted by the lesser Rulers.'[124] The Maharaja of Alwar warned that even those princes who had decided to attend the Chamber might abstain if they discovered 'that their views do not carry the amount of importance due to their position'.[125] Inevitably the Standing Committee of the Chamber, to all intents and purposes the Advisory Board recommended by the four princes in 1918, was tightly controlled by the medium-sized states. Initially it comprised five members: in addition to the Chancellor of the Chamber there was to be one representative from each of the four divisions of Bombay, Central India, Rajputana and the Punjab. During the first session of the Chamber, however, two changes were made: in future members were to be elected on merit, not on any territorial basis, and their number was to be increased from five to seven. In November 1921 the Committee consisted of the following princes - Bikaner (Chancellor), Scindia, Cutch, Patiala, Nawanagar, Alwar and Palanpur. Of these, Scindia was the odd man out. With the exceptions of Patiala, who was a Sidhu Jat, and Palanpur, who was a Pathan, all the others were descended from one of the numerous Rajput clans.[126] Scindia, however, was a lowly Maratha, and although he had sponsored their cause over the past six years, the others treated him as an outcaste.[127] He resigned in 1924 and never returned. In all subsequent personnel changes made on the Standing Committee, the predominance of the medium-sized states from Rajputana, Western India and the Punjab was perpetuated.[128]

The larger states also objected to the proposal to codify political practice. The Gaekwar of Baroda expressed their apprehensions when he said that codification would have a 'levelling and corroding influence upon the superior Treaty rights of individual States ... Uniformity of standards and codified methods of interpretation will tend to obscure these important distinctions of status no less than uniformity of nomenclature does now.'[129]

Montagu, who held but scant regard for the aloofness of the larger states, ignored these objections. At his insistence the Government of

India appointed a codification committee consisting of Bikaner, Alwar, Nawanagar, Patiala and Cutch, Sir George Lowndes (the Law Member of Council), and Robert Holland (the Deputy Political Secretary). The committee met first in September 1919 to discuss twenty-three points of political practice which the princes, in their replies to the government's inquiry about treaty infringments, alleged had encroached upon their rights and dignity. On this issue, however, the princes were unable to have things all their own way and a fundamental difference of opinion emerged between themselves and the British officials as to the procedure they should follow. The origin of this difference lay in the contents of a speech made by Alwar to the princes' conference in January 1919. He had argued that although the states could not claim a position of equality with the British Government, the fact of their internal sovereignty meant that their position was not one of subordination either. It was therefore necessary that any discussion on codification should be accompanied by a mutual definition regarding the relative position of the two partners in the relationship 'because without that we could not decide or discuss the abstract principles which shall guide and rule our treaty relations'.[130] What in fact Alwar was asking for was an authoritative definition of paramountcy which would involve the Government of India indicating the limits of its rights and prerogatives. This was precisely the possibility that Chamberlain had vetoed in his correspondence with the Government of India on the minorities issue, and not even Montagu could contemplate such a procedure.

Accordingly, when Alwar repeated his proposal in the codification committee, Lowndes countered by suggesting that as political practice was so well established and extensive, it would be more useful to examine the existing usage and principles underlying it in order to ascertain if any of them conflicted with the terms of the princes' treaties. Lowndes was prepared to concede that the reforms being introduced in British India made future political developments uncertain and that ultimately it might be equally in the interests of both parties to define their mutual positions. As yet, however, this contingency had not arisen. The problem was eventually solved by a compromise solution, suggested by the Maharao of Cutch. The committee would immediately concern itself with the examination of the twenty-three points of political practice, it being understood that this would not prejudice resort to Alwar's 'analytical' approach should this seem necessary.[131]

The Government of India was quite satisfied with the outcome. Four of the twenty-three points were successfully dealt with by the committee.[132] The government felt that the committee's proceedings had not only removed many misunderstandings but had also witnessed a 'marked growth of mutual confidence' between itself and the states.[133] This self-congratulation omitted one vital consideration: because no attempt had been made to define mutual rights and obligations, the princes concerned considered it necessary to append their own note to the general report of the codification committee. In their opinion it was hardly necessary to emphasise the inviolate character of our treaties, *sanads* and engagements. Suffice it to say that the treaties between the British Government and the Indian States provide the sole test of the latter's rights and the only correct standard for judging the obligations of the former. It must, however, be added that no laches, lapse of time or the growth of any practice in which the Princes had no voice can be admitted to modify the original relations of the States with the British Government as deducible from the treaties much less to render these treaties obsolete.[134]

Clearly these princes did not share the Government of India's satisfaction at the outcome of the negotiations.

A distinguished authority on the states wrote of the position confronting the princes in 1921: 'The paramount power continued to be paramount and paramountcy remained as vague and undefined as ever.'[135] Yet this did not mean, that by 1921, the princes were in a position analogous to the one they had experienced under Curzon. On the contrary, their contribution to the war effort had established them securely as Britain's principal allies. As Montagu had told Chelmsford in March 1918: 'I need not remind you, that after all, we owe a greater - or at any rate as great - a debt to the Princes than to British India, and it is equally incumbent upon us to try and satisfy them.'[136] The inauguration of the Chamber of Princes, despite its drawbacks, was the clearest indication that the days of isolation were over. Moreover, by 1921 a policy of non-interference was slowly beginning to pervade the Political Department of the Government of India, and it is to this that we shall next turn our attention. It is important to recognize, however, that over the fundamental issue of paramountcy, the process of removing the isolation had left one section of these princely allies with a grievance; a grievance which their imperial patron was most unwilling to redress. If this situation persisted, it was not inconceivable that in the future their effectiveness as allies would be subject to serious doubt.

NOTES TO CHAPTER II

1   Lee-Warner had served as political agent at Kolhapur, Resident at Mysore and also as a Secretary in the Political and Secret Department of the India Office before his appointment to the India Council.

2   'The Native States', draft of a chapter for the Imperial Gazetteer by W. Lee-Warner, 28 February 1903, PSCI, 1875-1911, Vol. 163, No. 694/1904.

3   Curzon's minute, 29 February 1904, ibid.

4   Fitzpatrick's minute, 28 May 1904, ibid.

5   Godley's revised draft, ibid.

6   Curzon's minute, 29 February 1904, ibid.

7   Curzon's speech, 20 July 1904, cited in G. Bennet (ed.), *The Concept of Empire from Burke to Attlee, 1774-1947*, London, 1953, pp. 345-348.

8   Fitzpatrick's minute, 28 May 1904, PSCI, 1875-1911, Vol. 163, No. 694/1904.

9   ibid.

10   ibid.

11   ibid.

12   Political Committee Resolution, 7 June 1904, ibid.

13   Godley to Brodrick, 31 October 1904, ibid.

14   Dane to Lee-Warner, 31 August 1904, ibid.

15   Godley to Dane, 4 November 1904, ibid.

16   Lamington to Minto, 9 October 1906, Minto Collection, No. 12765.

17   Ian Copland, 'Sayaji Rao Gaekwar and "Sedition" : the Dilemmas of an Indian Prince', in Peter Robb and David Taylor (eds.), *Rule, Protest, Identity : Aspects of Modern South Asia*, London, 1978, pp. 29-30.

18   Clarke to Minto, 8 December 1907, Minto Collection, No. 12767.

19   Clarke to Morley, 12 December 1907, Morley Collection, No. 42(c) and (d).

20   Ian Copland, op. cit., p.45.

21   Clarke to Morley, 25 December 1907, Morley Collection, No. 42(c) and (d).

22   Minto to Morley, 20 December 1905, Morley Collection, No. 9.

23   Minto to Morley, 29 August 1906, ibid.

24   Minto to Morley, 12 September 1907, Morley Collection, No. 12.

25   Morley to Minto, 30 November 1906, Minto Collection, No. 12736.

26   Clarke to Morley, 10 January 1908, Morley Collection, No. 42(c) and (d).

27   Barr's note, 12 December 1905, enclosed with J.F. Whyte to J. Dunlop Smith, 19 December 1905, Minto Collection, No. 12764.

28   *Summary of the Proceedings of the Government of India in the Foreign Department during the Viceroyalty of Lord Curzon, January 1899 - November 1905: Native States*, Calcutta:

Superintendent Government Printing, 1908, pp. 55-57, Minto Collection, No. 12589.

29   Dane's note, 25 November 1905, enclosed with Dane to Dunlop Smith, 23 January 1907, Minto Collection, No. 12766.

30   ibid.

31   ibid.

32   Barr's note, 12 December 1905, enclosed with J.F. Whyte to Dunlop Smith, 19 December 1905, Minto Collection, No. 12764.

33   Minto to Morley, 29 August 1906, Morley Collection, No. 9.

34   Minto to Morley, 15 August 1906, Minto Collection, No. 12736.

35   ibid.

36   Curzon to Hamilton, 29 August 1900, Curzon Collection, No. 159.

37   Morley to Minto, 11 October 1906, Morley Collection, No. 1. For British responses to the growth of extreme nationalism, see R.J. Moore, *Liberalism and Indian Politics 1872-1922*, London, 1966; and S.R. Wasti, *Lord Minto and the Indian Nationalist Movement, 1905-1910*, Oxford, 1964. For the nationalist movement itself, see D. Argov, *Moderates and Extremists in the Indian Nationalist Movement, 1883-1920*, London, 1967; and S.A. Wolpert, *Tilak and Gokhale: Revolution and Reform in the Making of Modern India*, Berkeley, 1962.

38   Minto to Morley, 28 May 1906, Morley Collection, No. 8.

39   ibid.

40   Butler's note, 11 March 1909, GOI, FPD, Confidential B, Internal Branch A, 1911, No. 3.

41   Cobb's note, 17 April 1909, ibid.

42   I.F.S. Copland, 'The Maharaja of Kolhapur and the Non-Brahmin Movement, 1902-1910', *Modern Asian Studies*, 7 (April 1973), pp. 209-225.

43   Measures desirable to prevent the spread of sedition in Native States, GOI, FPD, Secret-Internal, March 1910, Nos. 42-45.

44   Papers relating to a Council of Indian Princes, 1906-1907, Notes on the Report of the Committee appointed to consider reforms in the Indian Councils, Minto Collection, No.12621.

45   Minto's note, 19 December 1906, ibid.

46   Kitchener's note, 26 December 1906, ibid.

47   H.H. Risley's 'Summary of Proposals of Committee and Opinions Expressed on them', 27 February 1906, ibid.

48   Morley to Minto, 22 June 1906, Morley Collection, No.1.

49   GOI, Home Department, Despatch No. 7 to S/S, 21 March 1907, Minto Collection, No. 12621.

50   Minto to Morley, 14 November 1907, Morley Collection, No. 13.

51   Minto to Morley, 26 December 1907, ibid.

52   Minto to Morley, 12 August 1908, Morley Collection, No. 17.

53   Minto to Morley, 30 November 1908, Minto Collection, No. 12738.

54   ibid.

55   Hill to Dunlop Smith, 2 December 1907, Minto Collection, No. 12767.

56   Colvin to Dunlop Smith, 10 December 1907, ibid.

57 Hill to Dunlop Smith, 2 December 1907, ibid.
58 Hill to Dunlop Smith, 27 December 1907, ibid.
59 Colvin to Dunlop Smith, 14 January 1908, Minto Collection, No. 12768.
60 Clarke to Morley, 7 February 1908, Morley Collection, No. 42(c) and (d).
61 McMahon to Dunlop Smith, 21 January 1908, Minto Collection, No. 12768.
62 Minto to Morley, 29 January 1908, Minto Collection, No. 12738.
63 ibid.
64 Minto to Morley, 15 January 1908, ibid.
65 *Oudh Policy : The Policy of Sympathy*, p.39, Butler Collection, No. 63. For an earlier version of these views, see Butler's *Oudh Policy Considered Historically and with Reference to the Present Political Situation*, 1896, ibid.
66 Butler's memorandum, 'Reorganisation of the Foreign Office and the Political Department', 15 November 1910, Minto Collection, No. 12638.
67 ibid. Butler's views on the princes were not simply an outgrowth of his previous experience in Oudh, but a reflection of an attitude which was influencing policy makers in many other areas of the British empire. Professor D.A. Low has recently emphasised the similarity between the policy that Butler evolved towards the Indian princes and the system of indirect rule introduced by General Sir Frederick Lugard in relation to the chiefs of the emirates under his control when he served as High Commissioner of Northern Nigeria between 1900 and 1906. Butler and Lugard shared a common concern – to maintain stability and security in society by preserving traditional rulerships. D.A. Low, '*Laissez-Faire* and Traditional Rulership in Princely India', in Robin Jeffrey (ed.), *People, Princes and Paramount Power: Society and Politics in the Indian Princely States*, New Delhi, 1978, pp. 372-387.
68 Butler's memorandum, ibid.
69 ibid., emphasis in original.
70 Papers on relations between native dignatories and local political officers, Minto Collection, No. 12633.
71 Manual of Instructions to Officers of the Political Department of the Government of India, 1909, Minto Collection, No. 12629.
72 Butler's introduction, 15 June 1909, ibid.
73 ibid.
74 Butler's memorandum, 'Reorganisation of the Foreign Office and the Political Department', 15 November 1910, Minto Collection, No. 12638.
75 Minto to Morley, 26 December 1907, Morley Collection, No. 13.
76 Butler's memorandum, 15 November 1910.
77 Butler to his mother, 1 October 1908, Butler Collection, No. 6.
78 Lovat Frazer, *India Under Curzon and After*, London, 1911, p.209.
79 I.A. Butt, 'Lord Curzon and the Indian States, 1899-1905', unpublished Ph.D. Thesis, University of London, 1963, p.165.

[80] Curzon to Hamilton, 10 May 1899, Curzon Collection, No. 158.

[81] Curzon to Hamilton, 25 July 1900, Curzon Collection, No. 159.

[82] Butler to his mother, 18 February 1909, Butler Collection, No. 7.

[83] Installation of His Highness Maharaja Ganga Singh of Bikaner with Ruling Powers and removal of restrictions, Rajputana Residency Files, Box 182, No. 81, 1898-1907.

[84] K.M. Panikkar, *His Highness the Maharaja of Bikaner*, London, 1937, pp. 95-96.

[85] Bikaner's note, 14 January 1914, GOI, FPD, Confidential B, Internal Branch, Section A, 1914, No. 6.

[86] Hardinge to Wood, 19 January 1914, ibid.

[87] Wood to Hardinge, 21 January 1914, ibid.

[88] Hardinge to Wood, 19 January 1914, ibid.

[89] GOI, FPD, Letter No. 15 to S/S, 9 February 1917, Enclosure No. 2, PSSF, 1902-31, File 2811/1917, No. 930/1917.

[90] ibid.

[91] Enclosure No. 4, ibid.

[92] Many of the princes including Ganga Singh of Bikaner, served at the front during the war. Imperial Service Troops were fully employed and some princes, most notably Bhupinder Singh of Patiala, led recruitment drives within their states. Financial support was another contribution to the war effort. The Nizam of Hyderabad assumed pride of place with a donation of thirty-five *lakhs* of rupees, while some of the Rajputana princes made donations to a fund which was used to purchase air planes. For details, see Barbara N. Ramusack, *The Princes of India in the Twilight of Empire: Dissolution of a Patron-Client System, 1914-1939*, Columbus, Ohio, 1978, pp. 38-40.

[93] Wood's note, 27 May 1916, GOI, FPD, Secret-Internal, July 1916, No. 29.

[94] Notes by G.R. Lowndes, 3 June 1916, G.S. Barnes, 3 June 1916, and C.H.A. Hill, 29 June 1916, ibid.

[95] P.G. Robb, *The Government of India and Reform: Policies towards Politics and the Constitution 1916-1921*, Oxford, 1976, pp. 53-4.

[96] *Proceedings of the Conference of Ruling Princes and Chiefs held at Delhi on the 30th October 1916, 5th November 1917, 20th January 1919 and 3rd November 1919*, Delhi: Government of India Press, pp. 23-38, 40, 53-63, 84-90.

[97] Secret letter No. 9 to GGC, 15 September 1916, PSSF, 1902-31, File 2811/1917, No. 930/1917.

[98] It was common practice for political officers with distinguished careers to be appointed to the India Council. Bayley had risen to govern Bengal and Assam in 1912 and then Bihar and Orissa between 1912 and 1915 before his appointment to the India Council. It was significant that officials like Bayley maintained the beliefs that they had held as political officers, often to the irritation of their successors in India. See the case of Robert E. Holland in chapter three, The Policy of Non-Interference.

[99] Bayley's note, 23 August 1916, PSSF, 1902-31, File 2811/1917, No. 2328/1916.

100 Minute by Holderness, 31 March 1917, ibid.

101 Secret letter No. 15 to GGC, 27 April 1917, ibid.

102 GOI, FPD, Resolution No. 1894-I.A., 27 August 1917, No. P4209/1917, ibid.

103 Bikaner's memorandum, 17 April 1917, enclosed with Chamberlain to Chelmsford, 18 April 1917, Chelmsford Collection, No. 3.

104 Chelmsford to Chamberlain, 15 February 1917, Chelmsford Collection, No. 3. 1916 and 1917 were years of agitation by the Home Rule League in which Mrs. Annie Besant and Bal Gangadhar Tilak played prominent roles.

105 Chamberlain to Chelmsford, 8 May 1917, Chelmsford Collection, No. 3.

106 Bikaner's note, 14 January 1914, GOI, FPD, Confidential - B, Internal Branch, Section A, 1914, No. 6.

107 *Report on Indian Constitutional Reforms, 1918*, Cmd. 9109, 1918, para. 6 (hereinafter, *Montford Report*).

108 The error was corrected in the Government of India Act of 1919. As Parliament was not entitled to impose any constitutional enactments upon the states, the term 'India' was replaced by 'British India'. R. Coupland, *The Indian Problem, 1833-1935*, 5th impression, Oxford, 1968, p. 61.

109 *Conference of Ruling Princes*, pp. 288-289.

110 ibid., p.291.

111 Chelmsford to Chamberlain, 1 March 1917, Chelmsford Collection, No. 3.

112 Indian Diary, Vol. 2, Alwar, 14 January 1913, Montagu Collection, No. 39.

113 Montagu's views in this respect are discussed in chapter three, The Policy of Non-Interference.

114 *Montford Report*, para. 157.

115 ibid.

116 Minutes of meeting at Delhi, 4-5 February 1918, GOI, FPD, Secret-Internal, May 1918, No. 1.

117 ibid.

118 *Montford Report*, para. 305.

119 ibid.

120 ibid., para. 300.

121 *Conference of Ruling Princes*, pp. 588-9.

122 *Proceedings of the meetings of the Chamber of Princes (Narendra Mahal)*, February 1921.

123 *Conference of Ruling Princes*, p.507.

124 *Chamber of Princes*, February 1921.

125 ibid.

126 Details of the racial origins of the princes can be found in a Descriptive note on the Indian States, 1931, PIC, 1931-50, Coll. 11, File 4, No. 4.

127 Bosanquet to Holland, 8 August 1919, GOI, FPD, Deposit-Internal (Secret), 1919, No. 9.

128 U. Phadnis, *Towards the Integration of the Indian States, 1919-1947*, London, 1968, Appendix VII, Members of the Standing Committee.

[129] *Conference of Ruling Princes*, p.487.

[130] ibid., p.366.

[131] Proceedings of the Committee appointed by the Conference of Ruling Princes and Chiefs to examine the question of codification of existing political practice, 22 September 1919, GOI, FPD, Secret-Reforms, February 1920, Nos. 1-6.

[132] Report of the codification committee, November 1919, ibid. The four points were (1) Tours and visits abroad by princes, (2) The procedure for the examination in Indian States of commissions in criminal cases issued by British Indian courts, (3) The construction and maintenance of telephone lines in Indian States, (4) The acquisition of immovable residential property in British India by the princes.

[133] GOI, Secret-Internal Despatch No. 8 to S/S, 15 January 1920, ibid.

[134] Report of the codification committee, November 1919, ibid.

[135] V.P. Menon, *The Story of the Integration of the Indian States*, Calcutta, 1956, p.19.

[136] Montagu to Chelmsford, 3 March 1918, Chelmsford Collection, No. 4.

CHAPTER III

THE POLICY OF NON-INTERFERENCE: 1920-1934

Montagu and the Princes

The establishment of the Chamber of Princes was not only a major innovation in the evolution of British policy towards the states, it also represented a triumph for the eloquence and persistence of a select band of rulers of medium-sized states. Throughout the reform discussions the manner in which they had enchanted Montagu was indeed remarkable, but it was also rather surprising that a Liberal Secretary of State should have been able to establish such a harmonious rapport with some of India's leading autocrats. One of the principal reasons for this lay in the hostility they shared towards the bureaucracy of the Government of India. At the instigation of princes like Jey Singh of Alwar, Montagu repeatedly protested to Chelmsford at the 'petty acts of annoyance and interference by Political Agents'.[1] Such complaints were not new to the Viceroy: Chamberlain had reported a conversation with Bikaner in which the latter had complained that some political officers were less courteous to the princes then they should be.[2] Chelmsford confessed that he felt some concern about the quality of the political service but considered that 'the longer I am here the more reason I find for taking the stories of the Chiefs with more than a grain of salt'.[3] Montagu, however, was not to be put off and he voiced similar complaints at an interview he held with the Political Secretary, Wood. This annoyed Chelmsford who replied imploringly: 'Now I do earnestly ask you not to accept the tales which you get from the Chiefs on the subject.'[4] He reminded Montagu of an instance involving Patiala. The latter had constantly fulminated against what he considered to be unwarranted interference on the part of his Political Agent, L.M. Crump. From this Chelmsford deduced that Patiala would be particularly glad to see the back of this official, but when Crump was obliged to take his wife on leave to England, Patiala requested that he should be allowed to resume his duties as soon as possible as they had always been the best of friends.[5] Chelmsford was irritated and perplexed as he indicated to Montagu: 'I am left in doubt as to whether to take this as one more instance of the inconsistency of the human mind, or as a reflection on the rest of my Politicals, on the assumption that no change of Resident could possibly be for the better.'[6]

Chelmsford's confusion represented a dilemma for the Government of India and its Political Department which supervised the states. Despite his uncertainty, the Viceroy had at least identified the problem when, with reference to Bikaner's complaint, he had informed Chamberlain that rather than the prestige of the princes being lowered in recent years, the exact contrary was in fact nearer the truth.[7] Princes like Alwar, Bikaner and Patiala were now beginning to reap the full benefit from the freedom which Butler's policy of non-interference had intended for the rulers as a whole. A reversal of roles had in fact taken place: whereas in the time of Curzon political officers had resorted to every conceivable means of petty interference to emphasize their commanding position over the rulers and their states, by the end of the war the rulers, for their part, were prompted almost in a spirit of revenge and spite to protest against every petty indiscretion they encountered in order to emphasize their independence from political officers and to press for more. The difficulties of the Government of India were further increased by the precedent, established during the reform discussions, by which the princes now considered it their right to have direct access to the highest officials in London, particularly the Secretary of State. Montagu positively encouraged this because he believed it was the only means of avoiding the influence of political officers and ascertaining the real wishes of the princes. The opportunities for such contact were greatly increased in the post-war period. Bikaner was a frequent visitor to Europe in his capacity as an Indian representative at Imperial Conferences and the League of Nations. The lifting of restrictions on foreign travel meant that there was a continual stream of Indian princes seeking interviews at the India Office. As a purely formal matter of etiquette this would have been harmless but the manner in which the princes began to clamour for redress of their grievances in India was frustrating to the Government of India. A trend emerged whereby the princes assiduously cultivated their contacts in Britain, to whom they would extol the virtues of princely India and relate how they suffered under the iron hand of the Political Department. Many were completely taken in by the customary charms and graces of the princes; few bothered to inquire into what sort of men they really were, how they governed their states or what conditions in them were like. Few realized that Patiala's extravagant excursions to Europe were leading his state to bankruptcy.[8] Disbelief was often expressed when the authorities in India endeavoured to prove that some of the princes behaved quite differently when they were in their states as opposed to when they travelled abroad. By 1920, with greater freedom in India and influence in London, the triumvirate of Alwar, Bikaner and Patiala represented a formidable combination which even a Curzon would have had difficulty in dealing with.

The Issue of Direct Relations

One of the major recommendations of the Montagu-Chelmsford Report had been the institution of direct political relations between individual states and the Government of India. In its simplest form direct political relations meant that there should be only one intermediary between the states and the central government. When the report was published in 1918, with the exceptions of Hyderabad, Mysore, Baroda and Kashmir, the vast majority of states were subject to dual political control: AGGs and political agents in the agencies; provincial governments and political agents in the provinces. The authors of the joint report reached the conclusion that the presence of two intermediaries involved a somewhat long and cumbersome process in the relationship with the states and recommended that, where possible, one of them should be removed.[9] The principle of direct relations was welcomed by various princes for a significantly different reason: they saw it as a means to endorse their independence at the expense of the political officers who had been the symbols of their previous subordination.

For those states whose relations were with provincial governments it was not only a question of a single intermediary; they had also to be transferred to the Political Department of the Government of India. Although the Montagu-Chelmsford Report had given warning that the political hopes and aspirations of British India 'may overlap frontier lines like sparks across a street',[10] there was no intention to equate political advance in British territory with the same in the Indian States. Reforms in the latter could not be brought about as a result of the constitutional changes in British India and it was therefore essential to remove those states from the control of provincial governments which would soon embark upon the experiment of semi-responsibility known as dyarchy. When the question of direct relations had been discussed at the informal conference in February 1918, the Jam Sahib of Nawanager expressed the view that the Bombay Government was less liberal and broad-minded than the Government of India, and stressed that as relations with the states were a central subject it was essential that in the future the Government of India should decide all questions affecting them.[11] The Chief of Sangli considered that it would give the states a better 'perspective of Imperial sentiment' if they were under the Government of India and thought that the provincial system encouraged 'insular feeling'.[12]

The proposal, however, met with strong opposition from the provincial governments concerned. The Lieutenant-Governor of the Punjab, Sir Michael O'Dwyer, considered that it would be detrimental to the Punjab states if they were to sever their political, economic and social connections with the neighbouring British districts. The fact that the revenue and administrative arrangements in the most important states were based upon the Punjab model, the growth of communications, the long-standing partnership in such joint ventures as the Jirhind Canal, which was one of the 'pillars of prosperity of the Phulkian states', the closer co-operation in excise and police matters which had steadily been built up, all warranted the maintenance of the *status quo*.[13] O'Dwyer considered that, with his previous experience as Resident at Hyderabad and AGG in Central India, he himself could assume the mantle of AGG for the Punjab states, and assured the Government of India that he would not act in this capacity with either his official or popular advisers.[14] The Government of India remained unimpressed by these arguments and asked the Punjab for a tentative scheme of transfer. The Punjab's scheme, earmarking all the salute states and those which maintained Imperial Service Troops for transfer, was grudgingly forwarded by the Chief Secretary of that government, J.P. Thompson, who was still of a mind to question the utility of the proposal:

> The Lieutenant-Governor has done his best to advise the Government of India how the contemplated change could be carried out. But the question naturally arises - when there is in existence a system which has grown up with the Province, is in consonance with its history, traditions and geographical features, is working smoothly to the satisfaction of the Punjab Government and of the Punjab States generally - why should Government set up a novel organisation that will lack the weight which the above considerations give to the present system, or in other words why should it appoint a separate Agent to the Governor-General for the Punjab States, with all the administrative difficulties and risks of friction that such an appointment will involve, when the Lieutenant-Governor of the Punjab is already capable of discharging the functions of such an Agent smoothly and adequately.[15]

As negotiations proceeded O'Dwyer still hoped that he would become the new AGG, but his representations, like those of his Chief Secretary, were to no avail. In November 1920 preparations were made to transfer the states of Patiala, Jind, Nabha, Bahawalpur, Kapurthala, Faridkot, Sirmur, Malerkotla, Mandi, Suket, Chamba, Bilaspur and Loharu to the control of an independent AGG.[16] Only the very minor states, eighteen located in the Simla Hills and the two Plains states of Dujana and Pataudi were left to the supervision of the Punjab Government.

Objections to the transfer proposals were also raised by the Madras Government under Lord Pentland, and even the Political Department had to admit that, *prima facie*, there was little reason for taking these states into direct relations.[17] Montagu, however, urged that there should be no unnecessary delay and in May 1921 the new Governor of Madras, Lord Willingdon, agreed that the states of Cochin, Travancore, Pudokkottai, Banganapelle and Sandur could be transferred.[18]

The stiffest opposition came from Bombay. Here a special inquiry had recommended that it would be feasible to transfer fourteen of the sixteen first-class states and eight second-class states to the Government of India. The Bombay Government objected on the grounds that the transfer would be detrimental to the interests of the inhabitants since the provincial government was in a better position to supervise the administration of the states in the interests of their subjects than the central government. They argued further that the transfer would break the close economic and social association which had been built up between the majority of the Bombay states and the rest of the Presidency.[19] The Governor, Sir George Lloyd, reasoned that the transfer was inexpedient at a time when the Chamber of Princes was still in its 'earliest infancy' and when the reforms scheme which was only just being inaugurated in British India meant that 'new forces were at work, the effect of which upon the general administration of India could not be foreseen or measured'. He attributed the orderly administration of the Bombay states to the nature of his government's supervision and was convinced on administrative and political grounds that it was both unnecessary and undesirable to introduce so many and so great changes at the same time. He therefore suggested a postponement of the transfer until the Government of India had gained further experience of the effect of such changes elsewhere.[20]

Lloyd was obviously concerned that the prestige of the Bombay Government would be lowered if the states were removed from its control,[21] but the Government of India recommended to Montagu that, in deference to Lloyd's views, the transfer should be postponed for the present.[22] This was only partially true, for the issue had divided Chelmsford's Government in a most revealing manner. W.H. Vincent, the Home Member, was in complete agreement with Lloyd's arguments. He considered that even a partial transfer would lead to an over-centralization of authority which would impose an impossible burden on the Viceroy with the resultant loss in efficiency being detrimental to the states concerned. He doubted whether the Government of India would be able to deal with the repercussions and developments which the introduction of the reforms would produce in the states, with the same sympathy and knowledge of local conditions as the Bombay Government.[23] The Finance Member, W.M. Hailey, frankly admitted that:

> If I were the subject of a Native State, or were a *Thakur* or *Jagirdar*, I would rather on the whole that the States were in relation to the neighbouring Local Government than to the Government of India . . . My case would be considered in a more independent and judicial atmosphere, interested rather in the securing of justice than in the maintenance of the punctilio of political relations.[24]

However, at the same time, Hailey revealed that this was not the principal consideration:

> We cannot safely face a process which would contemplate putting the Chiefs on one side. The rapid growth of democracy will be inconvenient enough in many ways in our own territory; and it would seem to me wrong, in view of our previous relations with the Chiefs, to bring them against their wishes under the direct control of reformed Local Governments.[25]

In other words, Hailey had confirmed that, although the arguments of Bombay and the Punjab were valid, the necessity of preserving the princes as supporters of the Raj outweighed the consideration that the administration of the states should be conducted in accordance with the interests of their inhabitants. It was for this reason that Hailey had agreed to leave O'Dwyer and his government in control of the very minor Punjab states: 'The maintenance of large numbers of very small States is no gain to the country politically or economically: it is no particular source of strength or of stability to the Imperial Connection.   The larger States stand on an entirely different footing.'[26]   Hailey expected that in time the princes would have to undergo democratization of their own territories and experience a change from autocracy to at least constitutional monarchy, but for the present they should be allowed breathing space to work out their own destiny without having to face immediate contact with the popularly controlled executives which were being created in the provinces. He concluded that the princes would never agree that the Governor of a Province could act as an AGG because they would never be convinced that he would be entirely independent of the goodwill of his ministers.[27]

Hailey had, in fact, shrewdly anticipated the key factor which was to influence the attitudes of the princes to British Indian politics for the next twenty years.   What he did not anticipate was that the progress of reforms in the provinces would lead the princes in the opposite direction.   The princes responded to each stage in the constitutional process by insisting that, if the provinces of British India were to be granted greater autonomy, then they should receive greater freedom in the control of their internal affairs.   They justified their demands by reference to their treaty rights; but these rights made no mention of Hailey's process of democratization. Thus, while British India proceeded on the path of democracy, the majority of princes sought refuge in the principles of autocracy embodied in their treaties.   Any inducement there might have been for those princes who were supervised by provincial governments to keep in step with progress in British India, was lost when the process of transferring them to the Government of India began. For the Bombay states this was after Lloyd's departure in 1923.   The states in the Kathiawar, Cutch and Palanpur agencies were transferred to the Government of India in October 1924, and became the Western India States agency under an AGG stationed at Rajkot.[28]

Direct Relations in the Agencies of Central India and Rajputana

The question of establishing direct relations with the states of Central India and Rajputana which had not previously been supervised by provincial governments was, for this very reason, less immediate, but still of equal intricacy. Montagu had argued the case for direct relations with these states in 1913 when he had been Under Secretary of State for India.[29] His solution then had been to abolish the AGGs and split the two agencies into several subordinate charges under the direct control of the Government of India. The respective AGGs for Rajputana and Central India, Sir Elliot Colvin and Sir Oswald Bosanquet, saw the proposal as a direct threat to their own positions and objected strongly to it. However, they also reasoned more sensibly that the withdrawal of political officers would result in instances of gross misrule escaping notice, and the matter was therefore dropped by the Government of India.[30]

When Montagu returned to India in 1917 he still favoured the abolition of the AGGs, but the princes, particularly those in Rajputana, were undecided. When Montagu met them in February

1918 he found that although Alwar agreed with him, others like Bikaner, Jaipur and Jodhpur wanted to retain the AGG and abolish the political agents.[31] To accommodate these differences the authors of the Joint Report made three suggestions for the implementation of direct relations in Rajputana and Central India: the abolition of the political agent and the transfer of his functions to the AGG; the abolition of the AGG and the retention of the political agent; or the retention of both, while allowing the political agent to communicate direct with the Government of India, a copy of the communication being sent to the AGG.[32] Alwar remained committed to the second suggestion for a very significant reason: upon the abolition of the AGG he wanted the appointment of non-resident political agents for groups of states. Under this scheme the political agents would congregate together in Ajmer where, according to Alwar, they would find more 'society' than in a state. He also claimed that this system would minimize any risks of misunderstanding and obviate the risk of political agents favouring the states in which they resided.[33] Alwar's charming consideration for the welfare of political agents could not disguise the real purpose of his scheme: his aim was to consolidate the gains he had already made at the expense of paramountcy by actually removing the instruments of that paramountcy from the confines of the states. The princes would then be left with a completely free hand in the management of their internal affairs. In announcing this scheme to the Conference of Chiefs in January 1919, Alwar was also able to reveal that he had managed to convert Bikaner shortly before the latter left for Europe to attend the Paris Peace Conference.[34] Bikaner's conversion, however, came too late to prevent preparations being made, upon the basis of the opinion he had recorded in February 1918, to place his state in direct relations with the AGG. The transfer took place in March 1919,[35] while Bikaner was still in Europe and upon his return the Maharaja expressed his annoyance at the manner in which the proposal had been carried without his specific concurrence.[36] Consequently he joined forces with Alwar to campaign amongst the other Rajputana princes in favour of the non-resident scheme.

The activities of Alwar and Bikaner and the recommendations of the Montagu-Chelmsford Report were a source of serious concern to the former deputy political secretary and now AGG in Rajputana, Robert E. Holland. He was hardly enamoured with any of the three alternatives suggested in the report: the second would see him lose his position, the third would reduce him to the position of a mere functionary, while both the first and second were totally opposed to his political instincts. To undermine the work of Alwar and Bikaner he decided to ask all the Rajputana princes for their views and used the opportunity to impress upon them his opinion that, in the interests of preserving the unity of Rajputana, the abolition of the AGG was impracticable. According to Holland, the correct solution was the elimination of the local political agents but even this could be given effect to only gradually as the AGG could not immediately assume the duties of all the political agents in Rajputana; hence the experiment was being tried in Bikaner and Sirohi, and, if it proved successful, it might be extended if local circumstances proved favourable.[37]

The replies received by Holland were interesting in showing that at this stage only three states, Alwar, Bikaner and Banswana, wanted the abolition of the AGG, while the majority of the remainder not only expressed a clear preference for the retention of the AGG, but also admitted that there were good reasons for keeping the local political agent as well.[38] With this evidence Holland could become more precise in his reasons for wishing to preserve the *status quo*. His arguments were not only a commentary on the wishes of the princes but also a reflection upon the implications of the policy of non-interference, a policy to which Holland could never reconcile himself. There was a tendency to attach too much weight to the views of those princes who 'owing to their better knowledge of the English language and experience of public life command a hearing in the Conference of Princes and too little to those who, though they do not play so prominent a part in public, wield as great if not a greater influence in Rajputana'. The rulers of Udaipur, Dholpur, Jodhpur and Kotah, who were opposed to the abolition of the AGG, were as much entitled to consideration as those of Alwar and Bikaner, and the impression was being created that 'as in the politics of British India, attention will only be paid to the wishes of Princes who agitate'. Alwar and Bikaner were obviously influenced by 'overpaternal methods' adopted in the past. That they should strive to prevent a repetition of this was natural, but their manner of so doing had very grave implications:

> There are plain indications that some Darbars incline to the theory that political officers ought to be metamorphosed into diplomatic agents, the change typifying the purely reciprocal nature of the bond which unites the States with the Crown, and illustrating the Sovereign character of the Princes' powers. If the uniformity now asked for were granted, the change would, by weakening the political officer, tend to aggrandize the State *vis à vis* the Government of India.[39]

Furthermore, Holland believed there were dangers inherent in the policy of non-interference. There was a general trend of apprehension among the *jagirdars* of Rajputana that this policy might leave them to the 'unfettered caprice' of their rulers. There was no established public opinion nor any effective checks on the actions of a ruling prince. Holland also drew attention to the fact that the Rajput states differed both in origin and political constitution from the great majority of states in other parts of India, in that the nobles of the states claimed to be 'co-partners with the rulers in their right of dominion over the soil and to the fruits of it'. The frequent state of tension that existed between the rulers and the nobility, particularly in the older states, meant that the Government of India had a particular obligation to see that, as a result of the security conferred upon the rulers by British protection, the status of the great nobles did not deteriorate. Holland also had the exaggerated notion that measures of the type advocated by Alwar and Bikaner would enable the princes to arm their states with modern weapons, in which case any effective opposition to their authority in future would be practically impossible. If this synchronized with the withdrawal of political officers or a further diminution of the authority of the paramount power, public apprehension would inevitably increase. Therefore great caution was required in introducing any changes which might have the effect of converting political officers into 'postal agents'.[40]

Holland's arguments received additional support from Hailey, who commented that Bikaner had 'for some time considered that he occupies a position in which it is not consonant with his dignity to have relations with anyone below the rank of Governor-General'. He agreed that the 'tendency of the modern Indian Chief is to assume a position of autocracy which altogether neglects the historical basis on which, in Rajputana at all events, his personal position rests', and felt that the movement for the abolition of the AGG was in part due to a belief held by the princes that they would have clearer field in dealing in an arbitrary manner with their *Thakurs* and *Talukdars*.[41] The Government of India therefore decided to recommend to the Secretary of State that, in view of the wishes of the majority of Rajputana princes, the *status quo* would have to be maintained for the present.[42] It was no surprise that Montagu was not prepared to accept this. He felt it was a direct violation of the recommendations of the Joint Report and suspected that there was a conspiracy on the part of political officers to sabotage them. He frankly disbelieved Holland's analysis and commented naively to Chelmsford: 'Are you aware that some of the Princes, such as Alwar and Bikaner, deny the very existence of this majority as real?'[43] He insisted that the Viceroy should use the first available opportunity personally to ascertain the 'real wishes' of the princes. Chelmsford saw no reason to doubt Holland's word, but he was never able to undertake the proposed inquiry. Alwar and Bikaner were now to get unexpected assistance for their case from the least likely quarter – the Government of India itself.

Reductions in the Size of the Agencies

By 1922 the consequences of the dislocation which the Great War had imposed upon India's finances were becoming increasingly acute. The Government of India budget for 1922-23 showed a revenue deficit of Rs. 916 *lakhs*. This was the fifth of a succession of deficits amounting in aggregate to about Rs. 100 *crores* and it was anticipated that the deficit for 1922 could work out at a figure considerably higher than the budget estimate. Immediate steps, therefore, had to be taken to balance the budget.[44] The Foreign and Political Department was asked to make cuts in its establishments and also to institute inquiries into whether it was necessary to maintain all the subordinate agencies in Central India and Rajputana.[45]

Consequently in June 1922, Holland and his counterpart in Central

India, Colonel Denys Brooke Blakeway, were asked to consider the possibility of dividing Rajputana and Central India into five units along the following lines:

(1) A first-class appointment for Western Rajputana with up to three assistants,

(2) A second-class appointment for Eastern Rajputana with one assistant,

(3) A second-class appointment for Bundelkhand and Baghelkhand with one assistant,

(4) A second-class appointment for Gwalior and Bhopal with one assistant,

(5) A second (or possibly first) class appointment for the rest of Central India with two assistants.

It was estimated that such an arrangement would effect an annual saving of Rs. 1.34 *lakhs* in salaries of gazetted officers alone, while it would be possible to reduce the cadre of the Political Department by eight officers.[46]

The justification given by the Political Department for these proposals was not only economic. They would also enable the principle of direct relations to be implemented and conform with official policy towards the states. In their interpretation of that policy, the Political Department was clearly at variance with some of the more experienced officers serving in the states. Holland and Blakeway were informed that:

> Modern conditions of publicity and political organization render it unlikely, however, that the withdrawal of local officers will result in instances of gross misrule escaping notice, while their presence is the less necessary by reason of the inclination of the Government of India to interfere less and less with the internal affairs of the States.[47]

It was too late in the day to expect Holland readily to accept this thesis; his world was that of the supervisor, not that of the distant and casual onlooker. He was particularly at pains to point out that he stood by the arguments he had already made for preserving Rajputana and its political establishment intact, and that he was only prepared to consider the proposals in the interests of economy, not because of any 'new political factors'.[48] He was also alarmed at what he considered would be the consequences for Rajputana of amalgamating the existing seven agencies, supervised by an AGG, into only two, and the reduction of the political establishment from eleven officers to six.[49] Although these changes would afford an annual saving of Rs. 75,528, Holland judged that they would result in the 'occurrence of grave disorders, the settlement of which will be a far more costly business than the maintenance of establishments on their present footing'. Not only was there a possibility of grave misrule escaping notice 'but also the greater danger that agitators from British India, working insidiously among the people, will exploit their grievances, real or imaginary and estrange them from their Rulers, with the result of widespread disturbances which can only be quelled by our

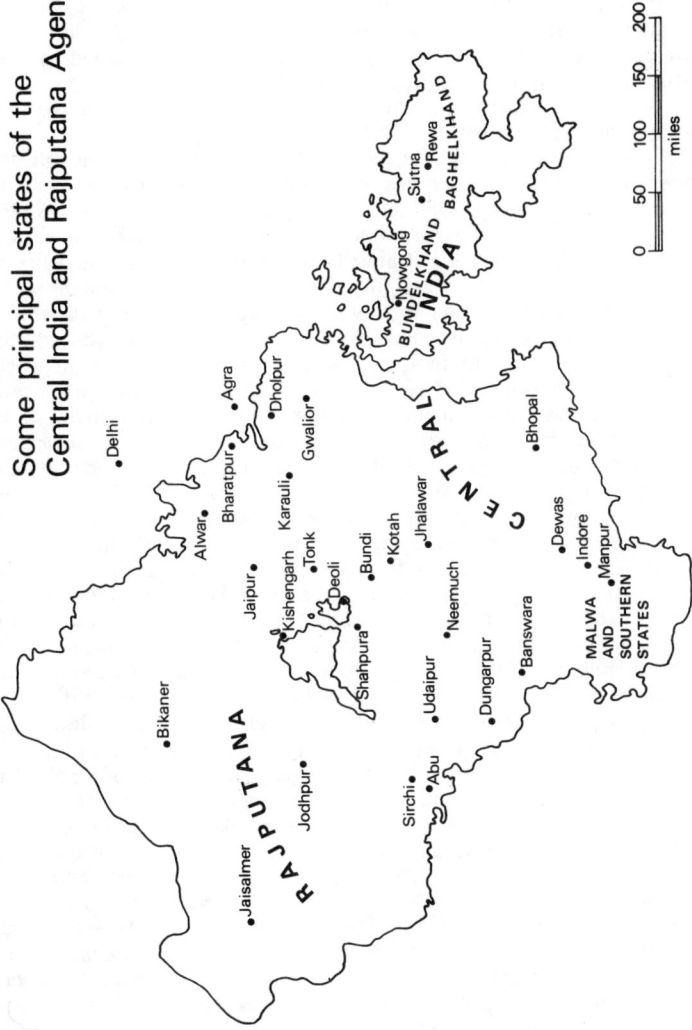

Some principal states of the Central India and Rajputana Agencies.

RAJPUTANA

Jaisalmer

Bikaner

Jodhpur

Sirohi
Abu

Udaipur

Dungarpur

Banswara

Shahpura

Kishengarh
Deoli
Tonk
Bundi
Kotah
Neemuch

Jaipur

Alwar
Bharatpur
Karauli
Dholpur
Gwalior
Agra

Delhi

Jhalawar

MALWA
AND
SOUTHERN
STATES

Dewas
Indore
Manpur

Bhopal

CENTRAL INDIA

BUNDELKHAND
Nowgong
Sutna
Rewa
BAGHELKHAND

0   50   100   150   200
miles

intervention'. Moreover, whether or not government interfered in internal affairs less and less, it still had an obligation to intervene to restore law and order if the stability of the administration was threatened: 'A policy of non-interference may lessen temporarily the work of political officers but, on the other hand, the withdrawal of the personal influence of the political officer and the trend of political affairs in British India, are likely to enhance the administrative difficulties of the Darbars and consequently to multiply the occasions on which they will need the advice and assistance of the political officer.'[50]

Holland was obviously conscious of the restrictions which the changes would impose upon his own authority, but in the case of Udaipur he had substantial evidence to support his arguments. In 1903 the AGG in Rajputana, Sir Arthur Martinade, had observed of the Maharana of Udaipur: 'As a Ruling Chief in the twentieth century of our era his administration and his qualifications leave much to be desired.' The Maharana was 'rigidly conservative, intensely suspicious and extremely sensitive to the least encroachment on his hereditary rights and dignity'. He had no advantages in the shape of early training or education and with these characteristics, Martinade concluded, 'the difficulty of inducing him to move in the direction of modern progress and reform will be admitted'.[51] Curzon's government had suggested that an improvement would be the introduction of an Executive Council, but in view of the fact that the Maharana was not unpopular and that petitions from his subjects were rare, no strong pressure had been exerted in this direction. Eighteen years later Holland was able to echo his predecessor: 'The administration of His Highness the Maharana is one of the worst in Rajputana, because his Highness will grant no delegation of his powers to any individual and insists on concentrating all authority in his own hands.'[52] The situation now, however, was fundamentally different because disaffection existed and there were indications of sympathy with the non-cooperation movement in British India. Four main causes of unrest were cited: the despotic and autocratic methods of the Maharana, corruption among subordinate officials, the tardiness of the administrative machinery and the complete inadequacy of the judicial system.[53] The relationship between ruler and nobility was far from satisfactory. The Maharana had endeavoured to curtail their judicial powers, a much needed reform in itself, but he had acted not with the intention of establishing a reformed and uniform judiciary, but rather in order to extend his autocratic control. This the British could not tolerate because they considered that without the co-operation of the nobility every scheme of internal reform - education, justice, police, irrigation and sanitation, would be only partial and unsuccessful. Above all, as long as serious difficulties existed between a ruler and his nobles 'the state, as a unit in alliance with the British Government, is practically valueless'.[54]

A serious agrarian problem had arisen within the state. In the districts of Bijolian, Parsoli, Begun and Basi, revenue had been withheld and attempts to collect it or to enforce official orders were met with threats of violence. In all four the villagers had refused to admit the direct authority of their *jagirdars* and independent tribunals had been established to decide civil, revenue and criminal cases. Large weekly meetings were held and all who attended were armed with *lathis*. From October to December 1921 volunteers had been posted in each village to disseminate notices of meetings and to refuse officials entry to the villages. These displays, although seemingly much more militant, resembled the campaign of non-cooperation which was being conducted across the border in British India and in December 1921 it was estimated that 250 villagers visited Ahmedabad to attend the session of the Indian National Congress. This so alarmed the *jagirdars* that one, the Rao of Bijolian, even wrote to the Resident in Udaipur, W.H.J. Wilkinson, asking whether they should send representatives to the Congress to counteract the influence of the agitators. Wilkinson was quick to advise against this as it would amount to a recognition that the Congress could interfere in the internal affairs of the states.[55]

The situation was restored when the Maharana was obliged to delegate his powers to his son, the Maharaj Kumar, but the case of Udaipur remains one of the most vivid illustrations of the consequences of the non-interference policy. The problem had been identified since 1903 but no attempt had been made to rectify it despite the fact that it was common knowledge that the situation could only become worse as the Maharana grew older. Instead, government policy had accorded to that laid down in the Political Department Manual of judging each case on its merits and refraining from intervention until misrule had reached a pitch which violated 'the elementary laws of civilization'. In practice this now proved to be the stage when the subjects of the state were on the verge of open rebellion, and by the time the government chose to interfere in Udaipur the state was virtually beyond redemption. Wilkinson was in no doubt as to where the blame lay:

> It is commonly said in Mewar that the administration took a steep downward curve from the time when Political Officers received instructions to leave the Darbars to their own devices, and in effect to refrain even from enquiries as to what was going on within the State. The news spread among the officials who were stimulated to fresh opposition. The nobles and cultivators alike lost their only hope of protection, and became easier victims ... The people, knowing the Resident's impotence, have been less and less inclined to acquaint him with their troubles, and he each year becomes less well informed of the condition of the State and its inhabitants.[56]

For Holland, this was ample justification to oppose the new amalgamation proposals; the policy of non-interference was bad enough but to abolish five appointments would be sheer folly. He therefore suggested as 'a less calamitous alternative' the creation of separate political groups. He considered that the Eastern Rajputana agency could be more easily 'lopped off' since the four states of Alwar,

Bharatpur, Dholpur and Karauli were in easy rail connection. To these he would add Kotah, Jhalawar and Jaipur and convert these seven states into a second-class Residency with headquarters at Jaipur. He estimated that this would secure an annual saving of Rs. 18,264. Holland wanted to draw the line here, but if the Government of India felt a greater saving was required, he suggested the creation of a group of the Southern states under a second-class Resident based at Udaipur. This would provide an additional saving of Rs. 15,864. Holland was obviously very reluctant to make these suggestions even though they fell well short, in terms of money saved, of those of the Political Department. The only advantage he could see in them was that they maintained the 'paramount necessity' of preserving resident political officers in the premier states of Udaipur, Jaipur and Jodhpur.[57]

In Central India, Blakeway shared Holland's concern about the amalgamation proposals. In deference to the seniority of Gwalior, that state had been accorded the status of a separate Residency in July 1920, but that was as far as the authorities in Central India wished to go. The new proposals now meant that the existing six agencies, supervised by an AGG, would be amalgamated into three, and the political establishment reduced from ten officers to seven.[58] Blakeway was disturbed because he felt that any real advance on the part of the princes of Central India towards a more 'liberal and democratic' conception of the theory of government could be achieved only through the persuasion and arguments of the political officers in touch with them. Like Holland, he was adamant that the position of the AGG could not be abolished and expressed his own concern at the effect which the changes would have on the future cadre of the political service: 'The number of junior posts where a young officer can obtain first-hand experience of Indian States is already lamentably small and the abolition of so many Political Agencies would make it impossible for all but a very small number of officers to obtain such experience even at a later stage of their service.'[59] Blakeway also clearly illustrated where he differed from official thinking: the latter considered that a policy of non-interference would induce the states to be more amenable in performing their role as imperial allies while Blakeway reasoned that some measure of control was necessary to ensure that they were capable of fulfilling that role:

> Ordered development in the administrative system of the States is, however, a great political desideratum. Their fortunes are bound up with ours. Their strength is our strength; their weakness ours. Misgovernment allied with corruption and incompetence is calculated not so much to furnish an object lesson of the benefits of British rule as a handle for our enemies' accusation that this state of affairs is due to our approval and connivance. The seditious movement of the last few years has fortunately not made much headway amongst the conservative peoples of Central India, but agitation has not left them entirely unaffected ... In view of the general political situation throughout India it is hardly

prudent to dispense with the best agency we possess for furthering
the cause of reform in Central India and avoiding the troubles
which may be anticipated sooner or later between democracy and
unrestrained absolutism.[60]

Moreover, Blakeway believed that there were serious practical
objections to the proposed amalgamations in Central India. The
location of agency headquarters would be vital if Bundelkhand and
Baghelkhand were amalgamated. There were two alternatives;
Nowgong in the former or Sutna in the latter. Nowgong would
probably be chosen because Bundelkhand was the charge with the
heaviest work, but this would deprive the state of Rewa in
Baghelkhand of a political officer. Rewa was 132 miles by road from
Nowgong and three unbridged rivers had to be crossed. The rail
journey took sixteen hours to which had to be added further road
journeys of thirty-one miles over two unbridged rivers at one end and
twenty miles at the other. The condition of Rewa itself was far from
satisfactory. In 1919 Bosanquet had expressed the view that 'the
State and its people are so backward in every respect that it will take
years of uninterrupted effort to raise its administration to the level
of ordinary efficiency even according to the standard of other States.
It remains to be seen, too, whether the young Maharaja when he gets
his powers will choose the path of progress'.[61] Blakeway therefore
considered that in the interests of Rewa alone, this particular
amalgamation was premature. Mutual jealousy and pride also made it
improbable that Gwalior and Bhopal would ever agree to form a joint
Residency. Accordingly, as Holland had done, Blakeway framed his
own alternatives: the Malwa and Southern states should be
amalgamated and Bhopal should amalgamate with the two Dewas
states. This would effect an annual saving of Rs. 1,772, as compared
with Rs. 3,022 in the Political Department's proposal, but it would
enable one political officer and his establishment to be retained.[62]

At the beginning of 1923, before a decision had been reached upon
either Holland's or Blakeway's alternatives, Alwar and Bikaner chose
this critical juncture to renew their attack upon the position of the
AGG. The Viceroy, Lord Reading, who had succeeded Chelmsford in
April 1921, was confronted with a deputation of Rajputana princes
consisting of Alwar, Bikaner, Bharatpur, Dholpur, Jaisalmer and
Jodhpur at Delhi on 7 February 1923 during the Chamber of Princes
session of that month. The deputation was totally manipulated by
Alwar and Bikaner; from the records on file of the meeting with
Reading, they were the only two princes who actually said anything.
Alwar reiterated his idea of local political officers for groups of
states, the salient feature of which was that they should reside in
neighbouring British districts. Together with Bikaner he urged that
Ajmer could replace Jodhpur for the Western Rajputana states, Agra
could replace Bharatpur for the Eastern states, the political agent for
Haraoti and Tonk could be located at Deoli, that of Jaipur and
Kishengarh at Ajmer and that of Udaipur at Neemuch.[63] These
proposals now received the unanimous support of all the princes at
the meeting. In the opinion of the Political Department this was not

surprising 'since it is natural that the masterful Bikaner and the subtle Alwar should have carried their less clever brethren along with them, especially when the reward held up before them was greater freedom from interference by Government and a raised status'.[64] An anxious Holland, however, urged Reading to make a definite pronouncement that the *status quo* would be preserved as even 'those Princes who are most firmly in favour of the maintenance of things as they are may waver if they think that the tide is really going to turn against them'.[65]

A final decision was eventually reached upon the basis of an important note written by the new Political Secretary, John P. Thompson, formerly Chief Secretary to the Punjab Government, who had succeeded Wood in March 1922. According to Thompson three fundamental questions were at issue: whether any definite promise had been given as regards the principle of a single intermediary, the general utility of the AGG and whether the same official increased the possibility of undue interference. On the first question, he correctly concluded that no such pledge had been given. Not only had the recommendations of the Joint Report envisaged the retention of both the AGG and the political agents, but it had also added the important phrase that direct political relations could only be introduced 'wherever possible'.[66] As regards the second, Thompson alluded to a point which he considered had been given less prominence in the discussions than it deserved. The Political branch of the Foreign and Political Department was unique in one respect. In all the other government departments, the Viceroy not only had a Member of Council and Secretary to advise him, but all important cases came up before his Council. On the Foreign side of the Political Department, although there was no Member of Council, the importance of international policy and frontier questions made it inevitable that most important cases would come up before the Viceroy in Council. On the Political side, however, only exceptional cases came up before the Council and the Political Secretary was the Viceroy's only adviser. Thompson considered that the AGG functioned as a valuable link in the government's information and advisory service and concluded therefore that, in this respect, the balance of argument now lay in favour of Holland. On the final point, Thompson had to agree that both Colvin and Holland, who between them had held the post of AGG in Rajputana with short intervals since 1905, had a reputation of being prone to interfere and that in some cases they had gone too far, but at the same time

> ... no Agent to the Governor-General who did his duty could possibly come up to the progressive Princes' ideal of non-interference. For the rest, interference is largely a matter of temperament. Some men cannot resist the natural instinct to protest when they see things going wrong; others can and do. Possibly among successful officials there are more of the former type than of the latter.

He concluded that the presence of the AGG probably did lead to a slightly greater degree of interference, but felt that the knowledge of his existence on the whole benefited both the princes and their subjects.[67]

Thompson's almost casual appraisal of this distinction between political officers was in fact the very essence of the policy of non-interference. It is recognized that the immediate retort to the theory that the proposals for amalgamations and service cuts would be detrimental to the interests of the states is that this would make no difference if, in any case, the political officers were pursuing a policy of non-interference. However, as Thompson recognized, interference was largely a question of temperament, which was entirely dependent upon the individual political officer. Whether or not an individual would interfere depended upon his political instincts which had been moulded by the length of time he had spent as a political officer, the number and different types of states that he had served in and the problems that had confronted him. There could be no set rules upon such a personal matter but the fact remains, as Thompson again recognized, that those who made it their business to know everything about their states often made more successful political officers than those who did not, and while there would always be some of the former, the nature of the non-interference policy was producing more of the latter.

On the issue of retaining the AGGs, Thompson's report had therefore vindicated the arguments of Holland and Blakeway. However, the amalgamations still remained. In Rajputana, much to the delight of Holland, preparations to create a second-class Residency for the Eastern states had to be suspended in November 1926 owing to disagreement among the states concerned over the location of a suitable headquarters. The Government of India suggested the existing establishment at Bharatpur, but the latter protested on the grounds that it would have to finance the new facilities that would be required. Of the remaining states only Jhalawar seemed satisfied with Bharatpur; Alwar, Kotah and Karauli all favoured Agra.[68] The suspension of the proposal infuriated Jey Singh of Alwar who, after six years of negotiating and scheming, still found himself confronted by two intermediaries. In an effort to remedy this he made a complete *volte face* and asked to be placed in direct relations with the AGG. To rub salt further into the wound, his claim was rejected on the grounds that his status in Rajputana did not warrant this and that it would encourage similar requests from other princes.[69] Central India was not so fortunate. Upon memorials from the two Dewas states their proposed merger with Bhopal was shelved but the amalgamation of the Malwa and Southern agencies was implemented in May 1925. The combined agency now consisted of 10 salute states and 34 minor and guaranteed estates with a population of 983,953 and an area of 8,150 square miles, all of which would come under the supervision of a single political officer.[70]

The first phase of amalgamations and establishment cuts were not as drastic as originally contemplated but the interplay of personalities and policies had been revealing. Economic difficulties and princely pressure had combined to pose a grave threat to the existence of the instruments of British paramountcy in the states. That these instruments had survived relatively intact by 1926 was largely due to the fact that in seeking complete independence, Alwar and Bikaner had pushed their demands too high. In retrospect, however, it is also clear that warnings about the implications of amalgamations and establishment cuts had been approached in the wrong way. These warnings had come from Holland and Blakeway, yet one must consider whose interests they claimed to be representing. They had argued for the preservation of the *status quo* by the retention of both the AGG and the local political agent, and had considered that, if either, the latter should be abolished. The Political Department had accepted this view but again the efficacy of their decision must be questioned. If the detection of misrule and the ability to give advice were the primary functions of a political establishment surely these functions could be best performed by the political agent who was the man on the spot. Holland and Blakeway had in fact argued very much from the point of view of their own interests because they had objected to a process which they envisaged would result in individual princes rising to a higher status than they possessed. Although the ideal solution would have been to maintain both officials, if one had to be removed it should have been the AGG who could have been transferred along the lines of Reading's compromise solution. The Viceroy considered that a great deal had been done to stimulate the princes' desire for direct relations but he had also been impressed with Thompson's comments upon the utility of the AGG. Consequently he suggested that an officer with specialist knowledge of Rajputana should be added to the secretariat of the Political Department.[71] His proposal was never seriously entertained because Holland was able to seal his already formidable battery of arguments with the information, supplied by the Regent of Jodhpur, Sir Sukhedo Pershad, that what Alwar and Bikaner really wanted was to get a member of the Diplomatic Service substituted for the Political Secretary, the underlying aim being to gain recognition of the princes as allies 'pure and simple' with no hint of subordination.[72] As a result Reading was obliged to submit to the view that the one official who possessed really intimate knowledge of local grievances within the states should become the target for future retrenchment proposals. Even Thompson had admitted that given a choice he would prefer the political agent 'as a protector of the interests of the subjects of the states', but he had refrained from advocating this because he considered that the AGG was in a position to speak with more authority to the rulers than the less experienced local officers.[73] This argument, however, took no account of the effect which the amalgamations would have upon the remaining political agents, and it was their position which would subsequently give cause for the gravest concern. The amount of work expected of an officer who was appointed political agent for an amalgamated charge like that of the Malwa and Southern states would now be double that to which he had been accustomed. Here in embryo was one of the major problems which would confront British policy ten years later when, in an effort to stem the tide of nationalist pressure directed from British India, the need for internal reforms in the states would be all-important: there were too many states in too backward a condition and not enough political agents to supervise them.

The Case of Hyderabad

There was one state to which the policy of non-interference could never be said to apply and it is initially surprising to learn that this was Hyderabad, the largest and most important of them all. In Hyderabad, intervention was the rule rather than the exception; the precedent had been established over the past 150 years with British intervention repeating itself at regular intervals of fifteen or twenty years. On each occasion, the reasons for such intervention, either conflict between the Ruler and his Chief Minister or between the Ruler and Resident and Viceroy, had been remarkably similar. The British attributed this perpetual state of friction to the person of the Nizam. They had never succeeded in establishing cordial relations with Hyderabad because of what they considered to be the idiosyncracies of successive generations of Nizams. Curzon described the Nizam of his generation as being 'utterly ignorant of, and completely indifferent to, the administration of his State or the welfare of his people'; as a ruler caring only 'for the gratification of his personal whims and desires, and ... surrounded by a horde of venal scribes and bloodsuckers of the worst description'.[74] Three years before the partition of India in 1947, the Political Adviser, Francis V. Wylie, wrote that the last Nizam 'must surely be the most freakish and disreputable person to be at this date placed in a position of authority over some 16 millions of his fellow human beings'.[75] These were not purely personal prejudices for it was true that, with the exception of the first Nizam and founder of the Osmania dynasty, Asaf Jah, there was not one really successful Nizam who emerged with any credit as an administrator. These opinions, however, do not explain the reverse side of the coin: the mistrust with which successive Nizams viewed the British. For this, as Wylie admitted, the paramount power had itself been responsible through the disgraceful conduct of early British officers in Hyderabad. This was the affair of William Palmer and Company, a banking firm which had been operating in Hyderabad since 1808 by charging exorbitant rates of interest for loans, thus compounding the already considerable financial difficulties of the Nizam's state. The crucial point for the future of Anglo-Hyderabad relations was the discovery that under the corrupt administration of the Nizam's cunning Chief Minister, Chandu Lal, certain British civilians and officers drew handsome profits from these underhand transactions. Indeed it has now been established that the Governor-General, Lord Hastings, had a vested interest in the firm and supported its operations. So too did the Resident at Hyderabad, Henry Russell, although in his case considerable pressure had been brought to bear by William Palmer's brother, John, a leading banker and merchant of Calcutta and an intimate friend of Hastings.[76] This episode certainly soured subsequent British relations with successive Nizams. In 1899 the Secretary of State, Lord Hamilton, informed Curzon that it was unfortunate that 'several of the Europeans who have been in Hyderabad have so conducted themselves and so done the Nizam that he has a natural detestation of the race'.[77] Future interference was henceforth viewed with a mixture of suspicion and resentment and any Chief Minister who showed signs of becoming too independent of his master was either summarily dismissed or subjected to such a campaign of intrigue and abuse that he would be forced to resign. Of more serious concern to the British was that although the manner in which the Nizams displayed their hostility increased the problems for the administration in Hyderabad, they were denied the one sure means of retrieving the situation. In 1900 the perennial financial difficulties of the state led Curzon to believe that 'some fine day we shall have to step in and cleanse this Augean stable of the premier Mahomedan State in India'.[78] Hamilton had to agree that Hyderabad was a 'sink of iniquity' but cautioned the Viceroy: 'The deposition of the Nizam would be so serious a matter that I would tolerate a good deal of oppression and maladministration before I had recourse to an act which would unquestionably frighten all the ruling princes.'[79]

The last Nizam of the Osmania dynasty, Mir Osman Ali Khan, succeeded in 1901 and although twenty-five at his accession he knew nothing about his own dominions outside the walls of King Kothi, his palace in Hyderabad. He was intensely suspicious and jealous and possessed an insatiable appetite for accumulating and hoarding riches in the form of money and jewellery. In November 1914, in accordance with Hyderabad tradition, he engineered the resignation of his popular Chief Minister, Salar Jang, and took it upon himself to be his own minister. Imperial necessity had dictated Hardinge's acquiescence in this ill-advised decision, for upon Turkey's entry into the First World War, the Nizam issued a manifesto declaring that the Indian Muslims should remain loyal to the allied cause. This won for the Nizam the title of 'His Exalted Highness' and confirmation of the traditional appellation of 'Faithful Ally of the British Government'. His gesture of friendship, at best only superficial, was certainly short-lived and by the end of the war the Nizam had renewed Hyderabad's anti-British bias. In 1918, largely at the instigation of a Bombay journalist, Abdullah Khan Khasmandi, who had previously been expelled from Hyderabad and was now attempting to regain the favour of his former patron, the Nizam was persuaded that being known as 'His Exalted Highness' was both meaningless and insufficient and that instead he should enjoy the title of 'King'. Suitably flattered, the Nizam became all that more desirous of replacing British and Hindu officials in his administration by Muslims, and he ordered the dismissal of two British officers who held the key posts of Revenue and Police in Hyderabad. Montagu reminded Chelmsford that he had always 'feared something of this kind because of the reverence which you and your Government felt it necessary to show the Nizam, not on his personal merits, not because of his short lineage, but having regard to the position which he holds among Muhammadans . . .', and doubted whether the Resident, Stuart Fraser, was the right man to deal with a person 'so liable to become swollen headed and dangerous from stupid vanity'.[80] The position of the Resident at Hyderabad, although the leading appointment in the political service, was hardly an enviable one, and Montagu's concern at the attitude which Fraser had adopted during his term of office from 1914 to 1919 was not the first time such misgivings had been expressed. In May 1900, at the time of the financial crisis in Hyderabad, Hamilton in agreeing with Curzon that the then Resident, T.J.C. Plowden, was quite unsuited to the work, had added his own reflection that 'very few of our officers who are quartered there contrive to leave it with as good a reputation as they had when they went there'.[81] For his part, Chelmsford chose the occasion of the Nizam's impertinence to deliver a vigorous indictment of the administration in Hyderabad, the result of which was that in June 1920 the Nizam was obliged to accept an Executive Council of between five and seven members with a Chief Minister or President who was to be given the fullest powers of control.[82]

From the beginning the experiment was doomed to failure for two basic reasons: the continued impotency of the Residency and the machinations of the Nizam. The first was itself largely due to the intransigence of the Nizam who adopted a policy of isolating himself as far as possible from the Residency and opposing anything in the nature of even friendly advice. In March 1922, Stuart Knox who was deputising for Sir Lennox Russell as Resident at Hyderabad, complained that he had not even been allowed a confidential conversation of five minutes with the Nizam.[83] He received no help from the Political Department who informed him that the Nizam was not obliged to speak to him and that 'if a Prince chooses to bury himself in his palace the Political Agent cannot dig him out merely for the purpose of cultivating his acquaintance, and however tactful and untiring he may be in his efforts, they will not always be crowned with success'.[84] This ridiculous state of affairs persisted until 1925 when the more forthright Sir William Barton was appointed Resident and in December of that year he produced evidence that conditions in Hyderabad had seriously and rapidly deteriorated. Corruption and oppression were now rampant and manifest in the Nizam's abuse of the practice of giving *nazars*, a form of tribute traditionally presented to a ruler to signify the loyalty of the donor. According to Barton, the receipt of *nazars* had poisoned every aspect of public life: 'The Revenue Department is honeycombed with corruption: Customs Officials are a by-word for rapacity: the Police are more concerned to line their pockets than to suppress crime.'[85] The heaviest demands were made upon the nobility who were constantly plagued by fear of their families being ruined by the seizure of their estates upon their death. The nobles in their turn, were forced to make heavier demands on the peasantry, the majority of which was Hindu, in order to meet the exactions. The Nizam had also succeeded in undermining the influence of the Council. Although the first President, Sir Ali Imam, had played a major role in enabling the Nizam to thwart the Residency, he soon aroused the jealousy of his master and, as a result of a deliberate campaign against him in the press, he was forced to resign in September 1922. From mid 1923 to 1925, the post had been held by a Paigah noble with no administrative capacity, Nawab Wali-ud-Daula, while two other Paigah nobles on the Council owed their positions to the Nizam's attempt to induce them to refrain from pressing their claims to their estates.[86] Basically the Council functioned as a 'mere constitutional camouflage designed to screen the arbitrary acts of the Ruler: if its advice registered the Nizam's approval it was accepted, if not it was ignored'. Finally, matters had been made worse by the attitude adopted by Barton's immediate predecessor, Sir Lennox Russell, who, being impressed with Sir Ali Imam's legalistic view of the Nizam's treaty rights, had deduced from it exaggerated theories as to the extent to which non-interference should be carried out. The result was not only that Russell had closed his eyes to many of the existing abuses, but also that the Nizam had now become intolerant of any interference from the Residency.[87]

Barton concluded that: 'We have to deal with the most complete absolutism in history, and absolutism untempered by fear of danger from within or without.'[88] Immediate steps had to be taken to prevent further deterioration and to restore the position of the Residency. Upon the basis of Barton's suggestions, the Government of India, with the concurrence of the Secretary of State, formulated the following measures: the Nizam was required to appoint an efficient President and Council, neither of whom were to be appointed or dismissed without the approval of the Government of India; there was to be a fixed division of responsibility between the Nizam and his Council; the Revenue and Police departments were to be placed under the control of lent British officers; and the system of giving *nazars* was to be regularized and limited to official occasions only.[89]

The imposition of these restrictions upon the authority of the Nizam in 1926 had the most profound impact upon the future course of Anglo-Hyderabad relations.   The British could justify their intervention not only by referring to the principles of non-interference, which had laid down that gross misrule could not be tolerated, but also by the precedent of their past policy towards Hyderabad. Yet previous experience taught them that the root of the problem lay in the person of the Nizam and everything now depended upon the attitude he would adopt. It was hoped that he would realize that the measures were not only designed to promote a spirit of reform within his administration but also to strengthen his position politically.   There were already signs that the majority Hindu population was beginning to react against the degeneracy of those who governed them. In a state with a working population of nearly twelve and a half million, just over ten and a half million were Hindus and just over one million were Muslims. Out of a total of 3,521 employed in public administration, 1,711 were Hindus and 1,376 were Muslims, which meant that while there was one Muslim offical for approximately every 900 of the Muslim population there was only one Hindu official for approximately every 6,000 of that community.[90] Even then these figures belie the fact that while Muslims held sixty per cent of the top administrative posts, the Hindus held only twenty per cent.[91] The attention of the Hindus was directed first towards the continual stream of Muslim immigrants from North India who were appointed to fill the leading administrative positions. Many of these were graduates of the Aligarh Muslim College which had been founded in the late nineteenth century and was intended to produce a class of Muslim leaders who, 'endowed with a consciousness of their claims to be the aristocracy of the country as much in British as in Mughal times', could be encouraged to work for the welfare of the Muslim community in India.[92] When they came to reform backward Hyderabad in the 1920s they brought with them many ties to the religious and political movements of North India which were being increasingly divided along communal lines. An attempt, therefore, to exert pressure for a reduction of the number of foreigners in the bureaucracy was made by a movement of Hyderabad natives known as Mulkis who had been displaced from administrative positions. The movement, although predominantly Hindu, did not possess a wide enough basis of support to make it a success. It was led by families who had themselves migrated from the north during the early years of the Osmania regime and who remained isolated in the old quarters of Hyderabad City treasuring the Persian traditions of the old court. They could not attract the support of rural Hindus because they continued to use Urdu and advocated it as the medium of education; and thus their ideology was correctly identified as being merely another 'thinly veiled argument for government jobs'. The remainder and majority of the Hindu population chose to express their dissatisfaction by forging links with the growing movements of linguistic nationalism in Andhra and Maharashtra.[93] Many wealthy Telugu *Desmukhs* and landlords, who had been particularly vulnerable to the exaction of *nazars,* sponsored the Andhra State Conference which had been established in Hyderabad in the early twenties and which put them in touch with the cultural-political association of Telugus outside the state, the Andhra *Mahasabha.* Similarly, in the Maharashtrian districts the merchants turned to communal organizations, in particular the *Arya Samaj* which became the vehicle for Hindu communalism within the state.[94] However, as Barton had indicated, the Nizam was oblivious to these as yet nascent threats to his regime. From 1926 he was determined at all costs to avoid the natural consequences of the scheme of quasi-constitutional government to which he had committed himself under pressure from the Government of India. He remained aloof from the Residency and continued his intrigue to paralyse the Council by attempting to enforce the appointment of his own nominees in the hope that this would neutralize the work of the British officers.[95] One of these, Theodore Tasker, who had been appointed Director-General and Secretary of the Revenue Department, considered that it was essential for the stability of his dynasty that the Nizam should himself head the reforms and gain the credit for any improvement that it might be possible to effect. The British officers should be seen to be 'eating his salt and wholeheartedly at his service'. That they were not seemed to be 'a political blunder of the first magnitude on his part: it confirms the belief that, although no ruler was worse advised or worse served during that period, he himself was in active sympathy with the old order of things'.[96]

By 1928, Barton had despaired of achieving any permanent remedy short of removing the Nizam[97] but by then the consequences of such a step would have been even graver than those envisaged by Hamilton at the turn of the century. In justifying intervention the Resident had confidently predicted that outside a few extremist circles there would be no general outcry among the Muslims of British India.[98] The Nizam, however, assiduously began to cultivate contacts among this community in the hope that propaganda on his behalf, if carried far enough, would induce the Government of India to leave him alone. Through the offices of Abdullah Khan Khasmandi the Nizam sent Rs. 25,000 to finance the 'Nizam Conference', a subsidiary of a conference of Muslim notables which was held at Lahore in October 1926 to discuss means of reviving the Caliphate. It was reported that, as a result, a deputation consisting of such leading Muslim notables as Sir Muhammad Shafi, Sir Abdur Rahim, Sir Fazalbhoy Currimbhoy, Dr. Hasan Imam, Dr. Kitchlew and the Maharaja of Mahmudabad should wait on the Viceroy.[99]   The deputation never actually materialized and Muslim interest in the Nizam's affairs was only short-lived, but it would evidently create serious misgivings in their minds if the premier Muslim prince in India were to be deposed. When to this is added the importance which Hyderabad would subsequently assume in the forthcoming constitutional negotiations, it can readily be seen how far the hands of the Government of India were tied in their dealings with the Nizam.

The much-vaunted intervention, which theoretically placed the most far-reaching restrictions upon the authority of a ruling prince, was therefore a conspicuous failure. The Nizam's one consuming ambition was to divest himself of British control and thus restore his independence and it is in this light that his prevarications up to the invasion by the new Indian Dominion in 1948 must be seen. For their part, the British had to be content with periodic remonstrances with the Nizam in the hope that, in time, fate might remove him for them. Unfortunately their prayers remained unanswered and in 1944, three years before the end of British rule, they were still lamenting the existence of the Nizam and longing for the day when 'His Exalted Highness may oblige us by joining his predecessors'.[100]

The Conference of Political Officers and the Policy of Lord Irwin

If the problems of British officers acting in a spirit of intervention in Hyderabad were considerable, those of their counterparts in the remaining states who were pursuing a policy of non-interference were even greater. Lord Irwin, who succeeded Reading as Viceroy in April 1926, was made aware of the situation early in 1927. In January of that year, the political agent for a minor charge in the states of Western India, Major A.S. Meek, forwarded a note to the Political Department with the remarkable title: 'British India is advancing along the lines of Evolution: The Indian States are on the road to Revolution.'[101]   Meek claimed that while British India was moving

towards self-government through education and a general raising of
the standard of living, with very few exceptions, there was no such
progress in the Indian States. The policy of non-interference was not
only causing the division between the two systems to become more
pronounced, it was also responsible for the increasingly frivolous
attitudes which were being adopted towards the states: 'There is
bitter criticism of the subject of State administration by many who
have knowledge of it; but a remarkable feature of the time is that
British officials who have the same knowledge condone with light
hearted good humour what the common judgement would hold
intolerable and a matter of grave disgrace.'[102] Meek attributed the
weakness of the Indian States system to the nature of the relationship
between the states and the paramount power. Prior to the British a
ruler had been obliged to consult the needs and desires of his subjects
in order to protect his own rule and life. There had been a common
interest in the safety of the state, rulers often being selected or
elected according to their qualifications, and those who failed in
their duty as protectors of the interests of their states were liable to
deposition. The British, however, in extending their paramountcy, had
divested the rulers of the responsibility for the safety of their states
and had themselves assumed this function. The result was that the
modern ruler now stood apart from his people.   Freed from any
anxiety as to the security of their states many rulers absorbed
themselves in luxury and in building up that strange phenomenon they
called their *izzat* (reputation). Meek concluded by recommending an
immediate reversal of the non-interference policy in two ways.
First, there should be more discussion between the Government of
India and political officers: many of the latter were completely in
the dark about official policy towards the states, while the former
would benefit from the specialist knowledge of the latter in devising
that policy. Secondly, political officers should cease to be held at
arm's length by the princes and be placed in actual contact with the
details of state administration in order to avoid the necessity for
drastic intervention when malpractices had been discovered too
late.[103]

  Irwin considered Meek's note to be very 'interesting and
suggestive'[104] and resolved to call an informal conference of
political officers to examine the methods by which the Viceroy,
within the framework of general policy, could induce improvement
when needed and also place the officers in fuller possession of the
mind of the central government. Discussion upon non-interference at
the conference, which was held at Simla in July 1927, varied
according to the experience of individual officers but most were in a
critical mood. Lieutenant-Colonel R.H. Chenevix-Trench, who had
spent just under a year as Revenue and Police Member of the Nizam's
Council in Hyderabad, strongly condemned the policy. He considered
that it had led to oppression and general misgovernment and that it
was therefore 'as short-sighted as it was unworthy of the Imperial
Government'.[105]   His views were supported by the Resident at
Baroda, Lieutenant-Colonel R.J.C. Burke, who declared that the
instructions in Butler's Political Department Manual left an officer

with 'little initiative' and seemed to imply that 'he should content himself by sitting in his Residency and listening to bazaar or club gossip'.[106] From Central India the AGG, E.H. Kealy, considered that even if the policy of non-interference was abandoned, the task of the Political Department would be doubly difficult as the princes would more than ever resent interference with what they believed to be their sovereign rights. Moreover, in that the Chamber had given some of the princes a greater sense of unity and provided increased opportunities for communication, it was conceivable that any suspected tendency to return to interference would 'close the remaining gaps in their ranks'.[107] In supporting this view, L.W. Reynolds, the AGG from Rajputana, considered that it was virtually impossible to make effective use of the Commission of Enquiry procedure which had been devised in October 1920 to investigate charges against princes:

> Before recourse is had to this remedy, the state of misrule must be so bad as to leave in no doubt what the verdict of the Commission, if appointed, will be. For obviously a verdict favourable to the defendant Prince would be disastrous. Consequently the probability is that the State concerned will be reduced to the verge of ruin, and the subjects to great misery before the remedy is applied.[108]

Reynolds was also of the opinion that 'we can hardly expect the administration of a State emerging from the "tribal" stage of evolution to approximate to that of British India'. He considered that the problems confronting the states of Rajputana were too deep-rooted for either a policy of interference or a well-intentioned ruler to make much progress. For this reason he was opposed to interference to improve an administration which was based upon indigenous talent. It was no use forcing the princes to adopt regular budgets and civil lists unless these measures were supervised by honest officials with some security of tenure. As such officials were rare in Rajputana, Reynolds concluded that the only solution was for the Government of India to lend to the princes the services of trained British Indian administrators until such time as the advance of education in the states had created the necessary indigenous supply.[109]

The opinions recorded by the representatives of Central India and Rajputana at the conference revealed yet a further dilemma for British policy. Kealy had indicated that a return to interference would meet with formidable opposition from the Chamber of Princes while Reynolds had declared that the only solution lay in going beyond the norm of interference by urging the states to employ British Indian officials. Lord Irwin was confronted with the task of resolving the dilemma.

From the beginning the Viceroy determined to steer a middle course. He was himself of the opinion that the instructions to political officers outlined in Butler's Manual went too far, and was rather surprised at the conference to learn that the more junior officers thought that the government wished them to interfere as little as possible.[110] He agreed with Kealy's analysis but not with that of Reynolds: the princes would never submit to the bureaucratic control of British Indian officials. Intervention there would have to be, but it should be pursued respectfully and tactfully and with the acquiescence of the general body of princes. In order to win them over, Irwin chose to work in close co-operation with the Chamber of Princes and more particularly with the Standing Committee of that organization. As in his approach to the problems of British India, he adopted the principles of conciliation and consultation towards those of the states. Historians have since applauded his statesmanship in dealing with the conflicting elements of the nationalist movement in British India, but a similar judgement cannot be passed on his handling of the princes. His tactics made none of the necessary modifications to the non-interference policy and served only to elevate still further the members of the Standing Committee to a position of influence out of all proportion to the importance of their states.

An aristocrat himself, Irwin felt a natural empathy with the princes and found welcome relief from the complexities of Indian politics during the many hours of leisure he spent among them in their states. However, it was the affluence of palace society which made him realize that all was not well in princely India. The lavish expenditure of the princes must have affected his conscience for he considered that the first 'great reform' would be to induce them to have a regulated civil list for what they spent on themselves. He did not expect a great response: 'I do not conceal from myself that we are not likely to get them all to adopt this principle very quickly, or that even if they did they would still no doubt, as some do today, be able to wangle their accounts. But if one could get the principle into their minds, it would begin to create a public opinion in its favour and would gradually bear increasing fruit.'[111] He spoke to Patiala about it in November 1926 and suggested that two leading princes might move a resolution to this effect in the Chamber of Princes. Irwin's reasoning was typical of his approach: 'They would get the full credit of this public-spirited action and I should, on behalf of the Government of India, congratulate them on their progressive inclinations.'[112] When informal discussions were held with the Standing Committee in May 1927, Irwin again hinted at the need for internal reforms in the states and, at his request, Bikaner agreed to move a resolution on the subject at the forthcoming Chamber session. Again the Viceroy was content in the knowledge that although there would be a 'gulf between profession and practice', it would be a great step forward to have secured a recognition of 'sound principles'.[113] Accordingly, at the Chamber session in February 1928, Bikaner called for a definite code of law, guaranteeing liberty of person and safety of property, to be administered by a judiciary independent of the executive, and the settlement, upon a reasonable basis, of the purely personal expenditure of the ruler as distinguished from the public charges of his administration.[114] The Maharaja was clear that there should be no misunderstanding about the intention of such reforms: 'We naturally cherish, and desire to preserve intact, and to render secure for all time, our internal autonomy; and we resent ... undue intervention or interference from any source outside our States in our internal and domestic affairs, or any encroachment on our Sovereign powers.'[115]   In seconding the resolution, Patiala chose to be more explicit. Reforms in the states were not to be confused with those pending in British India:

> In the States our institutions are framed upon certain traditional lines, the position of the Ruler is fixed in accordance with the dictates of religion and morality. I for one believe that the position of Kingship in India is every bit as constitutional as that of the monarchies in the West, for which reason, I want to tell your Highnesses that in lending our support to his Highness of Bikaner's resolution, we are, I am sure, in no way committing ourselves upon the vexed question as to whether democracy is or is not a good thing, either for India in general or our States in particular.[116]

The speeches of Bikaner and Patiala made it clear that in contemplating reforms, the princes would not be obliged to consider the introduction of representative institutions. On the contrary, it was their positive duty to maintain the traditions of autocracy within their states. For his part, Irwin made no attempt to encourage the growth of democracy within the states. He recognized that only Mysore, Cochin and Travancore in the south, and possibly Baroda, possessed representative bodies exercising any degree of popular influence on the administration, and considered that the events of the last ten years in British India had not convinced the princes that democracy was a worthwhile experiment. In 1930, in the midst of constitutional negotiations in London, he confided to the Secretary of State, Wedgwood Benn, that 'it might even do harm if they suspected us of trying to stampede them towards responsible representative institutions', and concluded that it would be better to leave such reforms to the growth of public opinion both within and without the states once the constitutional position of British India had been settled.[117] Irwin's contribution to reform was a note he prepared for circulation to those princes who requested it on the general principles of 'Administration and Government'. In it the Viceroy stressed the need for an administration conducted in accordance with the law, an efficient and uncorrupt police force and an efficient judicial system whose personnel should be secure from arbitrary executive interference and who should be secure in the tenure of their office provided they continued to do their duty. He also drew attention to the fact that taxation should be proportionate to the ability of the tax-payer to pay and that the personal expenditure of the ruler should be fixed either at a definite sum or a definite percentage, preferably not more than ten, of the total income of the state. Reference was made to the need for every government to have some machinery, not necessarily 'representative (or elective)', whereby it could inform itself of the wishes of its subjects and whereby the latter could make their voice heard. Finally, Irwin emphasized: 'Perhaps the principal necessity for a personal ruler is that he should be able to choose wise counsellors, and having chosen them that he should trust them, and encourage them to tell him the truth, whether or not this is always palatable.'[118] The initiative for this note did not rest with the Viceroy. It had been written at Patiala's request[119] and the circulation it achieved created more problems than it purported to solve. Many princes completely misunderstood the purpose of the document. Some, like the Maharaja of Jind, thought it was intended as a criticism of their own administrations and replied with notes of their own in which they attempted to prove that they governed in accordance with the principles laid down by the Viceroy.[120] This had never been Irwin's intention and he had to reassure many princes that the note merely expressed his personal views and was not to be regarded as an official document.[121] In so doing, Irwin had let slip a rare opportunity of closing the gap in administrative standards between British India and the states. He appreciated that: 'In the last resort and in the fullness of time I am certain no doubt that an even more effective security for the States than assurances of goodwill on the part of either Viceroys or Secretaries of State will in the long run be found to consist in the quality and in the calibre of their administrations.'[122] However, the lack of sanction behind his note, which meant that it soon became a dead letter as far as the princes were concerned, and his repeated assurances as to the sanctity of treaty rights and Britain's obligation to uphold them, served only to confirm the belief held by many princes that these rights would be sufficient to protect them from what they considered to be revolutionary influences across their borders. It would have been more to the point had Irwin made this support and defence of the princes contingent upon their reforming their administrations in accordance with the principles he himself laid down.

The Case of Alwar

Irwin's tactics were more than complemented by those of a new Political Secretary, Charles Watson, who succeeded Thompson shortly after the conference of political officers. Watson, who had attended the conference in his capacity as AGG for the states of Western India, was a firm believer in the policy of non-interference. It was significant that he was one of the few officers at the conference who considered that administrative conditions in many of the states compared favourably with those in British India.[123] It was also no coincidence that the most disastrous consequence of the non-interference policy occurred when Watson was head of the Political Department.

The issue was once again that of direct relations and amalgamations. At the July Conference, Kealy had expressed his opinion that it was essential to restore those agencies which had been abandoned or amalgamated in recent years. He considered that the amalgamation of the Malwa and Southern states in Central India had proved to be a very great mistake because the combined agency was too large for the political agent ever to get to know the states or use his personal influence with their rulers. As a result several of the states had not been visited for many years. He concluded: 'If non-interference continues, however, these defects are immaterial.'[124] Kealy in fact emerged from the conference under the impression that Irwin meant to abandon non-interference and therefore recommended the separation of the Malwa and Southern states.[125] He was informed by the Political Department that there was no question of departing from that policy and that it was Irwin's desire to diminish the instances of intervention by encouraging political officers to secure the confidence of the princes.[126] To this Kealy quite justifiably replied that the size of the new agency made it impossible for the political agent to achieve such a rapport. It was 200 miles from end to end with the headquarters station at Manpur being tucked away in one corner. The states, over forty in number, were almost inaccessible by road which made touring even more difficult. Many of them were hopelessly backward and in desperate need of more constant help and advice.[127] These misgivings, however, fell on deaf ears in the Political Department.

Of more immediate concern to Watson when he became Political Secretary was a renewed campaign for the conversion of the states in Eastern Rajputana into a second-class Residency. Not surprisingly, the initiative rested with Alwar. In February 1929, Watson approved the proposal[128] but he met with formidable opposition from the then Secretary of State, Lord Peel, who objected for reasons which stood in marked contrast to those which Montagu had used in making the original proposal for direct relations: 'In seeking direct relations main object of Princes is to reduce control of Paramount Power.' The Secretary of State considered that as this was one of the underlying issues of policy arising out of the report of the Indian States Committee, it was desirable to avoid any premature action which might appear even slightly to prejudge this question. Furthermore, there was a danger that the princes might connect the proposal with the wider question of the retention of the AGG.[129] These arguments were reminiscent of those which had been used by Holland and indeed he was responsible for them, having been appointed to the Secretary of State's Council upon the expiry of his term of office in Rajputana. Watson was furious; he considered that the 'desire of the Princes to get rid of Paramountcy is an ever present bogey to the India Office', and again, after Peel had refused to reconsider, that the decision was 'a typical example of the rigid conservatism of the India Office and their want of touch with the feelings of the Princes'.[130] Alwar shared Watson's anger but he was able to take advantage of his presence in London for the first Round Table Conference to petition Wedgwood Benn, the new Secretary of State. The latter eventually relented and proposed that while preparations were being made for the conversion of all the states in Eastern Rajputana, Alwar should be placed in direct relations with the AGG.[131] This took effect from July 1931, the month Holland left the India Council.

The arrangement for Alwar lasted under two years. In January

1933 British troops were moved into the state to suppress a rebellion by a tribe of Muslim peasantry known as Meos. An inquiry into the revolt revealed a sickening catalogue of financial oppression, corruption, torture and misery unparalleled in any other state.[132] The sinister personality of the Maharaja had pervaded every aspect of life in Alwar. Arthur Lothian, who was Prime Minister in Alwar during February and March 1933, wrote of Jey Singh:

> When to his arrogance there is allied a vindictive, capricious, and cruel temperament, his officials and attendants never dare put up any proposals that are unpalatable to him or they would get savagely punished by dismissal or fine, or at the least get held up to ridicule or approbium in files or in the State Gazette. As a result there is a cringing, frightened atmosphere in Alwar amongst the Maharaja's staff such as I have never seen in any other State.[133]

Lothian acknowledged that the Maharaja was something of a Jekyll and Hyde: '. . . when he chooses to show the charming side of his character, a more intelligent man than even the late Mr. Edwin Montagu might well be taken in'.[134] As a result of the inquiry, Jey Singh was forced to leave his state which was hurriedly re-incorporated on a temporary basis into the Eastern Rajputana states agency in the summer of 1933.[135]

Responsibility for the sordid state of affairs that had arisen in Alwar lay not only with Jey Singh but also with the policy of non-interference. The Political Department had been aware of the existence of grave oppression and maladministration in the state for the past ten or twelve years and Watson reported of the Maharaja that there had 'for some time been a general impression that his rule represents autocracy in its worst form'.[136] He appreciated that the case would lead to criticism of the department but felt that this could be faced with 'equanimity'. He reasoned that officials could only intervene if there were complaints from the oppressed, and in Alwar fear of the Maharaja had prevented this. He had himself been political agent in Alwar from 1918 to 1921 and had never heard of any complaints either by letter or when he toured with the Maharaja.[137] He completely ignored the fact that because of the non-interference policy neither he nor his successors in Alwar made it their business to question how the state was governed. If they had, the calamity of 1933 might have been avoided. Furthermore, in support of Alwar's claim for the upgrading of the Eastern Rajputana states in 1929, Watson had written:

> As the States administrations improve – as they gradually must – the Rulers are inclined to prefer that the exercise of Paramountcy should take place from a reasonable distance outside. The immediate presence of a Political Officer does tend to minor complaints being made by aggrieved persons, and the knowledge that such complaints are being received tends to make the Darbar suspicious of the local Political Officer even though he may take no action upon them. Where complaints are serious and

widespread, justifying intervention, they will always reach the Agent to the Governor-General even although his headquarters are outside the State.   In the case of States therefore with reasonably modern and efficient systems of administration it may be preferable that the Political Officer in relation with them should have his headquarters outside.   The same does not of course apply where the administration is notoriously backward or inefficient or where there are special conditions, such as a minority, requiring closer and more detailed attention on the part of the Central Government.[138]

What could be more notoriously backward or inefficient and in greater need of closer and more detailed supervision than the state of Alwar?   By their literal and rigid adherence to the instructions laid down in the departmental manual the officials within the hierarchy of the Political Department had scaled new heights of incompetence.

To make matters worse that policy received further confirmation from the financial crisis of 1929 to 1931 which necessitated even more widespread retrenchment.   This time the Bundelkhand and Baghelkhand agencies in Central India could not escape and were amalgamated in June 1933.[139]   In July of the following year, Rajputana was reorganized upon the following basis: the Eastern Rajputana states, the Western Rajputana states, the Residency at Udaipur, and the Residency at Jaipur to which Alwar was now transferred.[140]   This meant that in the period from 1920 to 1934 the number of subordinate agencies in Central India had been halved, from six to three, and those in Rajputana reduced from seven to four. Concurrently, the number of local agents expected to cope with the increase in work resulting from these amalgamations had been reduced from six to three in Central India, and from eight to five in Rajputana.   A future Viceroy would have cause bitterly to regret the policies that had been adopted in these fourteen years.

NOTES TO CHAPTER III

[1] Montagu to Chelmsford, 4 February and 4 March 1919, Montagu Collection, No. 3.

[2] Chamberlain to Chelmsford, 8 May 1917, Chelmsford Collection, No. 3.

[3] Chelmsford to Montagu, 1 April 1919, Montagu Collection, No. 8.

[4] Chelmsford to Montagu, 18 June 1919, ibid.

[5] Chelmsford to Montagu, 1 April 1919, ibid.

[6] ibid.

[7] Chelmsford to Chamberlain, 22 June 1917, Chelmsford Collection, No. 3.

[8] Financial difficulties of the Patiala state, GOI, FPD, No. 105 - Political, 1929.

[9] *Montford Report*, para. 310.

[10] ibid., para. 157.

[11] GOI, FPD, No. 30 - Political, 1923, p.23.

[12] ibid.

[13] J.P. Thompson, Chief Secretary to the Punjab Government, to Wood, 21 September 1918, GOI, FPD, Secret-Internal, August 1921, Nos. 1-21, No. 3.

[14] ibid.

[15] Thompson to Wood, 12 October 1918, No. 5, ibid.

[16] Wood to Thompson, 3 November 1920, No. 12, ibid.

[17] Proposal for the Establishment of direct relations between the Government of India and Indian States in the Madras Presidency, GOI, FPD, Secret-Internal, July 1921, Nos. 24-31, p.5.

[18] ibid., p.7.

[19] Secret-Internal Despatch No. 8 to S/S, 20 January 1921, GOI, FPD, Secret-Internal, January 1921, Nos. 19-21.

[20] ibid.

[21] Chelmsford to Montagu, 31 March 1920, Montagu Collection, No. 10.

[22] Secret-Internal Despatch No. 8 to S/S, 20 January 1921, GOI, FPD, Secret-Internal, January 1921, Nos. 19-22.

[23] Minute of dissent by W.H. Vincent, 22 December 1920, ibid.

[24] Hailey's note, 15 August 1920, pp. 17-18, ibid.

[25] ibid.

[26] ibid.

[27] ibid.

[28] Viceroy to S/S, telg., 25 September 1924, GOI, FPD, No.186 - Political (Secret), 1924-5, Nos. 1-28, No. 19(a).

[29] Indian Diary, Vol. II, Alwar, 14 January 1913, Montagu Collection, No. 39.

[30] Proposed Establishment of direct political relations between the Government of India and the States in the Central Indian Agency, GOI, FPD, No. 226 - Political (Secret), 1924-5, Nos. 1-9, p.9.

[31] Establishment of direct political relations between the

Government of India and the Indian States in Rajputana, GOI, FPD, No. 30 - Political, 1923, p.23.

[32] *Montford Report*, para. 310.

[33] GOI, FPD, No. 30 - Political, 1923, p.23.

[34] ibid.

[35] The state of Sirohi, which ranked fourteenth in the precedence of Rajputana states, was also placed in direct relations with the AGG on the grounds of its proximity to agency headquarters at Abu.

[36] Bikaner's 'Note on the Question of Simplification of Political Relations between the British Government and the Princes and the States of Rajputana', 11 September 1923, GOI, FPD, No.30 - Political, 1923.

[37] Holland to Rajputana Chiefs, 27 March 1920, GOI, FPD, Secret-Internal, July 1921, Nos. 13-23, No. 14, Enclosure No. 1.

[38] Holland to Wood, 13 May 1920, No. 14, ibid.

[39] ibid.

[40] ibid.

[41] Hailey's note, 18 August 1920, ibid.

[42] Secret-Internal Despatch No. 82 to S/S, 2 September 1920, No. 16, ibid.

[43] S/S to Viceroy, telg., 23 December 1920, p.7, ibid.

[44] *Report of the Indian Retrenchment Committee, 1922-1923*, p.291.

[45] ibid., pp. 158-159.

[46] Re-arrangement of political charges in Central India and Rajputana, 29 June 1922, GOI, FPD, No. 226 - Political (Secret), 1924-25, Nos. 1-9, pp. 8-9.

[47] ibid.

[48] Holland to Thompson, 9 July 1922, GOI, FPD, No. 30 - Political, 1923.

[49] In 1922 Rajputana was served by an AGG with two assistants; a second-class Resident at Udaipur; a second-class Resident at Jaipur; a political agent for the Eastern Rajputana states with one assistant; a second-class Resident for the Western Rajputana states; a political agent for the Southern Rajputana states; a political agent for Haraoti and Tonk; and a political agent for Kotah and Jhalawar.

[50] Holland to Thompson, 9 July 1922, GOI, FPD, No. 30 - Political, 1923.

[51] Cited in Holland to Wood, 7 June 1921, GOI, FPD, Secret-Internal, May 1922, Nos. 1-35, No. 3.

[52] ibid.

[53] W.H.J. Wilkinson to Holland, 18 May 1921, Enclosure No. 3, ibid.

[54] ibid.

[55] Wilkinson to Holland, 24 December 1921, No. 33, ibid.

[56] Wilkinson to Holland, 18 May 1921, Enclosure No. 3, ibid.

[57] Holland to Thompson, 9 July 1922, GOI, FPD, No. 30 - Political, 1923.

[58] In 1922 Central India was served by an AGG with two assistants; a Resident at Gwalior; a political agent at Bhopal; a political

agent for Baghelkhand; a political agent for Bundelkhand with one assistant; a political agent for the Southern states; and a political agent for the Malwa states.

[59] Blakeway to Political Department, 16 August 1922, GOI, FPD, No. 226 - Political (Secret), 1924-25, Nos. 1-9.

[60] ibid.

[61] ibid.

[62] ibid.

[63] Proceedings of the informal discussion on the subject of direct political relations between the Rajputana States and the Government of India, 7 February 1923, GOI, FPD, No. 30 - Political, 1923.

[64] ibid.

[65] ibid.

[66] *Montford Report*, para. 310.

[67] Thompson's note, 7 May 1923, GOI, FPD, No. 30 - Political, 1923.

[68] Proposal to establish a Second Class Residency to be styled the Eastern Rajputana States Agency. Questions connected with the location of the headquarters of the proposed Agency, GOI, FPD, No. 195 - Political (Secret), 1925-27, Nos. 1-6, p.9.

[69] ibid., p.23.

[70] Proposals for the abolition of the Malwa Political Agency and its amalgamation with neighbouring Agencies in Central India, GOI, FPD, No.226 - Political (Secret), 1924-25, Nos. 1-9, No. 2.

[71] Viceroy to S/S, telg., 18 June 1924, No. 195-P (Secret), 1924-5.

[72] Holland to Political Department, 20 June 1924, ibid.

[73] Thompson's note, 7 May 1923, ibid, No. 30 - Political, 1923.

[74] Curzon to Hamilton, 28 December 1899, Curzon Collection, No. 158.

[75] Wylie's note, 17 November 1944, GOI, Political Branch, No. 80 - Political (Secret), 1944. The position of Political Adviser was created in 1937. For details, see chapter six, The End of the Non-Interference Policy.

[76] Zubaida Yazdani, *Hyderabad During the Residency of Henry Russell 1811-1820: A Case Study of the Subsidiary Alliance System*, Oxford, 1976, pp. 48-69.

[77] Hamilton to Curzon, 14 April 1899, Curzon Collection, No. 158.

[78] Curzon to Hamilton, 1 April 1900, ibid.

[79] Hamilton to Curzon, 10 May 1900, Curzon Collection, No. 159.

[80] Montagu to Chelmsford, 7 November 1918, Montagu Collection, No. 2.

[81] Hamilton to Curzon, 10 May 1900, Curzon Collection, No. 159.

[82] For an analysis of the period 1914-1919, see Fraser's 'Note on the Hyderabad Residency', 1 February 1948, Lothian Collection, No. 10.

[83] Knox to Wood, 11 March 1922, GOI, FPD, No. 663 - Internal, 1922.

[84] Thompson to Knox, 31 May 1922, ibid.

[85] Barton's 'Memorandum on Hyderabad Affairs and suggestions for future policy', 11 December 1925, GOI, FPD, No.13(5) -

Political (Secret), 1924-26, Nos. 1-40.
[86] One of the Nizam's favourite devices for squeezing money was to keep succession cases involving the Paigahs pending while his minions moved in to administer, in effect plunder, the estates. In the meantime the Nizam would wait to see who would pay him the biggest bribe. For details, see Wylie's note, 17 November 1944, GOI, Political Branch, No. 80 - Political (Secret), 1944.
[87] Barton's 'Memorandum on Hyderabad Affairs and suggestions for future policy', 11 December 1925, GOI, FPD, No. 13(5) - Political (Secret), 1924-26, Nos. 1-40.
[88] ibid.
[89] Secret-Political Letter No. 5 to S/S, 27 May 1926, ibid.
[90] *Census of India, 1921*, Vol. XXI, Pt. II, Table 10.
[91] Carolyn M. Elliott, 'Decline of a Patrimonial Regime: The Telengana Rebellion in India, 1946-1951', *Journal of Asian Studies*, 34 (November 1974), p.31.
[92] P. Hardy, *The Muslims of British India*, Cambridge, 1972, pp. 103-104.
[93] The Hindus of Hyderabad were divided into three regions by language. In the north and east were Telugu speakers, in the west, bordering on Bombay, those who spoke Marathi, and in the south-west those who spoke Kannada. Forty-eight per cent of the population of Hyderabad spoke Telugu, twenty-six per cent Marathi and eleven per cent Kannada. Elliott, op. cit., p.32.
[94] For an analysis of Hindu political movements in this period, see ibid., pp. 32-35.
[95] Barton to Political Department, 23 December 1927, GOI, FPD, No. 610 - Political (Secret), 1927.
[96] Tasker's note, 'From the point of view of the British Officers lent to the Government of Hyderabad', 1928, Tasker Collection, No. 5.
[97] Barton to Political Department, 17 April 1928, PSSF, 1902-31, File 906/1925, No. P2764/1928.
[98] Barton's 'Memorandum on Hyderabad Affairs and suggestions for future policy', 11 December 1925, GOI, FPD, No. 13(5) - Political (Secret), 1924-26, Nos. 1-40.
[99] Barton to Political Department, 23 October 1926, GOI, FPD, No. 13(17) - Political (Secret), 1926.
[100] Wylie's note, 9 August 1944, GOI, Political Branch, No. 80 - Political (Secret), 1944.
[101] Note by Major A.S. Meek, Political Agent, Mahi Kantha, 29 January 1927, GOI, FPD, No. 48 - Political (Secret), 1927.
[102] ibid.
[103] ibid.
[104] Irwin's note, 9 February 1927, ibid.
[105] Proceedings of an informal conference of Political Officers held at Simla, July 1927, opinion recorded by Lt.Col. R.H. Chenevix-Trench, GOI, FPD, No. 557 - Political (Secret) , 1927.
[106] Opinion recorded by Lt.Col. R.J.C. Burke, ibid.
[107] Opinion recorded by E.H. Kealy, ibid.
[108] Opinion recorded by L.W. Reynolds, ibid. The regulations which

governed the Commission procedure made it virtually impossible to convict a prince. The Government of India would normally be expected to appoint a panel of ruling princes to assist the Commission in its investigation, and the Commission itself would require actual proof, as distinct from evidence, of misconduct or maladministration. In 1942 the powers of Gulab Singh, the Maharaja of Rewa, were suspended and he was obliged to leave his state while a Commission investigated allegations that he was implicated in a murder and that he had employed agents to bribe staff employed in the office of the Resident for Central India. The Commission, which consisted of the Maharaja of Jhalawar, the Nawab of Rampur, Sir S. Shankar Rangrekar (a former judge of the Bombay High Court), Mr. Justice F.W. Gentle (a judge of the Calcutta High Court), and Colonel de la Hay Gordon (formerly the Resident at Mysore), was not unanimous in its verdict when it reported in January 1943. The three Indian members absolved Gulab Singh of guilt while the British members concluded that the charges had been proved. The Maharaja was required to remain outside the state until certain reforms had been introduced by Sir Edward Wakefield, a newly appointed British Prime Minister. Wakefield described Rewa as having 'much in common with the England of Henry III. At the Court, jealousy and intrigue among the ruler's favourites, all of them seeking influence and grants of land; among the nobles, determination to cling to their privileges, and resentment at the way in which they were treated by their Sovereign.' Furthermore, according to Wakefield, the administration of Rewa was 'corrupt, or inefficient, or both'. The police had only one method of detecting crime. They lodged all suspects in a cell and beat them until one or other confessed. If no confession was forthcoming, beating was followed by torture. Gulab Singh was allowed to return to Rewa in 1944 but was eventually deposed in 1946. The case of Rewa was one of the few occasions when a Commission was appointed with other princes in attendance. In the cases of Udaipur (1921), Hyderabad (1926), Kashmir (1931) and Alwar (1933), none of the princes concerned requested an inquiry. In Alwar and Kashmir independent inquiries were undertaken by officials of the Political Department. The case of Alwar is examined at the end of the present chapter. In Kashmir in the summer of 1931, the grievances of the Muslim population exploded into rioting and forced the Government of India to intervene with troops. The Hindu prince, Hari Singh, was subsequently obliged to inaugurate a council system of government and to appoint a commission headed by a British official to investigate the Muslim grievances. In 1926 the Maharaja of Indore, who was implicated in a murder which had been committed in British India, declined the offer of a Commission and offered to abdicate provided an investigation into his involvement was abandoned. This was accepted by the Government of India. In 1927, a Commisison was offered to the Maharaja of Bharatpur whose state was bankrupt. The offer was declined and the Maharaja was required to appoint a European Dewan, selected by the Government of India, with full administrative powers. The Maharaja's subsequent refusal to cooperate with this measure led to his expulsion from Bharatpur. In 1922 a Special Commissioner was appointed to investigate serious allegations of misgovernment and oppression against the Maharaja of Nabha. As a result of the inquiry the Maharaja was required to reside outside Nabha and the Government of India took over the administration. The Maharaja was eventually deposed in 1928. All these examples illustrate the consequences of the non-interference policy in the sense that the Government of India would only intervene when, as a result of years of misrule, the situation in a state had become desperate. For details of the situation in Rewa, see GOI, Political Department, Political Branch No. 18(2) - P(S)/1942, Rewa Affairs, and Sir Edward Wakefield, *Past Imperative : My Life in India 1927-1947*, London, 1966, pp. 195-207. A brief synopsis of intervention in the 1920s can be found in GOI, FPD, No. 19 - Special (Secret), 1931, Nos. 1-2, 'Recent cases illustrative of the exercise of paramountcy', pp. 5-7. For an account of the situation in Kashmir, see Prem Nath Bazaz, *The History of the Struggle for Freedom in Kashmir : From the Earliest Times to the Present Day*, New Delhi, 1954, pp. 151-171. For the situation in Nabha, see Barbara N. Ramusack, 'Incident at Nabha : Interaction between Indian States and British Indian Politics', *Journal of Asian Studies*, 28 (May 1969), pp. 563-577.

[109] ibid.

[110] Irwin to Birkenhead, 7 July and 31 August 1927, Halifax Collection, No. 3. (The Viceroy had been created Baron Irwin in 1925 and succeeded his father as Viscount Halifax in 1934).

[111] Irwin to Birkenhead, 7 July 1926, Halifax Collection, No. 2.

[112] Irwin to Birkenhead, 17 November 1926, ibid.

[113] Irwin to Birkenhead, 11 May 1927, Halifax Collection, No. 3.

[114] *Chamber of Princes*, February 1928.

[115] ibid.

[116] ibid.

[117] Irwin to Benn, 18 January 1930, Halifax Collection, No. 6.

[118] Irwin's 'Note on Administration and Government', 14 June 1927, enclosed with Irwin to Benn, 18 January 1930, Halifax Collection, No. 6.

[119] Irwin to Sir L. Wilson, Governor of Bombay, 4 October 1927, Halifax Collection, No. 21.

[120] Maharaja of Jind to Irwin, 22 September 1927, ibid.

[121] Irwin to Maharaja of Panna, 24 September 1927, ibid.

[122] *Chamber of Princes*, February 1928.

[123] Proceedings of an informal conference of Political officers held at Simla, July 1927, opinion recorded by C.C. Watson, GOI, FPD, No. 577 - Political (Secret), 1927.

[124] Opinion recorded by E.H. Kealy, ibid.

[125] Kealy to Watson, 25 July 1927, GOI, FPD, No. 177 - Confidential/Establishment, 1930.

[126] Thompson to Kealy, 29 August 1927, ibid.

[127] Kealy to Thompson, 31 August 1927, ibid.

[128] Watson's note, 18 February 1929, GOI, FPD, No. 177 - Political (Secret), 1929.

[129] S/S to Viceroy, telg., 19 April 1929, ibid.

[130] Watson's notes, 23 April and 22 May 1929, ibid.

[131] S/S to Viceroy, telg., 10 January 1931, GOI, FPD, No. 53 - Political (Secret), 1931.

[132] Notes on the financial position, oppression and maladministration in the Alwar State, GOI, FPD, No. 223 - Political (Secret), 1933, Nos. 1-6. A.W. Ibbotson, a British Liaison officer who assisted in the investigation into the causes of the rebellion, was shown an instrument of torture known as a *Kat* or *Katta* which had been used during police investigations and in the collection of revenue. A *Kat* consisted of two heavy beams each with about eight semi-cylindrical grooves cut crosswise. The following is an extract from Ibbotson's report: 'The method of use which was displayed to me forthwith by the Meos is that one beam is placed on the ground with grooves uppermost and a man's legs widely separated and placed shins downwards in two of the grooves. The other beam is then placed on top so that the legs from knee to ankle are in cylindrical holes just big enough to contain them and not quite in the line of the leg, the grooves being kept at right angles to the beams while the legs being separated are at angles to it. The man under torture thus supports himself face downwards on the ground and in some cases cannot lie with his chest on the earth as the height of the horizontal grooves would involve breaking his shinbones to do so. He therefore has to support himself with his hands and forearms and these are placed wide apart sometimes with sharp stones under them and a man made to stand on each hand'. Ibbotson to Political Department, 21 April 1933, Enclosure to No. 3, ibid.

[133] Lothian's report, 19 April 1933, Enclosure to No. 2, ibid.

[134] ibid.

[135] Question of reverting to the original position by which the Alwar State was in relations with the Political Agent, Eastern Rajputana States, GOI, FPD, No. 112 - Political (Secret) 1933.

[136] Watson's note, 27 April 1933, GOI, FPD, No. 233 - Political (Secret), 1933, Nos. 1-6, p.6.

[137] ibid.

[138] Watson's note, 23 April 1929, GOI, FPD, No. 177 - Political (Secret), 1929.

[139] Question of the reduction of Political Agencies in Central India in view of the urgent need for economy in expenditure, GOI, FPD, No. 339 - Political (Secret), 1931, Nos. 1-39.

[140] Redistribution of political charges in Rajputana, GOI, FPD, No. 693 - Political (Secret), 1933, Nos. 1-10.

CHAPTER IV

THE INDIAN STATES COMMITTEE: 1921-1929

Upon the establishment of the Chamber of Princes, the main concern of the princes on the Standing Committee was to achieve a suitable definition of paramountcy. By 1921 this had assumed a new dimension. The progress of the non-cooperation movement in British India had created grave misgivings in the minds of the princes. Only a few were directly affected by agitation within their territories but all were particularly vulnerable to the increasingly hostile attitudes which were being adopted towards the states and their rulers in the vernacular press. The princes sought protection by lobbying for press legislation and an assurance that in future they would conduct their relations solely with the Viceroy rather than with the Governor-General in Council who was head of a government that could become increasingly susceptible to popular opinion. At the same time, however, the princes remained anxious to prevent encroachments by the Political Department on their sovereignty and continued to press for a codification of political practice which would recognize that the exercise of paramountcy depended solely upon the terms of their treaties and not upon the vagaries of usage. These twin objectives were really incompatible for while the former depended upon the strength of paramountcy, the latter sought to weaken it. This chapter is concerned with the attempts by the Standing Committee to achieve a subtle balance whereby the paramount power would be strong enough to protect the princes from any threats posed by British India but not to infringe their cherished rights.

Press Protection for the Princes

Although the non-cooperation movement of 1920 to 1922 was India's first experience of mass involvement in politics, for some princes, like the Maharaja of Kolhapur, it revived bitter memories of the old anti-Brahmin campaigns of Minto's day. As early as January 1920, Kolhapur was advising Chelmsford to take stern measures to repress 'the wild abuse of speech at Congress meetings'.[1] The Nizam of Hyderabad was equally perturbed by the Khilafat agitation which existed as part of the non-cooperation movement. This agitation had been inspired by Muslim hostility towards the allied intention, revealed in the Treaty of Sèvres of May 1920, to dismember the old Turkish Empire. The Nizam responded by prohibiting all Khilafat meetings within Hyderabad and attacking Khilafat theory as both disloyal and unjustified by historical circumstances. As a result he was vilified as a traitor of Islam in certain Lahore-based Urdu papers like the *Zandur*, *Siyasat* and *Zamana*. In July 1920, the Nizam warned Chelmsford that 'the virulence of the Urdu Press had broken all bounds' and that it would become increasingly difficult for him to give the right lead to the Indian Muslims if these 'scurrilous attacks' continued.[2]

The question of press legislation to protect the princes was first raised by Kolhapur during the informal meetings held concurrently with the inauguration of the Chamber of Princes in February 1921. Accordingly, Bikaner was deputed to raise the issue with the Political Secretary. By November 1921, when the second session of the Chamber was held, princely concern had been increased by the knowledge that the restrictive Press Act of 1910 would probably be repealed. This Act, designed to afford protection to both the government and the princes against such press criticism as the government considered would lead to 'disaffection or hatred', had been widely condemned by nationalist politicians because the proprietors and editors of accused papers were denied the opportunity to defend themselves in court. Montagu was anxious to see a revision of some of the more objectionable features of the Act in order to ensure that the government would have the support of moderate politicians in working the new constitution. Chelmsford responded by appointing a nine-man Press Act Committee in March 1921 to consider if any modifications were necessary. Sir Tej Bahadur Sapru, the Law Member of the Government of India, and W.H. Vincent, the Home Member, were the only official members of the Committee, which reported in July 1921. The princes were disturbed to find that it had unreservedly advocated total repeal of the Press Act. If this recommendation were accepted, the only protection available to the princes would be for them to prosecute offending newspapers. This, however, was precisely what they wished to avoid as they considered court actions to be beneath their dignity and status.[3]

Chelmsford had been on the point of retirement when he appointed the Committee. His successor, Lord Reading, was quickly informed by Alwar that no prince would allow his name to be mentioned in connection with court proceedings.[4] In August 1921, Montagu gave his approval to the introduction of legislation to repeal the Press Act but asked the Government of India to consider whether it would be possible to protect the princes by some means which would overcome their objections to appearing in court.[5] According to Sir Ali Imam, the Nizam of Hyderabad had very definite views on how to protect himself. During an interview with Sir John Wood in September 1921, Imam confided that for the Nizam, it was not only a question of aversion to court appearances; the damage would have been done once a newspaper had published. The Nizam would never agree to abdicate his despotic powers and would inevitably be driven to take strong measures to protect his reputation and to prevent the penetration of democratic ideas into Hyderabad from British India.[6] As for the other princes, when the Chamber assembled for its second session in November 1921, Alwar moved a resolution calling for protective press legislation. Scindia objected because he thought that the princes would be emphasizing the weakness of their position by asking for special protection. Scindia's influence, however, was rapidly declining in the Standing Committee and his was the only voice of dissent.[7]

In March 1922, Montagu was forced to resign over his handling of the Government of India's protest against the post-war Treaty of Sèvres with Turkey. His Conservative successor, Lord Peel, refused to approve the repeal of the Press Act until he had received definite assurances that the princes would be protected.[8] The Government of India was therefore obliged to reconsider the question of special press legislation for the princes. Sapru remained adamant that legislation to this effect was unnecessary, but Vincent had now changed his mind on the grounds that if the princes were not protected, some of them might react by encouraging sedition in their own states against the Government of India.[9] On 23 September, just six months after the repeal of the Press Act, Vincent asked leave to introduce a bill in the Legislative Assembly to prevent the dissemination of news calculated to excite disaffection against the princes and their governments. The Assembly rejected the motion but on the following day Reading used his powers of certification to enable the bill to become law. On 3 October Peel wrote to Reading expressing satisfaction that certification under the Act of 1919 had first occurred in a matter which was one between Indians and Indians.[10]

The Standing Committee in Negotiation with Lord Reading and the Political Department

The princes of the Standing Committee had sufficient political acumen to realize that special press legislation could not, of itself, secure adequate provision for the protection of the states and their rulers. Even before Reading's certification they realized that any Press Act could, like its predecessor, become the subject of a debate demanding its repeal. Moreover, it was not inconceivable that a future Government of India might consider it more politic to submit to nationalist opinion in British India than to endorse the claims of its less numerous princely clients. It was this possibility that led the princes to seek an assurance that in future they would conduct their relations with the Viceroy rather than the Governor-General in Council. The offices of Viceroy and Governor-General in Council were held by the same person. The term Viceroy was used to describe the representative of the Crown in India and it was through the Viceroy that the Indian States owed allegiance to the British monarch. As the states were not constitutionally part of British India it was extremely rare for the Viceroy to act in his capacity as Governor-General and thereby consult his Council on matters concerning the states. However, fearing that the logical development of the Government of India Act 1919 would be the responsibility of the central executive to the central legislature, many princes now sought an assurance that the Viceroy would never consult his Council on matters concerning the states. In this way the princes hoped to gain immunity against interference by the British Indian executive and legislature.

This issue had in fact been the subject of a controversy between two members of Chelmsford's Council in 1920. Sir George Lowndes, the Law Member, had been in favour of making the Viceroy immediately responsible for all the affairs of the states which did not directly affect the administration of British India. He argued that the change should have been made in 1870 when the Indian Empire had been constituted because all the matters involved referred to suzerainty which, in his opinion, was definitely a relationship concerning only the states and the British Crown. He considered that the princes did not contemplate the change as an attempt at 'aggrandisement' but rather out of a 'genuine fear of the effect of a popular government of India upon the rights and privileges which we have guaranteed them'. Lowndes concluded: 'The ruling Chiefs all want this, and, if we are to be able to consolidate the Indian Empire, which is to me of the greatest possible importance at the present time, I feel that we must carry them with us.'[11]

A different view had been expressed by the Finance Member, Sir Malcolm Hailey. He considered that it would be wrong to lend any encouragement to what he believed was a mistaken theory that the states were dependent only on the Crown and entirely independent of the Government of India. He saw the problem in terms of central responsibility and argued that the position could only be reconsidered if a radical change were contemplated in the constitution of the Government of India whereby the Viceroy's executive gave way to a popularly elected ministry. In these circumstances Hailey admitted that it would be impossible to make the princes subordinate to an authority elected by British India.[12]

Hailey's opinion was the one that prevailed. In July 1921, when Alwar asked if it would be possible to amend the wording of the 1919 Act to the effect that the states were in relation only with the Viceroy, he was informed by Reading that as it was extremely rare for the Viceroy to consult his Council on matters concerning the states, no such action was necessary. Alwar, although expressing misgivings as to the attitude of a future Viceroy, was reluctantly obliged to let matters rest there.[13]

The princes were similarly disappointed with the promised negotiations on the codification of political practice. Although in the codification committee of 1919 Lowndes had conceded that future political developments could necessitate a definition of mutual rights and obligations, the Political Department remained convinced that there was nothing to be gained by Alwar's analytical approach. When the Standing Committee met Thompson in January 1924, Patiala argued that the government itself would benefit by increasing the powers of the princes who had always been loyal and who had no wish to become subservient to the democracy of British India. It was therefore in the government's own interest to adopt Alwar's method.[14] To this Thompson replied that numerous difficulties would arise if an attempt were made to extract principles from treaties and *sanads*, many of which had been concluded over a century ago. Moreover, the Political Secretary thought that it was not inconceivable that a thorough examination of these treaties and *sanads* might result in a case being made for an even stricter interpretation of political practice.[15] By August 1924, Thompson had slightly modified his position in that he was prepared to work with Alwar in formulating a set of principles based upon treaties, provided that due recognition was given to usage and that such an examination would not be binding on the government or the princes.[16] By then, however, the princes' reflections on events which had accompanied the first three years of the reforms in British India, had persuaded them that something far more substantial than a codification of political practice was required.

In May 1922 Bikaner had written to Reading asking for a 'round-table conference with a selected number of princes' to enable the Viceroy to 'understand at first hand the difficulties, hopes and aspirations of the princes and the remedies they suggest'.[17] Bikaner could possibly have been influenced by the knowledge that in December of the previous year Reading had been prepared to convene a round-table conference with moderate nationalist politicians and Gandhi as a means to end the non-cooperation movement. To the relief of Reading's advisers and the exasperation of some of Gandhi's lieutenants the conference never met because Gandhi imposed certain conditions upon his attendance which were completely unacceptable to the government. By the time Bikaner made his request the government's position had been considerably strengthened. The violence of Chauri Chaura brought non-cooperation to an end in February 1922 and in the following month Gandhi was arrested and sentenced to six years' imprisonment. Thereafter the Indian national movement fell into sad disarray. While the Congress split into various factions over the adoption of a new political strategy the Khilafat agitation began to appear pointless in view of the enthusiasm which greeted the movement by Kemal Ataturk in Turkey to abolish the Caliphate. By the summer of 1922 the confidence of the Government of India led to a summary rejection of Bikaner's suggestion: 'The idea underlying a round-table conference is that all meet on a footing of equality and this alone is sufficient to show that it is impossible where the Princes and the Viceroy are concerned.'[18] Bikaner was informed that as the princes now had a regular organ of expression in the Chamber of Princes, they should make use of it for the purpose of bringing matters to the attention of the Viceroy.

Two years later Bikaner tried again. In July 1924 he presented Reading with two lengthy and detailed notes. In the first the Maharaja dropped the idea of a round-table conference and wrote instead of the 'urgent need' for informal discussions between the Viceroy and the princes. He explained that since the constitutional negotiations of 1918 the states had been able to reflect upon how matters stood and to focus upon the great difficulties that lay ahead of them. As a result:

> The time would therefore appear to be fully ripe now when, in the best interests of both parties, the British Government and the States ought to take stock of the whole situation and without loss of time concentrate, during the period of transition in British India, on measures leading to a settled line of action and with the goal clearly defined and the future position of the Indian States clearly in view when a new condition of affairs will prevail in British India. Otherwise the position of the Princes and States will be an

unenviable one and in many respects probably even worse off than that of the Loyalists in Ireland.[19]

Bikaner emphasized that his suggestion would not undermine the Chamber of Princes and that the proposed discussions would not take place regularly 'but, as in this case, when special circumstances demand them, or at the outset of each new Viceroyalty'. What then, were the special circumstances of this particular case? It was clear that Bikaner, in common with many other Chamber members, had been unnerved by the campaign of non-cooperation, the controversy that had surrounded the special press legislation, and the reluctance of the Political Department to recognize the importance of treaty rights. These princes feared that unless their position was defined before the next stage of constitutional advance, they could find themselves at the mercy of the democratic movement in British India. Thus, 'in order to eliminate all elements and risk of surprise, uncertainty and haste', Bikaner considered that it was imperative to give the princes sufficient time to consider their future well in advance of the Statutory Commission which was due to report on the progress of the British Indian constitution in 1929.[20]

In his second note Bikaner chose to be rather more explicit:

> The day may be near or distant when India attains full Self-Government but, without the least hostility to constitutional advance in British India . . ., the instinct of self-preservation urgently demands every timely effort and precaution to preserve the entity and to safeguard the rights and autonomy of our States and, wherever possible, even to strengthen our position.[21]

Bikaner again emphasized the need for informal discussions but this time his proposals went further because he felt that the result of any 'stock-taking' would be to reveal the multiplicity of inter-dependent subjects requiring thorough investigation. He considered that this work would be beyond the capacity of either the Viceroy or the Standing Committee and therefore requested the appointment of an 'important Committee' to go into the whole matter and report to the Viceroy. The committee would have to be chaired by someone who was 'endowed with statesmanlike qualities and imagination and a broad outlook and genuine sympathies with the legitimate aims and aspirations of the Princes and States . . .' Bikaner had even prepared a time-table: informal discussions would be held immediately prior to the Chamber session in November 1924; the committee would be appointed either in December 1924 or January 1925; approximately three months would be allowed for the investigation with the committee thus submitting a report in March or April 1925.[22] Bikaner was in fact anticipating that if an Indian States Committee reported in the spring of 1925, the British Government would be in a position to settle the future position of the Indian States four years before it was due to examine the future of British India.

Reading and the Political Department reacted to Bikaner's suggestions in two very different ways. Thompson welcomed the proposal for informal discussions because he believed that: 'Private conversations do not give them (the princes) quite the opportunity that they want, and do not inspire the same degree of confidence in the minds of the Princes as a body, as informal discussions with a few selected rulers.'[23]   As for the subsequent inquiry he considered that although a committee would eventually have to be appointed, there was no immediate urgency about it.[24]   In viewing the informal discussions and the appointment of a committee as two quite separate issues, Thompson appears to have entirely missed the point. The very idea of informal discussions was that they would give the princes an opportunity to present their case in readiness for the investigation to be undertaken by a committee. Informal discussions by themselves would, for the princes, be useless. Reading, however, appears to have been more aware of Bikaner's intentions. Realizing the implications of the type of committee that Bikaner had anticipated would follow the informal discussions, the Viceroy refused even to contemplate the latter. He argued that they would create a 'camarilla' in the Chamber of Princes.[25]   Reading must have been aware that his argument made little sense in view of the fact that the Chamber was already controlled by a camarilla. He was, however, prepared to use any excuse in order to prevent discussions on the constitutional future of the states preceding similar discussions on British India by four years. As far as Reading was concerned the situation was similar to the one in 1916 when Wood had suggested a Council of Princes: no decision could be taken on the future of the states until British Indian policy had been settled.

The attitudes of Reading and Thompson were also responsible for their differing responses to a suggestion made by Scindia when the Chamber of Princes met in November 1924. Scindia put forward the idea of an 'Advisory Committee of the Princes' which the Viceroy could consult periodically.[26]   He suggested that it could be consulted on matters such as the economic development and fiscal interests of the states, the organization of minority administrations and the reconciliation of communal differences. Reading looked more favourably on this idea for it was intended only to discuss 'matters of the moment' rather than the larger issue of the constitutional position of the states.[27]   Thompson, however, saw Scindia's suggestion as an attempt to circumvent the Chamber and considered that it was therefore 'nothing but unreasonable on the part of the Princes to ask for the constitution of another Committee which could not but prove unnecessarily embarrassing, much less of any real benefit either to the States or to the Government'.[28]   In the event no action was taken upon the basis of an Advisory Committee, for an issue which originated with Hyderabad's claim for the restoration of Berar convinced the princes that they would gain nothing from negotiations with the Reading administration.

Lord Reading's Paramountcy Letter to the Nizam of Hyderabad

Berar was a tract of country to the north of Hyderabad consisting of the four districts of Amraoti, Yeotmal, Akola and Baldana.   For administrative purposes these districts had been part of the Central Provinces since 1853. Their three million inhabitants, however, were not British Indian subjects, but subjects of the Nizam whose sovereignty over Berar had been acknowledged by Dalhousie in the same year. In 1902 the then Nizam of Hyderabad had been forced by a severe financial crisis to conclude an agreement with Curzon's government whereby the British held Berar on perpetual lease in return for a fixed annual payment of twenty-five *lakhs* of rupees. In 1918, in pursuit of his ambition to divest himself of British control, Mir Osman Ali Khan employed Sir Ali Imam, at a fee reported to be in the region of 1,000 rupees a day, to prepare a case justifying the reincorporation of Berar into his dominions. Eventually, in October 1923, the Nizam presented Reading with an enormous and extraordinary document. It contained a survey of the past 150 years of Anglo-Hyderabad relations and concluded by suggesting that if Berar was restored to Hyderabad, the Nizam would grant its inhabitants a constitution for responsible government with complete popular control save in matters relating to his relations with the Crown and the Hyderabad Army Department. Copies of this document, together with a covering letter from Sir Ali Imam asking for support, were also sent to Peel and several other members of Prime Minister Baldwin's cabinet. Peel expressed his surprise that the Nizam should have appealed over the head of the Government of India, and it was this audacity, together with a recognition of his ultimate objective, that lead Reading to reject the claim in March 1925.[29]

The Nizam, however, was not prepared to let matters rest there. In September 1925 he wrote to Reading requesting the appointment of a Court of Arbitration to examine the Berar controversy. He justified his request upon the following basis:

> Save and except matters relating to foreign powers and policies, the Nizams of Hyderabad have been independent in the internal affairs of their state just as much as the British Government in British India. With the reservation mentioned by me, the two parties have on all occasions acted with complete freedom and independence in all inter-Government questions that naturally arise from time to time between neighbours. Now, the Berar question is not and cannot be covered by that reservation. No foreign power or policy is concerned or involved in its examination, and thus the subject comes to be a controversy between the two Governments that stand on the same plane without any limitations or subordination of one to the other.[30]

In deriving a theory of internal independence from the fact that he was the equal of the British Government in this respect, the Nizam was striking at the very essence of paramountcy. For the Resident, Barton, this served only to compound the already considerable difficulties he was facing in dealing with the Nizam. He produced a lengthy note of his own in which he described how the numerous occasions of British interference in Hyderabad proved beyond all doubt that the state had never been internally independent. He concluded with a remark made by a previous Resident in 1903: 'If I may say so I think the tendency is to treat Hyderabad with undue importance; to place the State too much on an equality with the Government of India.'[31] Barton recommended a clear and definite assertion of the government's right to interfere in Hyderabad in order to impress upon the Nizam 'that his position is more in accord with history than with his own interests'.[32] Reading, however, saw the issue in a much wider perspective. In January 1926, the Viceroy took the decision to publish all correspondence relating to Berar once a reply had been officially sent to the Nizam. Reading thought this necessary

> not only for the purpose of publicly refusing the Nizam's claim, but also because there is an underlying current of thought among the Princes ... to claim that under their treaties and engagements, they or most of them, are Allies of His Majesty and consequently should be in a position of complete internal independence whatever may happen regarding foreign relations.[33]

Moreover in view of the princes' recent concern to gain acceptance of this theory in any consideration of their constitutional future, Reading saw the occasion as an opportunity to inform them all exactly where they stood in relation to the paramount power. In March 1926 the following statement was made in a letter to the Nizam:

> The Sovereignty of the British Crown is supreme in India, and therefore no Ruler of an Indian State can justifiably claim to negotiate with the British Government on an equal footing. Its supremacy is not based only on Treaties and Engagements but exists independently of them and, quite apart from its prerogative in matters relating to Foreign Powers and policies, it is the right and duty of the British Government, while scrupulously respecting all Treaties and Engagements with the Indian States, to preserve peace and good order throughout India . . . The right of the British Government to intervene in the internal affairs of Indian States is another instance of the consequences necessarily involved in the supremacy of the British Crown. The British Government have indeed shown again and again that they have no desire to exercise this right without grave reason. But the internal no less than the external security which the Ruling Princes enjoy is due ultimately to the protecting power of the British Government, and where Imperial interests are concerned or the general welfare of the people of a State is seriously and grievously affected by the action of its Government, it is with the Paramount Power that the ultimate responsibility of taking remedial action must lie. The varying degrees of internal sovereignty which the Rulers enjoy are all subject to the due exercise by the Paramount Power of this responsibility.[34]

Reading's statement came as a shock to the princes. While respect for treaties had been mentioned, the degree of intervention now claimed seemed almost to invalidate the rights which the princes believed to be embodied in them. A stronger declaration of the omnipotence of the paramount power could not be imagined.

Lord Irwin and the Princes:
The Origins of the Indian States Committee

In April 1926, a month after the publication of the Berar correspondence, the viceroyalty changed hands. For the princes, the circumstances in which Irwin succeeded Reading were similar to those in which Minto had succeeded Curzon. They hoped that the new Viceroy would, like Minto, prove to be more sympathetic to their interests than his predecessor. In this respect Irwin did not disappoint them. In sharp contrast to Reading he was immediately prepared to consider the future of the states. At the end of June 1926, after a mere exchange of pleasantries with the Standing Committee, he confided to Lord Birkenhead, Peel's successor at the India Office: 'I think myself it is quite vital that we should seek to clear our minds on this problem in advance of the Statutory Commission. It must be faced sooner or later and failure to do so will inevitably breed uneasiness in the minds of the general body of the princes.'[35] Irwin proposed to institute a preliminary inquiry through a sub-committee of his Executive Council following which he hoped to be in a position to hold informal talks of an exploratory nature with the Standing Committee. Birkenhead was dubious about any informal talks: 'It is always a danger in discussion with the Princes that even the most informal remarks may be brought up again subsequently as "pledges", and in a matter of this importance to the Princes we should have to be specially cautious on this point.'[36] He gave his reluctant consent on condition that nothing was said which could be construed as a commitment.

Irwin commissioned Thompson to write a note which would form the basis of discussion in the sub-committee of his Council. Before considering Thompson's remarks, however, it is worthwhile to recall that some important conclusions had already been reached on one aspect of the future relationship between the states and British India. At the Chamber session of January 1926, the princes had expressed dissatisfaction with the existing economic and financial policy of the government which they considered to be totally biased in favour of British India. According to the Maharaja of Bharatpur this was due to the failure to initiate the kind of joint deliberations between the Council of State and the Chamber of Princes which had been recommended in the Montagu-Chelmsford Report.[37] As a result a situation had arisen in which, although the princes were theoretically independent of the British Indian legislature and free to tax their subjects as they saw fit, in practice acts passed by the legislature applied with equal force in the states as in British India. Bharatpur cited the example of the salt tax. Despite the fact that most states had salt treaties with the Government of India, they were all equally

affected by the periodic increases and decreases in the salt tax
sanctioned by the legislature. If this practice were to continue, then
Bharatpur argued that the states were entitled to a share of the salt
revenues of the Government of India. He also complained that the
states had not been consulted on such major questions as the adoption
of a tariff policy and the establishment of a tariff board. Moreover,
as the customs revenue derived from the tariff policy should legally
be used for the benefit of India as a whole, the states, as in the case
of salt, were entitled to receive a share of it.[38]

Bharatpur's views were endorsed unanimously by the Chamber
with the result that Reading was obliged to appoint a committee of
his Council, consisting of Sir Basil Blackett, S.R. Das, C.A. Innes and
B.N. Mitra, together with Thompson, to consider the states' claim to
a share in the customs and salt revenues of the Government of
India.[39] The committee was also asked to frame the substance of a
reply which would be given to the princes in the event of their claims
being found unacceptable. In their evidence before the committee
the princes added a further argument to their customs claim: as the
Government of India had no right to impose taxes within their states,
it also had no right to continue the existing practice of levying
customs duties on goods which, although imported through British
Indian ports, were intended for consumption in the states. Thompson
thought that these claims were justified in view of the enormous
increase in customs duties which had been occasioned by the adoption
of a protective tariff in 1922. He also believed that the
backwardness of many state administrations was due to their lack of
funds. The Government of India was therefore hardly helping the
states by forcing them to pay such heavy customs duties.[40] The
other members of the committee disagreed with Thompson. They
argued that the states derived considerable revenue from other
sources such as income tax, the proceeds of which in the provinces
went completely to the central government. They also considered
that it would be impossible to admit the claim to a share of the
customs revenue unless the inland customs duties, levied by a large
number of states, were abolished.[41] Moreover, as long as the princes
occupied a position in which they stood strictly by the terms of their
treaties and held themselves as far aloof as possible from British
India, there could be no justification for giving them a voice in
decisions concerning the fiscal policy of the Government of India. If
the states wished to obtain such a voice they would have to agree to
the formation of a Zollverein or Customs Federation with British
India. This in itself would involve something more than the mere
adoption of a common tariff. Representatives from the states would
have to be directly associated with representatives from British India
for the purpose of determining customs policy. Hence:

> It should be regarded as a cardinal principle that any step taken
> to alter the *status quo* of the relations, particularly the financial
> relations between the Government of India and the Indian States,
> should be a step in the direction of federal unity, and this
> proposal, unless combined with far-reaching changes of other

kinds, offends against this cardinal principle.[42]

Thus the committee's conclusion was that economic considerations alone could not determine the basis upon which the states could be given a voice in financial policy. They would have to enter some form of political, as well as economic federation with British India. Yet it was by no means certain that the princes would agree to this. Would they, for instance, agree to rescind their sovereignty in the administration of matters deemed federal when they had persistently argued that this sovereignty derived from inviolable treaty rights?[43]

The committee did not feel competent to predict the possible reaction of the princes and therefore concluded that the claim to a share of the customs and salt revenues was an aspect of the much larger question of the future political relationship between the states and the Government of India. According to the committee, this was

> ... one of the most difficult problems which will have to be faced in working out a scheme for self-government in India. It will no doubt be reviewed in all its aspects by the Statutory Commission, and we do not think any useful purpose would be served by our attempting to anticipate the conclusions of the Commission.[44]

Reading had departed by the time the committee presented its report in June 1926. Irwin was therefore informed that the question of a reply to the princes should be decided by the Secretary of State in consultation with the Government of India.

Thompson was mindful of these conclusions when he prepared his note for Irwin. He began with an appraisal of princely apprehensions:

> The princes are afraid of the future ... They are the last congenital autocrats in the world. Democracy has swept away others before their eyes. The reflection that it may end in dictatorship brings them no balm. Such a dictatorship would mean their downfall. With the examples of Ireland and Egypt before them, they discount our assurances of protection, and they are terrified lest out of deference to clamour or fetish of the people's will we should let all the powers of the Government of India pass to a responsible Government composed of the type dominant among politicians, a type they dislike and distrust.[45]

The Political Secretary suggested two ways in which these fears could be overcome. First, as soon as an element of responsibility was contemplated in the central government, the Viceroy would have to act apart from his Council on matters concerning the states. This had been advocated by Hailey in 1921 but Thompson now added that while it would give satisfaction to the princes it would also distinguish the viceroyalty in India from a governorship in the other dominions in that a permanent portfolio would be left in the hands of the Crown Representative. Secondly, Thompson suggested that the recent idea of a Customs Union should be extended to all matters of common concern by the establishment of a 'union' legislature. He contemplated that the representatives from the states and British India would participate in a unitary legislature, the former being nominated by the princes. Rejecting the misgivings of the other members of the customs committee, Thompson was of the opinion that this scheme would in fact appeal to the princes. Although education and the growth of democracy were destined 'to bring the despot down', the scheme would 'break his fall and tend to keep him on his throne with powers equal in extent to those of the "autonomous" provincial governments of the future, and with his ceremonial position safeguarded permanently'.[46]

Irwin endorsed Thompson's conclusions and expressed his own view that he had no wish to see the disappearance of the states as independent entities into British India by forcing compulsory constitutional progress upon them.[47] The Viceroy, however, was also of the opinion that it would take many years before India achieved self-government and therefore asked his Political Secretary for a further opinion on the immediate necessity of devising means for discussion of matters of common concern. Thompson's reply was extremely subtle for in arguing that there was such a need he was also now able to make out a case for the Viceroy's acting independently of his Council well in advance of British India achieving responsible government. He argued that provision should be made for the Viceroy to act independently and for the establishment of a Union Legislature in 1929, the year the Statutory Commission would be appointed. This would not only remove the princes' apprehensions that the 'progress of British India towards responsibility will be marked by a steady growth in the influence of popular representatives on the policy of the Central Government', but also make them even more amenable to participation in the Union Legislature.[48]

Thompson's views were debated in September 1926 by a sub-committee consisting of Irwin, Blackett, Sir Alexander Muddiman, Das and Thompson.[49] Blackett, the Finance Member, and Muddiman, the Home Member, objected strongly to the Political Secretary's hypothesis. They both considered that it would be wrong to protect the states in this manner from the pressure of popular opinion. Muddiman also thought that there was a tendency to think only in terms of the princes and asked whether their subjects would welcome the states conducting their relations only with the Viceroy. Moreover, the Home Member considered that in ignoring the probable reaction of British Indian politicians, Thompson had failed to realize that the existing Legislative Assembly would never agree to the change. Eventually a compromise was reached upon the basis of the suggestion made by Thompson in his first note: the principle of the Viceroy acting independently of his Council was endorsed but it was agreed that, as a matter of tactics, the change could only be effected simultaneously with a change to responsible government in British India.[50]

The sub-committee was, however, unanimous in its approval of the idea of a Union Legislature. Due recognition was given to the fact that the British Indian representatives would be likely to take exception to their association with state representatives who were nominated by the princes and not elected by popular vote. The committee therefore considered that 'something in the shape of federation' would be the only satisfactory solution. Such an association would involve a substantial sacrifice of sovereignty on the part of the princes with the Union Legislature exercising direct and indirect powers of taxation and powers of federal execution within the states. Despite Thompson's optimism, the other members of the committee still thought that this would be a highly contentious issue as far as the states were concerned. It was recognized, therefore, that it might be necessary to begin with a less ambitious scheme of association, but the details of the form this would take were not discussed.[51]

Before these preliminary investigations had been completed, the Government of India felt ready to reply to the claims made by the princes, particularly in respect of customs policy. In September 1926 Birkenhead was informed that when the Chamber of Princes assembled in November, Irwin proposed to make a statement to the effect that although customs policy could only be considered as but one aspect of the future political evolution of India

> ... Parliament has provided machinery for the timely consideration of future developments and he (the Viceroy) hopes that it will be found possible to bring the larger questions here involved within the scope of that enquiry ... The solution to be aimed at must be one which will tend to unity and not to dissidence among the various elements which go to make up the Indian Empire. In this sphere of customs duties there may appear to exist already the beginnings of a federal unity which may be of the greatest value in working towards the solution which all must desire.[52]

Here the Government of India had officially recommended that an investigation into the relationship between the states and British India should be undertaken by the Statutory Commission. It was upon this basis that Irwin wished to initiate informal discussions with the Standing Committee. Birkenhead, however, doubted the wisdom of the Government of India's suggestion. The Statutory Commission would be required to report only on British Indian matters. Moreover: 'We cannot feel certain that combined inquiry would be acceptable either to Princes or to British Indian opinion, since no-one knows what composition of Commission may be.'[53] He also deprecated any mention of federation as this 'raises large questions and may perhaps frighten the princes'. Birkenhead in fact thought that it would prove more convenient to dispose first of any inquiry concerning the states in order that the conclusions resulting therefrom could be available for the Statutory Commission as a basis for its separate investigations.[54] This idea was almost exactly the same as the one Bikaner had suggested to Reading in 1924, the essential difference being that at this stage Birkenhead was not prepared to commit himself as to how such an inquiry would be conducted or indeed what it would discuss. The Government of India accepted the observations of the Secretary of State. When Irwin addressed the Chamber in November he invited the Standing Committee to hold informal discussions with him. He emphasized that it would be premature for the Government of India to commit itself in regard to the question of customs policy but did express the hope that the ultimate solution to the problem would be one tending 'to unity and not to dissidence among the various elements which go to make up the Indian Empire'.[55]

The informal discussions took place at Simla in May 1927. Present were the Maharajas of Alwar, Bikaner, Kashmir and Patiala, the Jam Sahib of Nawanagar, and the Nawab of Bhopal. They were assisted by Sir Mirza Ismail, the Dewan of Mysore, Sir Prabhashankar Pattani, the Dewan of Bhavnagar, Sir Manubhai Mehta, the Dewan of Bikaner who also acted as representative for Baroda, Kailas Haksar on behalf of Gwalior, and L.F. Rushbrook Williams on behalf of Patiala.[56]

Discussion focused upon an Aide-Memoire which had been prepared by the princes. In it they ascribed their feelings of insecurity to two reasons: the infringement of their treaty rights by the paramount power and their uncertain position with regard to their future relations with a self-governing British India. 'The result of our stock-taking' said the Aide-Memoire, 'has been increased realization of the fact that our position, during the last ten years of intensive developments in British India, has been adversely affected to a degree not generally appreciated.' Thus in view of the forthcoming Statutory Commission on constitutional reform in British India it was essential that the position of the states should be investigated by a committee whose personnel 'should be such as would be welcome to, and inspire confidence amongst the Indian States'.[57]

In preparing the Aide-Memoire, the princes were unaware of the Government of India's opinion that they were not to be transferred to a responsible Indian government. They knew only of Reading's reluctance to commit himself to this view. They therefore devised a formula which made the Secretary of State and not the Viceroy the final authority on matters concerning the states. Moreover, they suggested that if the powers of the Secretary of State were curtailed or even removed altogether by a further devolution of power in British India, there should be statutory machinery competent to adjudicate on disputes between the states and British India. The princes also wanted the suggested committee to report upon methods of harmonizing political practice and to recommend means of effective co-operation with British India on matters of common concern whereby the disabilities under which the states were labouring as a result of the financial policy of the Government of India would be removed. Finally, the princes suggested that a distinguished British statesman like Lord Ronaldshay should preside over the committee which would consist of the following personnel: an eminent jurist, a member of the Secretary of State's Council, representatives of the Government of India, an economist and financier of 'European repute', some ruling princes and some ministers from the states.[58]

There was a fundamental contradiction in these proposals. While the princes sought legal protection in matters of dispute with British India, they also wanted an effective voice in matters of common concern. The princes were prepared to consider some form of economic merger with British India but wanted to maintain their distance politically. Evidently they were as yet unaware that an economic union was to a large extent dependent upon the consummation of some form of political association.

In reporting the informal discussions to Birkenhead, Irwin confided that the princes were unclear as to what they really wanted not only because of the complexity of the problem but also because 'they are undoubtedly hampered by lack of ability in their Counsels (sic) and by their temperamental incapacity to agree among themselves'.[59] Indeed he believed that the only unanimity reached at the meeting was a 'cordial dislike of Alwar'.[60] The immediate problem confronting the Viceroy was to devise some means of making the princes realize that it was impossible to divorce their economic from their political future. He considered that while it would be premature to consider the hypothetical case of the relationship between the states and a responsible Indian government, 'it might not be impossible to approach the main political problem more indirectly through an enquiry ostensibly directed to economic and financial issues'. He therefore suggested that an Indian States Committee should be appointed to inquire not only into the relationship between the states and the paramount power but also into the economic relations between British India and the states, and to make any recommendations considered desirable for their more satisfactory adjustment.[61] Irwin's idea was not for the committee to suggest a new constitutional relationship between the states and British India but for it to present its report on economic and financial issues in such a way as to impress upon the princes that ultimately such a relationship would be necessary.

In his response to Irwin's suggestions, Birkenhead appeared at first to be contradicting himself. Having previously considered that it might be wise to dispense first with a states' inquiry, he now began to express doubts.[62] Apparently when Birkenhead had suggested a separate states' inquiry in 1926, he had expected that it would serve only as a preliminary investigation into the economic and financial relations between the states and British India. He had not anticipated that it would discuss paramountcy. Indeed it was clear that the Viceroy and Secretary of State had different views about the possible results of a states' inquiry: whereas the former believed that it would above all induce the states to be more realistic in their attitude towards relations with British India, the latter was more concerned at the effect it might have on the paramountcy issue.

In December 1927 Birkenhead confessed that he was agreeing to the appointment of a states' committee as a matter of expediency only in order to show the princes that the government was not unaware of their anxieties.[63] His greatest fear was that the paramountcy findings of the committee might satisfy the princes. On the one hand this would seriously hamper the conduct of the government's relations with the states, while, on the other, 'giving them a written constitution on their relationship with the paramount power' would in all probability 'impede the adjustment of the states to any future developments in British India'.[64] Birkenhead's approval of a states' committee was therefore dependent upon Irwin impressing these considerations upon its designated chairman, Sir Harcourt Butler. Realizing that Butler was likely to be 'out of touch'[65] with the states, Birkenhead instructed Irwin to inform the former Foreign Secretary that there could be no weakening of the paramountcy question as expressed in Reading's letter to the Nizam. The Secretary of State concluded:

> Even granted that it may be in the interests of Great Britain (as many people think), no less than of the States themselves that they should be entrenched against an Indianized Government of India responsible to an Indian legislature, the dreaded day is remote, and we cannot afford in the meantime to entrench them against ourselves.[66]

It is clear, therefore, that the subsequent paramountcy recommendations of the Indian States Committee had been effectively prejudged before the Committee began its deliberations.

The Report of the Indian States Committee

The personnel of the States' Committee, which arrived in India at the beginning of 1928, were a disappointment to the princes. Besides Butler, it consisted of two other members only: Professor W.S. Holdsworth, an eminent jurist, and Sidney Peel, a financier. The princes, however, were not as one in presenting their evidence before the Committee. The Standing Committee of the Chamber of Princes established a Special Organization, briefed by Sir Leslie Scott, K.C. and four other constitutional lawyers, to prepare a case on its behalf. Approximately three-quarters of the Chamber states associated themselves with the activities of the Special Organization which functioned under the guidance of Haksar, Rushbrook Williams and K.M. Panikkar. The larger states, however, continued to maintain their distance from the Chamber. Hyderabad, Mysore, Baroda and Travancore chose to present their cases before the Committee independently. Rampur, Junagadh and some of the Kathiawar states adopted a similar course.[67]

The case prepared by Sir Leslie Scott on behalf of the Standing Committee monopolized the proceedings of the Indian States Committee. Birkenhead's fears of what was likely to happen should the princes gain satisfaction on paramountcy were immediately confirmed by the strategy of the Standing Committee's advisers. Scott and his colleagues sought a positive assurance that paramountcy derived literally from the treaties between the government and the states. This was essential in order to secure for the princes permanent protection against interference either from the Political Department or subsequently from a self-governing British India. From this virtually unassailable position the princes would then be able to dictate the terms upon which they were prepared to reach an understanding concerning their relations with British India.

Scott's work consisted of three parts, the first being an interpretation of paramountcy. He claimed that the states had originally been independent and that they had remained as such save to the extent that they had transferred any part of their sovereignty to the Crown. All sovereign rights not so transferred were vested in the ruler of the state. As it was only in respect of foreign affairs and internal and external security that any sovereignty had been surrendered, the states were therefore fully independent in matters concerning their internal administrations.[68]

The second part concerned proposals for the Political Department. Scott recommended the virtual abolition of the department and its replacement by an 'Indian States Council' consisting of the Viceroy, three princes or ministers, two 'impartial' Englishmen and the Political Secretary. Each member of the council would subscribe to a solemn obligation to protect the interests and rights of the states. Future Viceroys would take a separate oath to this effect upon assuming office. Political officers would operate under the direction of the princes and there would be a royal proclamation limiting interference in the affairs of the states. Finally, the Viceroy's intervention in the event of gross misgovernment in a state would be subject to the condition that he first consulted and took advice from the Indian States Council.[69]

The third and final part concerned the relations between the states and British India. Scott suggested the creation of a 'Union Council' for discussion of matters of common concern. It would consist of representatives from the Indian States Council together with representatives from the Governor-General's executive. The interests of the states would be safeguarded by stipulations that the Governor-General's executive could not outvote the Indian States Council and that any proposal to which the latter objected would be withdrawn.[70]

Irwin was cynical in his response to these proposals. He believed that Scott was not only misleading the princes but also suffering from delusions of grandeur: 'I am afraid that his trouble really is that he has convinced himself that his intervention at this juncture is one of the direct attempts of Providence to bring order into a disordered world and his critical faculty has suffered some obliteration under his enthusiasm.'[71] The Indian States Committee proceeded to dismantle Scott's contentions.

Acting upon instructions, Butler and his colleagues declared: 'The relationship of the Paramount Power with the states is not merely a contractual relationship, resting on treaties made more than a century ago. It is a living, growing relationship shaped by circumstances and policy, resting ... on a mixture of history, theory and modern fact'. Moreover it was not true that the states were originally independent: 'Nearly all of them were subordinate or tributary to the Moghul empire, the Maratha supremacy or the Sikh kingdom, and dependent on them. Some were rescued, others were created by the British.'[72] The Committee therefore concluded: 'Paramountcy must remain paramount; it must fulfil its obligations, defining or adapting itself according to the shifting necessities of the time and the progressive development of the States.'[73]

The Commitee rejected the idea of an Indian States Council although it did suggest that more frequent discussion between the Standing Committee of the Chamber and the Political Department might lessen the friction between the two.[74] However, the Committee also suggested a new and novel theory of intervention. If an insurrection which occurred in a state was due, not to misgovernment on the part of the ruler, but to a widespread popular demand for a change in the form of government, then the paramount power would be bound to take such measures as would satisfy this demand without eliminating the prince.[75] The Political Department's acquiescence in this recommendation was typical. Watson thought it 'unthinkable for many years to come' that the government would be required to act in this manner provided the autocratic rule of the princes was 'tolerably just and efficient'. Moreover, agitators who might stir up discontent 'could always be won over by a prudent ruler who gave them employment in the state service'.[76]

In considering relations between the states and British India, Butler's Committee recommended the appointment of an expert body to inquire into the 'reasonable claims' of the states to a share in that part of the government's revenue which was derived from matters of common concern to the states and British India.[77] It also suggested that policy on such matters as excise and postal arrangements should henceforth be decided after joint consultation between the states and British India.[78] These proposals were designed to prod the states in the direction intended by Irwin. Anything in advance of them, particularly any scheme of a 'federal character', was deemed by the Committee to be wholly premature.[79] Endorsing the opinion reached by Irwin's executive in 1926 the Committee concluded:

> For the present it is a practical necessity to recognise the existence of two Indias ... there is need for great caution in dealing with any question of federation at the present time so passionately are the Princes as a whole attached to the maintenance in its entirety and unimpaired of their individual sovereignty within their states.[80]

Irwin's expectation of the Indian States Committee never materialized. The reason was that when the Committee presented its report in March 1929 the attention of the princes was riveted upon its paramountcy recommendations. Needless to say this aspect of the report horrified the princes of the Standing Committee. For them it represented a complete repudiation of nine years prolonged, and often expensive, labour.[81] Yet they were not the only ones to feel aggrieved. The princes in general were alarmed at the suggestion that the government could suggest changes in the form of their governments should popular demands for such arise. This appeared to be an open invitation to their political opponents to encourage agitation for change. Moreover, in this respect it was significant that in December 1927 the first meeting of an All-India States' People's Conference had been convened at Bombay. The conference had been partly inspired by the government's refusal to allow the forthcoming States Committee to receive deputations from subjects of the states on grounds that this would exceed its terms of reference. The conference, which subsequently attracted the support of such prominent Indian politicians as C.Y. Chintamani and N.C. Kelkar, moved a resolution urging 'responsible government for the people of the Indian States through representative institutions under the aegis of their Rulers'.[82]

The only consolation for the princes in the Butler Report was its recommendation, also advocated by Irwin's executive in 1926, that the states could not be transferred to a responsible Government of India and that accordingly relations with the princes should be conducted through the Viceroy and not the Governor-General in Council.[83] For the princes, however, events in British India seemed to emphasize the uncertainty of this solitary gain.

In February and March 1928 an All-Parties Conference had been convened in British India with the object of devising a constitution for an Indian Dominion. In the following August, Motilal Nehru and Tej Bahadur Sapru presented the conference with details of such a constitution which became known as the Nehru Report. With reference to the Indian States, the report proposed that the new Indian Commonwealth would have the same rights and obligations towards the states arising out of the treaties as were exercised and discharged by the Government of India.[84]

For the princes a more alarming prospect could not be imagined. Moreover, by 1929 it appeared to them that an attempt might be made to give effect to this threat. Jawaharlal Nehru and the radical wing of the Indian National Congress were annoyed that the Nehru Report had advocated Dominion Status instead of complete independence for India. With their attitude threatening to split the Congress, Gandhi emerged from his self-enforced political retirement to effect a compromise. At Calcutta in December 1928 the Congress confirmed Dominion Status as its goal, but threatened to resort to civil disobedience in order to achieve complete independence if dominionhood was not conceded by 31 December 1929.[85]

When seen in the context of the report of the Indian States Committee, the Congress decision at Calcutta had placed the princes, particularly those on the Standing Committee, in an extremely invidious position. These princes had completely failed in their efforts to achieve that subtle balance whereby the paramount power would be strong enough to protect the states from a hostile British India but not to impinge upon their cherished rights. On the contrary, the Indian States Committee's definition of paramountcy seemed to invalidate these rights; its novel theory of intervention seemed to invite hostile action from British India; while the Congress decision at Calcutta seemed to confirm the imminent possibility of such action taking place. It was these considerations which prompted the latest recruit to the Standing Committee, Hamidullah, the Nawab of Bhopal, to inform Irwin that the time had come for the British to distinguish between friends and enemies. Appealing for a rejection of the conclusions of the Indian States Committee and for the princes to be freed from all the restraints of intervention so that they could appear as effective rulers in the eyes of their subjects, Bhopal declared:

You will, I am sure, find amongst the Princes of India certain Rulers who could be fully trusted and taken into confidence and who, in their turn, if they are well supported, would be of far greater use to you than any of the most influential and clever politicians in British India. I will go as far as to say that you will find them more useful and more tactful than many of the responsible Englishmen who are today guiding the destinies of the Indian Empire. These Rulers will be ready to stand by you through thick and thin; and they will be able to collect behind them a power which none of the politicians would dare to flout or ignore, and which would always be at the disposal of the British. After all the fact remains that the utility of the Indian Princes has stood the test of time and trial. Is it therefore in the best interests of the Empire to create a position for them whereby they should cease to be a real factor in guiding the destinies of the country and thus strengthen the position of the British Indian politicians whose loyalty and allegiance to the Empire is not only debatable but is unquestionably non-existent? If you would only give us a chance and trust us, we would, God willing, prove ourselves worthy of the confidence reposed in us.[86]

NOTES TO CHAPTER IV

[1] Kolhapur to Chelmsford, 19 January 1920, Chelmsford Collection, No. 24.

[2] Nizam to Chelmsford, 8 July 1920, Chelmsford Collection, No.25.

[3] For a full discussion of the question of press legislation for the princes, see Barbara N. Ramusack, *The Princes of India in the Twilight of Empire: Dissolution of a Patron - Client System, 1914-1939*, Columbus, Ohio, 1978, pp. 122-128.

[4] Reading to Montagu, 21 July 1921, Reading Collection, No. 1.

[5] Ramusack, op. cit., p.124.

[6] Wood's 'Memorandum of conversations with Sir Ali Imam', 16 September 1921, GOI, FPD, Secret-Internal, January 1922, No. 3.

[7] *Chamber of Princes*, November 1921.

[8] Ramusack, op. cit., p.126.

[9] ibid., p.127.

[10] ibid., p.128.

[11] Note by Lowndes, 20 August 1920, GOI, FPD, Secret-Internal, January 1921, Nos. 1-22.

[12] Hailey's note, 15 August 1920, ibid.

[13] Reading to Montagu, 21 July 1921, Reading Collection, No. 1.

[14] Ramusack, op. cit., p.130.

[15] ibid.

[16] Political Department's 'Memorandum regarding the relationship between the Paramount Power and the States', GOI, FPD, No. 73 - Reforms, 1928, Nos. 1-4, Appendix 1.

[17] Bikaner to Reading, 18 May 1922, GOI, FPD, No. 179 - Political (Secret), 1924-25.

[18] Thompson's note, 3 August 1922, ibid.

[19] Bikaner to Reading, 27 July 1924, ibid.

[20] ibid.

[21] Bikaner to Reading, 29 July 1924, ibid.

[22] ibid.

[23] Thompson's note, 3 August 1924, ibid.

[24] ibid.

[25] Reading's note, 7 August 1924, ibid.

[26] *Chamber of Princes*, November 1924.

[27] Patterson's note, 3 March 1926, GOI, FPD, No. 179 - Political (Secret), 1924-25.

[28] Thompson's undated note, p.33, ibid.

[29] For a brief *résumé* of the Berar case up to 1925, see 'Question of retrocession of Berar to His Exalted Highness, the Nizam of Hyderabad', GOI, FPD, No. 13 - Political (Secret), 1924-26, Nos. 1-49, pp. 7-9.

[30] Nizam to Reading, 25 September 1925, ibid.

[31] Barton's note, 14 February 1926, ibid. The remark was made by Sir David Barr who was the Resident at Hyderabad between 1900 and 1905.

[32] ibid.

[33] Reading to Birkenhead, 14 January 1926, Reading Collection, No. 6.

[34] Reading to Nizam, 27 March 1926, GOI, FPD, No. 13 - Political (Secret), 1924-26, Nos. 1-49.

[35] Irwin to Birkenhead, 30 June 1926, Halifax Collection, No. 2.

[36] Birkenhead to Irwin, 22 July 1926, ibid.

[37] *Montford Report*, para. 326.

[38] *Chamber of Princes*, January 1926.

[39] GOI, FPD, Secret-Internal Despatch No. 8 to S/S, 9 September 1926, Claim of the Indian States to a share in the customs and salt revenues of the Government of India, PSSF, 1902-31, File 2764/1927, pts. 1 and 2, No. 1747/1927.

[40] Report of the Committee appointed by His Excellency Lord Reading to enquire into the claims of the Ruling Princes to a share of the customs and salt revenues of the Government of India, 4 June 1926, para. 11, Enclosure No. 4, ibid.

[41] ibid., para. 12.

[42] ibid.

[43] The adoption of a common tariff was a case in point. It would have to be administered by federal officials.

[44] Report of the customs and salt Committee appointed by Lord Reading, para. 15.

[45] Thompson's note, 17 July 1926, GOI, FPD, No. 302 - Political, 1926.

[46] ibid.

[47] Irwin's undated note, ibid.

[48] Thompson's note, 28 August 1926, ibid.

[49] Minutes of the proceedings of the sub-committee appointed by the Viceroy to discuss future relations between British India and the Indian States, 17 September 1926, ibid.

[50] ibid.

[51] ibid.

[52] GOI, FPD, Secret-Internal Despatch, No. 8 to S/S, 9 September 1926, Claim of the Indian States to a share in the customs and salt revenues of the Government of India, PSSF, 1902-31, File 2764/1927, pts. 1 and 2, No. 1747/1927.

[53] S/S to Viceroy, telg., 13 November 1926, ibid.

[54] S/S to Viceroy, telg., 14 November 1926, ibid.

[55] *Chamber of Princes*, November 1926.

[56] Minutes of the proceedings of an informal conference which took place at Viceregal Lodge, 4 May 1927, GOI, FPD, No. 654 - Political (Secret), 1927, Nos. 1-8.

[57] ibid.

[58] ibid.

[59] Irwin to Birkenhead, 5 May 1927, Halifax Collection, No. 3.

[60] Irwin to Birkenhead, 11 May 1927, ibid.

[61] Irwin to Birkenhead, 26 May 1927, ibid.

[62] Birkenhead to Irwin, 16 June 1927, ibid.

[63] Birkenhead to Irwin, 15 December 1927, ibid.

[64] ibid.

[65] Butler's views on the states had not changed since he had been Foreign Secretary during Minto's Viceroyalty. In June 1927 he wrote to Irwin: 'I should be very sorry myself to see any popular body in British India interfere in any way with the Native States. They existed long before there was any idea of democratic institutions in India and they are an excellent foil. Also the Indian Princes are likely to be the best friends that we shall ever have ... Democratic institutions have not succeeded anywhere in the East as yet, and although I am by no means a pessimist as regards India, I think it is a very large assumption to expect that they will blossom at an early date.' Butler to Irwin, 1 June 1927, Butler Collection, No. 61.

[66] Birkenhead to Irwin, 15 December 1927, Halifax Collection, No. 3.

[67] *Report of the Indian States Committee, 1928-1929*, Cmd. 3302, 1929, para. 6.

[68] Joint Opinion of Sir Leslie Scott, K.C.; Mr. Stuart Bevan, K.C.; Mr. Wilfred Greene, K.C.; Mr. Valentine Holmes; and Mr. Donald Somervell, Appendix 111, ibid.

[69] Private Office Papers, L/PO/401, Indian States Committee, 1927-29.

[70] ibid.

[71] Irwin to Birkenhead, 9 August 1928, Halifax Collection, No. 4.

[72] *Report of the Indian States Committee*, para. 39.

[73] ibid., para. 57.

[74] ibid., para. 73.

[75] ibid., para. 50.

[76] Watson's undated note on the 'Position of the Government of India in supporting a Ruler against a demand of his subjects for a change in the methods of State Government', GOI, FPD, No. 73 - Reforms, 1928, Nos. 1-4.

[77] *Report of the Indian States Committee*, para. 80.

[78] ibid.

[79] ibid., para. 66.

[80] ibid., paras. 67 and 68.

[81] Scott's fees were estimated at £100,000.

[82] R.L. Handa, *History of the Freedom Struggle in the Princely States*, New Delhi, 1968, p.31.

[83] *Report of the Indian States Committee*, paras. 58 and 67.

[84] All Parties Conference, 1928, Report of the Committee appointed by the Conference to determine the principles of the Constitution for India, 1928, cited in C.H. Philips (ed.), *The Evolution of India and Pakistan, 1858-1947 : Select Documents*, London, 1962, p.233.

[85] S.R. Mehrotra, *India and the Commonwealth, 1885-1929*, London, 1965, p.140.

[86] Bhopal to Irwin, 4 September 1929, Halifax Collection, No. 28.

CHAPTER V

THE POLITICS OF AN ALL-INDIA
FEDERATION: 1930-1935

The Paramountcy Strategy of the Standing Committee

Irwin used the opportunity of his mid-term leave in the summer of 1929 to take soundings from political opinion in Britain on proposals which he believed might forestall the Congress threat of civil disobedience. His intention was first to gain an assurance from the recently elected Labour Government that ultimate Dominion Status was implicit in the Montagu declaration of 1917, and secondly, to secure a promise that Indian leaders would be consulted on any conclusions the Government might reach upon the basis of the Statutory Commission's report before they were included in a new Government of India Act.[1] Of the two, Irwin considered the latter to be the more problematical. It would be difficult to devise a suitable occasion for making such a declaration without implying a change in policy and also impairing to some extent the position of the Statutory Commission. Ultimately the questions raised by the report of the Indian States Committee and the obvious necessity of considering the future of the Indian States provided the only feasible opening.[2] In London Irwin met with formidable opposition from spokesmen for the Conservative and Liberal parties who believed that both parts of the Viceroy's strategy would persuade Indians to believe that far-reaching constitutional changes were imminent. However, on 31 October 1929 a statement was issued to the effect that Dominion Status was implicit in the declaration of 1917, and representatives from British India and the Indian States were invited to convene a conference in London with the British Government for the purpose of discussing both British Indian and All-Indian problems.[3]

Irwin was subsequently disappointed to find that his initiative had failed to prevent civil disobedience. In part this was due to the uproar which greeted the statement in Britain. The hostility displayed during the debates in both the House of Commons and House of Lords was sufficient to convince many Indians of British insincerity. Above all, however, when Gandhi and Motilal Nehru met the Viceroy on 23 December they informed him that they would only attend the conference on the understanding that its task would be to draft a Dominion constitution. Irwin was in no position to give such an assurance with the result that when the Congress assembled at Lahore on 31 December 1929 it opted for civil disobedience and declared its goal to be complete independence.[4]

For the princes of the Standing Committee, however, the October statement represented a possible solution to their dilemma. The obduracy of Gandhi and Motilal had not doomed the London conference. On the contrary, it was now more than ever essential that it should be a success. Moreover, as the princes were seen as an integral part of the conference, its success was in no small measure dependent upon the attitude that they would adopt. The Standing Committee princes therefore considered that they were in an exceptionally strong bargaining position. They would make their co-operation in any constitutional scheme that might result from the conference conditional upon a satisfactory settlement of paramountcy. Thus when these princes expressed readiness to reconsider their relationship with British India they did so purely with the intention of subverting paramountcy.

This became apparent at the Chamber session of February 1930. The proceedings were monopolized by a deliberate assault upon paramountcy. In his opening speech as Chancellor, Patiala welcomed the conference invitation but quickly moved on to accuse the Indian States Committee of 'having gone further than the most ardent champion of the Political Department'. He also declared that the 'findings of the Committee, unless they are agreed to by the Chamber, should not be considered as authoritative pronouncements or interpreted as political practice binding against the States'.[5] Similar sentiments were voiced in speeches by Alwar, Bikaner, Kashmir and the Jam Sahib of Nawanagar.

Irwin was surprised by the vehemence of the onslaught, particularly as this was the first occasion upon which the proceedings of the Chamber had been made public. He considered that the princes had committed a 'tactical error' in attacking paramountcy in this manner because he believed that in the absence of popular government in the states many people in British India regarded the protection afforded by paramountcy as the sole refuge for the subjects of the princes. The Viceroy subsequently asked for authority to meet the princes in the near future in order to dissuade them from disputing paramountcy any further.[6]

It was evident from Irwin's reaction to the Chamber session that he was unaware of the Standing Committee's motives. This was not the case with the more astute Sir Robert Holland in the India Office. Holland realized that the princes were not concerned with conciliating British Indian opinion because they were convinced that paragraph 58 of the Butler Report (which declared that the states should not be transferred to a responsible Indian government) would be accepted. Holland argued that from this starting point the Committee's tactics were to divide sovereignty between themselves and the Crown, thus restricting the paramount power's intervention in their internal affairs and eliminating its discretionary element: 'They regard this as the bargain issue upon which their co-operation in a Federal scheme depends.' This analysis led the former AGG to believe that the only way of countering the Committee's 'carefully thought out strategical plan' was to inform them that just as the question of paramountcy was *sub judice* so the same applied to paragraph 58 of the Butler Report.[7] Wedgwood Benn, the Labour Secretary of State, accepted this conclusion and advised Irwin to communicate it to the princes.[8]

Holland's analysis, though undoubtedly correct, was slightly premature in its assumption that the Standing Committee was contemplating federation. In May 1930 the Statutory Commission reported that the evolution of a federal association 'will be slow and cannot be rashly pressed'. The Commission therefore limited its recommendation to the establishment of a Council of Greater India with consultative and deliberative functions on matters of common concern to the states and British India.[9]

It was upon the basis of this recommendation that the Standing Committee initially approached the subject of constitutional reform. During an informal conference held at Simla in July 1930, members of the Committee, together with representatives from Baroda, Hyderabad and Mysore, told Irwin that although the princes realized that an 'All-India Federation may possibly prove the most satisfactory solution of India's problem', they considered that the offer of a 'Council of Greater India should be accepted without hesitation, subject to safeguards . . . dealing with matters of common concern'.[10] Reference was also made to the need for a satisfactory settlement of the paramountcy question which, according to the Standing Committee, would be essential even if the forthcoming round table conference left the position of the central government unchanged.[11]

Irwin's role at the July conference was based upon the assumption that the princes were not contemplating immediate federation. Despite the reference to paramountcy the Viceroy did not therefore consider that the Standing Committee was in a bargaining position. Moreover, this being the case, he saw no need to inform the princes that paragraph 58 of the Butler report was still *sub judice*. Instead Irwin virtually assured them on this point by indicating that in future the Viceroy would act apart from his Council on matters concerning the states. He also agreed to discuss questions relating to paramountcy with the Standing Committee upon their return from the round table conference, an agreement which convinced Irwin that there was no danger of paramountcy being raised at the conference.[12]

The Viceroy maintained his belief that neither federation, nor consequently paramountcy, would be discussed at the round table conference throughout the remainder of the summer and the autumn of 1930. In a Reforms Despatch of September 1930, the Government of India endorsed the Statutory Commission's 'distant ideal of an All-India Federation' but recognized that 'the time had not yet come when the general body of Indian States would be prepared to take a step so far-reaching in its character as to enter any federal relations with British India'.[13] On 1 October Irwin wrote of the princes: 'Whatever lip-service (they) may pay to the federal idea, they will, when it comes to the point, want to begin through some consultative machinery before they burn any boats.'[14] Within a month it was evident that Irwin had miscalculated. From London, Sapru explained why to his son: 'The only organized party here is that of the Princes and they are taking very progressive lines. They are ready to join the All-India Federation . . . at once.'[15]

*The Genesis of Federation
and Preparations for the First Round Table Conference*

The initiative for an immediate All-India Federation came from Hyderabad. Responsibility for it lay with Lieutenant-Colonel Terence H. Keyes who became the Resident in the state in February 1930. Keyes was disturbed by that part of the Statutory Commission's report which dealt with British Indian reform. The prospect of autonomous provinces growing into a powerful British-Indian Federation was not one that could be recommended to the princes, particularly to the Nizam. According to Keyes this type of political development would strengthen the regional movements in Maharashtra, Andhra and Berar and enable them to seize the first available opportunity of attacking the Muslim oligarchy in Hyderabad. Furthermore, Hyderabad had to consider its economic interests. Unlike the states of Rajputana and Central and Western India, Hyderabad, in common with Mysore, the other major southern state, was landlocked. Whereas the former category of states could maintain their economic survival upon the basis of the ports of the Kathiawar peninsula, Hyderabad and Mysore were totally dependent for their economic existence upon the goodwill of the neighbouring provinces. Keyes concluded that the only salvation for Hyderabad lay in its recognition of British paramountcy and its immediate entry into an organic All-India Federation. By doing so the Nizam would not only be able to prevent 'plots' being 'hatched' against Hyderabad but also to secure a more favourable economic future for his state.[16]

The Nizam was impressed by these arguments for two reasons. First, by 1930 he was beginning to realize the implications of the fact that his state was landlocked. When Keyes arrived as Resident he found the Nizam busily re-examining Hyderabad's commercial treaty of 1802 with its promise of a free port at Masulipatam on the Madras coast.[17] Secondly, it made a pleasant change for the Nizam to have a Resident more interested in securing a stable future for Hyderabad than in condemning his personal conduct. Keyes subsequently assumed that the Nizam had agreed to favour an All-India Federation and to admit British paramountcy. His first assumption was correct but his second required an important qualification. The precarious position of his state made the Nizam realize that it would be impracticable to impose general restrictions upon the exercise of paramountcy. At the same time, however, his determination to rid himself of the restrictions upon his own ruling powers remained unchanged. The result was an ambiguous situation in which the Nizam approved the principles of an omnipotent paramountcy provided that they were not applied within his state.

Evidently Keyes, who was quite taken with the Nizam,[18] did not realize this. In the month preceding the Simla conference he continually petitioned both Viceroy and Political Department to lend their support to his proposals. He was also anxious to be present at Simla because he was deeply concerned at the calibre of the delegation Hyderabad was sending to the informal conference. It was to be led by Sir Akbar Hydari, Finance Member of Hyderabad's

Executive Council. Keyes had nothing but contempt for Hydari. He confided to Sir George Cunningham, Irwin's private secretary, that although Hydari had originally been in favour of federation, he had changed his mind as a result of Congress threats to his mill-owning interests in Bombay. According to Keyes these had 'frightened the wits out of that chicken-hearted little creature' with the result that the Hyderabad delegation at Simla would pursue 'a timorous course of wait and see in the hope that an opportunity will occur of bargaining in the true baniah spirit'.[19]

Much to his annoyance, Keyes was refused permission to be present at Simla, although on the eve of the conference he was able to persuade the Nizam to telegraph instructions to his delegation that he was prepared to enter an All-India Federation under due safeguards.[20] The telegram, however, arrived too late to influence the conference proceedings. On hearing of this, Keyes was furious. He subsequently attributed the fact that he had not been allowed to attend to an attempt by the Political Department to sabotage the idea of a federation before it got off the ground. Of an equally serious nature, he also accused the department of deliberately misrepresenting Irwin's views. In a letter to Sir Denys Bray, Foreign Secretary to the Government of India, Keyes declared that the department was so obsessed by the picture of an Indian India and a British India portrayed in the report of the Indian States Committee that they were working in a way that would make an All-India Federation impossible:

> To me this is the madness that the gods send before destruction ... What Butler calls British India is just that part of India that is trying to repudiate all that is British ... What he calls Indian India is that part that wants to retain the British connection. Swaraj India and Maharaja's India are mixed up like the bits of a jigsaw puzzle, and everywhere they touch there will be continued friction.

In the same letter, Keyes restated his belief in federation as the only means to avoid such friction and expressed his disquiet that Irwin was being unwittingly 'manoeuvred' into accepting the Political Department's point of view.[21]

The idea that an attempt had been made to sabotage the federal idea in the summer of 1930 reappeared six years later in the India Office. In April 1936 the Political Department of the India Office was astonished to read the following extract from the appendix to an Administration Report from Hyderabad for the year October 1932 to October 1933:

> Rightly anticipating in the light of the discussions with certain Princes and representatives of other States that took place in Simla in July 1930 that Federation was likely to become an immediate issue, Sir Akbar Hydari, in consultation with his colleagues, drew up on the voyage to England a federal scheme in broad outline.[22]

Paul J. Patrick, the Political Secretary at the India Office, commented that this was the first time his department had heard of any reference to federation at the Simla conference.[23] Sir Findlater Stewart, the Permanent Under Secretary of State for India, remarked that it was the first time *any* department in London had heard mention of it.[24] The Parliamentary Under Secretary of State, R.A. Butler, summed up the general impression in the India Office: 'Presumably there were persons in official circles in India at the time who hoped to see the idea overlaid at birth.'[25] Evidently the Government of India had not seen fit to inform the India Office in July 1930 that the Nizam was prepared to contemplate federation.

However, the accusations made by Keyes cannot be accepted at face-value. His claim that the Political Department was 'manoeuvering' Irwin was certainly false. The Viceroy was just as much impressed by the notion of 'two Indias' as was the Political Department. He was quite content with the recommendation for a Council of Greater India because this accorded with the conclusions reached by the sub-committee of his Council in 1926. In the meantime Irwin wanted to deal with the more pressing problem of the British Indian centre. Hence the recommendation in the Government of India's Reforms Despatch to make the government 'responsive' to the central legislature except on matters such as defence, foreign relations, internal security, finance, protection of minorities and the protection of services recruited by the Secretary of State.[26] As for the Political Department itself, Watson had already recorded his views on federation at the time of Holland's warning about the paramountcy strategy of the Standing Committee. Although the Political Secretary realized that the princes would welcome, and indeed press, for a federation with British India which would leave their internal administrations unchanged and intact, he doubted if any, with the possible exceptions of the Maharajas of Mysore and Travancore, would agree to a federation which involved the grant of constitutional government to their subjects. Moreover, Watson was of the opinion that without constitutional government in the states, a genuine federation with British India seemed impracticable.[27] It would appear therefore that the Political Department was not going to lend any encouragement to federation while the paramountcy issue remained unsettled. Finally, it is significant that Irwin and the Political Department shared a profound mistrust of both Keyes and the Nizam. The Resident was not liked in official circles. Irwin's successor, Lord Willingdon, described him as 'one of those people who rather like spreading themselves and has to be watched pretty closely'.[28] Statements emanating jointly from Keyes and the Nizam were thus inevitably suspect to Irwin and Watson. Indeed it appears that in July 1930 both Viceroy and Political Department had preconceived ideas on federation which they saw no need to change in view of the opinion expressed by the general body of princes and ministers present at Simla. They therefore dismissed the recommendation for an immediate federation as the work of two misfits.

Between the Simla conference and the opening in November of

the first round table conference in London, certain representatives of the states began to reconsider their attitude towards federation. The first to do so were Haksar and Panikkar on behalf of the Special Organisation of the Chamber. In August 1930 they completed the first draft of a book, later to appear on the opening day of the London conference with the title *Federal India*, which contemplated the grant of complete responsible government to British India save for the transfer to a federal council of matters of common concern to the states and British India. This conception of federation was precisely that which Holland had warned against. A large part of *Federal India* was devoted to describing how, in return for British India achieving central responsibility, the states would obtain complete internal autonomy safeguarded by a supreme court.[29] The scheme therefore had obvious attractions to the Standing Committee princes.

In late August 1930 a similar scheme of federation was produced by Sir Mirza Ismail, Dewan of Mysore. At a conference of South Indian states held at Bangalore, Ismail declared himself to be at variance with the way the Statutory Commission had surrounded their vision of a federal India 'with the misty twilight of a distant future'. In his concluding remarks at the conference Ismail recommended 'a constitution which provides full autonomy in the Provinces, responsibility at the Centre (subject to such transitional safeguards as may be unavoidable) and a closer association between British India and the States in matters of common concern'.[30] Ismail, however, was not influenced by paramountcy considerations. He was concerned at the growth of vocal opinion among the subjects of the states against the continuation of autocracy and his suggestion was largely inspired by a States' People's Conference which had met simultaneously with that of the South India states at Bangalore.[31] Ismail was also influenced by the consideration that if Mysore entered a federation it might gain relief from the heavy burden of tribute which it paid to the British Government.[32]

In September 1930 a yet further scheme of federation appeared from Hyderabad. The initiative this time rested with Sir Akbar Hydari who had real cause to reconsider his previous attitude. The responsible British Indian centre envisaged in the Haksar-Panikkar and Ismail schemes was, as Keyes had indicated, a serious threat to Hyderabad's existence and the autocracy of the Nizam. Hydari therefore sketched a plan for federation which involved the abolition of the British Indian centre and its replacement by a small 'aristocratic' federal assembly consisting of thirty-six provincial representatives, twenty-four state representatives and twelve Crown nominees. All matters of common concern would come under federal jurisdiction, while all remaining British Indian subjects would be completely provincialized. Reserved subjects, particularly foreign affairs, political relations with the states, defence, finance and law and order would remain as such under the jurisdiction of the Crown.[33] Hydari explained his scheme to Sir George Schuster, Finance Member of the Government of India, on the voyage to London for the opening of the conference. Schuster, though appreciative of Hydari's concern to eliminate 'the popular demagogues from British India', pointed out that British Indian politicians would never accept the abolition of their 'central political stage'.[34] Hydari therefore revised his scheme to accommodate a British Indian centre. However, he was emphatic that the activities of this centre were in no way to influence those of the federal assembly. Thus the British Indian representatives in the assembly were not to be indirectly elected from those who held seats in the British Indian centre but directly from the individual provinces.[35]

Despite the varying motives which had produced these schemes, the delegation of princes and their advisers arrived in London in late October 1930 and appointed a committee to consider the attitude that they should adopt towards federation.[36] At the beginning of November they reached agreement that the states should join with British India in a federal structure for joint control of matters of common concern.[37] This attitude had a marked effect upon the other delegations to the conference, both British and Indian.

Sir Malcolm Hailey had been sent to London as a constitutional adviser. On 14 November he wrote back to Irwin:

If the movement of the Princes can be guided on to really useful lines, there is something of real substance behind it, because if we could obtain a Federal Assembly in which they were well represented, and in which the Viceroy would have a wide nomination in order to discharge his responsibilities to Parliament, then we should all of us be prepared to go further in the way of responsible Government than we should if matters took their ordinary line in development of the proposals of Simon or the Government of India. As I suggested to a friend the other day, the proposal may possibly be merely a good red herring but, if we are lucky, it may actually turn out to be a good 'fishable salmon'.[38]

This was an accurate appraisal of the official British mind. The Conservative and Liberal parties in particular were agreed that the princes' initiative had given them the basis for a twofold strategy to pursue at the conference. During the preliminary stages of the conference spokesmen for these two parties had been obsessed with the fear that when discussion commenced the British Government would be confronted with a united demand for Dominion Status. Now, however, the princes' federal initiative could be used on the one hand to divert attention from Dominion Status, while on the other it could prove of more lasting value in dealing with the vexed problem of how much power should be transferred to Indian control in the central government. Lord Reading, Liberal spokesman on India, remarked: 'If the Simon Commission and the Government of India had known what we now know they'd have written very different reports.'[39] For the Conservatives, Samuel Hoare subsequently submitted a memorandum for the consideration of his party's Business Committee in which he spoke of federation extricating British India 'from the morass into which the doctrinaire liberalism of Montagu had plunged it'. Moreover, with a federal constitution Britain could 'yield a semblance of responsible government and yet retain ... the realities and verities of ... control'.[40] Clearly for the Conservatives federation was indeed to become another 'good red herring'.

The final link in the federal chain was Sapru, head of the Indian Liberal delegation. According to Hailey, Sapru had in fact arrived in London with the intention of demanding a declaration in favour of Dominion Status. He did not succeed because the Muslim delegates refused to contemplate such action without corresponding guarantees for their own position.[41] Sapru was therefore obliged to consider federation with the states as the only means of acquiring some form of central responsibility. At the end of November he wrote to a colleague in India: '. . . if we leave the States out, we shall get nothing, and certainly responsibility at the Centre, with a unitary form of Government is not going to come to us'.[42] Indeed it was Sapru who helped Bikaner write his speech agreeing to join a federation, which the Maharaja delivered on behalf of the princes when the conference opened on 17 November 1930.

The Problem of Paramountcy and the Confederation Scheme

Irwin was astonished when he received news of events in London. He wrote to his father that he doubted if the princes realized what they were doing.[43] Certainly in the case of Hyderabad it was clear that when the conference closed in January 1931, Hydari had been manoeuvred into a position which he had not intended. Largely at the insistence of Sapru and the Hindu Liberals, the Federal Structure Committee which had been appointed by the conference recommended that the federal authority should ultimately inherit such central subjects as income tax, civil and criminal law, and law and order from the Government of India. Sapru and his colleagues sought a strong federal authority with a wide range of powers in order to make a reality of central responsibility. The Muslim delegates objected to this because they wanted to avoid a Hindu-dominated centre and preferred that these subjects should be devolved upon the provinces. Having previously envisaged that the federal authority would discuss only a limited number of subjects of common concern, Hydari had similar misgivings. Furthermore, the Federal Structure Committee recommended a bicameral federal legislature with representatives from British India and the states in both chambers to replace the existing central legislature. Hydari was thus confronted with a much closer association with British India than he had originally intended. In India, the Nizam responded to this situation by insisting that his accession to federation would be conditional upon receipt of a written assurance that the Crown would possess the 'moral and material means' of protecting his state in accordance with the terms of his treaties.[44] Whether or not Britain could give the Nizam such an assurance subsequently became a key factor in determining Hyderabad's attitude towards federation.

Hydari's misgivings did not influence the princes of the Standing Committee. Federation for them was primarily a means to gain autonomy in their internal affairs. This was just beginning to dawn upon Irwin: 'I am not sure . . . that they may not have some ideas in their minds of using federation to get rid of the exercise of paramountcy.'[45] Hailey confirmed the impression: 'They seem to be out for the extinction of the Political Department, rather than the creation of a Federal constitution.'[46] The princes of the Committee revealed their true colours at meetings they held with the Prime Minister, Ramsay MacDonald, on 3 December 1930 and 9 January 1931. At the first Bikaner threatened that the princes would be unable to federate until they knew what their position was regarding paramountcy.[47] At the second Bikaner, supported by Alwar and Patiala, declared that the princes were 'up against a stone-wall of departmental prejudice' in India and that a 'high legal luminary' from Britain was required to supplement the personnel of the Political Department.[48]

From India, Watson's response to these discussions was truly remarkable. The Political Secretary declared that he might even be prepared to abandon non-interference in order to counter the Standing Committee's assault upon paramountcy. Moreover, in stark contrast to his previous utterances, Watson now considered that the policy of non-interference had resulted in 'an increase of irresponsible autocracy and lessened protection and benefit to the states subjects'. He concluded: 'The more the Paramountcy presses upon the States, forcing them to improve the conditions of their subjects, the more ready they will be to welcome a Federation on really effective terms as an alternative or to escape the rigours of intervention by granting their people some effective voice in the administration.'[49] This was not the first occasion upon which the Political Department had used the truth about non-interference merely to justify its own authority in the states.

Irwin's reaction to the discussions was essentially to repeat the foreboding expressed three years previously by Birkenhead when he had authorized the appointment of an Indian States Committee. It was only now that the Viceroy became fully conversant with the tactics of the Standing Committee. He realized that if, in addition to an assurance being given that the states would never be transferred to a responsible Indian government, large concessions were made over paramountcy, then the princes would have no need for federation.[50] Irwin anticipated difficulties during the paramountcy discussions he had promised the Standing Committee when they returned from London. However, at the Committee's own request, these discussions were postponed.

One of the reasons for this postponement was that Irwin's term of office would expire in April 1931 and the Committee felt that the issue could not be fully discussed in the short time before he was due to leave. The main reason, however, was that personal rivalries were beginning to disrupt the Committee. Bikaner and Patiala had always felt a mutual antipathy. Their close co-operation for a decade could not conceal the fact that Patiala greatly resented Bikaner's reputation as a more capable and experienced statesman. Friction between the two came to a head in March 1931 when Bikaner's support for the Nawab of Bhopal enabled the latter to defeat Patiala by a narrow margin in the elections for the Chancellorship of the Chamber of Princes.[51]

Patiala's reaction to his defeat took the form of an attack upon the federal scheme adopted at the first round table conference. On 15 June 1931 he published a pamphlet entitled *Federation and the Indian States*. Denouncing federation as a 'radical innovation' which 'subverts the very basis of the well-tried and time-honoured political institutions of the states', Patiala suggested instead that the Chamber of Princes should be enlarged into a 'Union of States' from which a Standing Committee would confer with a Standing Committee of the British Indian legislature on matters of common concern.[52] Patiala was undeterred when a meeting of princes in Bombay in July rejected his scheme. In August he joined forces with his cousin, the Maharaja of Dholpur, to produce a further scheme for a confederation of states. This envisaged that an enlarged Chamber of Princes would operate as an electoral college for the purpose of electing state representatives to the federal legislatures. Provision was made for responsibility to be exercised in a federal executive but only in respect of matters which were strictly of common concern to the states and British India.[53]

Neither Patiala nor Dholpur could claim to have originated the confederation scheme. This honour rested with Sir Prabhashankar Pattani, regent to the Maharaja of Bhavnagar, ruler of one of the Kathiawar states. Pattani had recommended confederation at the first round table conference on the grounds that it would enable the states to 'perpetuate their existence, for, standing together as a collective body, they can induce British India to take account of their united strength'. For the states to federate individually would 'only result in the individual state being swallowed up'.[54]

Pattani's ideas appealed particularly to the smaller states and to their principal spokesmen, the Chief of Sangli and the Raja of Sarila. Their size and collective number meant that the small states would never gain individual representation in an All-India Federation. Confederation, however, would provide them with an opportunity of influencing the election of state delegates to the federal legislatures. The attraction that confederation held for the smaller states was primarily responsible for Patiala's support for the confederate cause. By championing the interests of the smaller states he hoped to strengthen his chances of regaining the Chancellorship of the Chamber. Patiala's maneouvres infuriated Bikaner and Bhopal who found themselves bombarded with demands from the smaller states that they were entitled to individual representation in an enlarged Chamber of Princes. Bikaner spent a large part of the summer of 1931 threatening the smaller states that if they persisted their larger brethren would have to 'seek protection by securing a plurality of votes for themselves in the Chamber, and also in both Federal Houses and elsewhere, which might be more proportionate to their size and importance'.[55]

Confederation also appealed to those states whose geographical location made them particularly susceptible to agitation directed from British India. Indeed this was Dholpur's main reason for supporting confederation. The Maharaja was said to stand in 'great dread' of the influx of democratic propaganda from the contiguous district of Agra.[56] In this respect confederation had attractions for a conservative prince like Gulab Singh, the Maharaja of Rewa. The state of Rewa was less than one hundred miles from Allahabad in the United Provinces, a point which Gulab Singh had stressed to Watson in 1930 when some of his more recalcitrant *thakurs* had attempted to settle a dispute by securing the mediation of Jawaharlal Nehru.[57] However, Rewa could never become firmly entrenched in the Patiala-Dholpur camp. As a conservative prince he greatly resented the domination of the Chamber princes and the facilities they enjoyed for appearing to represent the states as a whole. He would never tolerate dictation from the Chamber princes which the electoral college implied. Moreover, Rewa did not share Patiala's paramountcy views which had remained unchanged by his support for confederation. Unlike Patiala, Rewa believed that an unrestricted paramountcy would still be necessary to protect the states from British Indian agitation whatever form the future Government of India might take. Rewa was therefore prepared to accept that he could never be completely independent in the conduct of his internal affairs.[58] On paper confederation should have held attractions for Hyderabad, particularly in view of the recommendation to limit discussion at the responsible centre to matters of common concern. Yet like Rewa, the Nizam would not submit to Chamber dictation nor did he subscribe to the Chamber version of paramountcy. Rewa and the Nizam differed only in respect of the latter's belief that he could still be internally independent.

In reality therefore confederation could never be considered as a viable alternative to federation. Other important states like Mysore, Baroda and Travancore would never accept an electoral college. The three premier states of Rajputana, Udaipur, Jodhpur and Jaipur had always maintained their distance from the Chamber and moreover accepted the Rewa version of paramountcy. Confederation therefore served not only to emphasize the bitterness and divisions within the Standing Committee, but also to show how unrepresentative the Committee was of the princes as a whole. It was, however, also significant in that it represented the first recoil among the princes from the federal ideal.

Further Princely Recoils from Federation and British Pressure

In August 1931, Ramsay MacDonald formed a National Government with a 'doctor's mandate' to deal with the economic crisis in Britain. His cabinet consisted of only ten members - four Conservatives, four Labour and two Liberals. Among the Conservatives was Samuel Hoare who became the new Secretary of State for India. Within a month of the opening of the second round table conference in September 1931, Hoare recorded the following impression of the princely mind:

I have been terribly depressed by the individual talks I have had
with almost all the members of the Conference, and particularly
with the Princes, for I have found that we have scarcely a friend
amongst them. This makes me think that however the Conference
ends, we must somehow keep the princes happy ... the princes
talk to me as if it were certain that we were leaving India in the
next five years.[59]

This latter remark was a reference to the Gandhi-Irwin pact of the
previous April which had brought a temporary cessation to civil
disobedience. The new Viceroy, Lord Willingdon, confirmed that he
had spent the first five months of office disabusing the princes of the
idea that a 'Gandhi Raj' was imminent.[60] In August, the Nawab of
Bhopal had written to Willingdon: 'The people of British India, as a
result of intense agitation, are being given and promised powers
which they never possessed, whilst the princes cannot get ratification
even in regard to their rights which "inviolate and inviolable"
Treaties had secured for them more than a century ago.'[61] In order
to go some way towards removing the anxieties of the princes Hoare
suggested to Willingdon: 'Would it not ... be practicable at once to
refer to arbitration some question of fact that may be outstanding
between the Government of India and one of the princes.' Hoare was
sure that the effect this would have upon the princes would be 'out of
all proportion to the magnitude of the question referred to
arbitration'.[62] It was obvious that the Secretary of State had in mind
the customs dispute of the Jam Sahib of Nawanagar.

The Jam Sahib was in dispute with the Government of India over
the reimposition of a customs barrier known as the Viramgam Line in
1927. Between 1917, when the line had ceased to operate, and 1927,
Nawanagar had been permitted to retain all customs receipts on
goods, including those on goods destined for British India, which were
imported through his port at Bedi Bander. During these ten years,
however, extensions to the port had resulted in an enormous increase
in Nawanagar's customs receipts. From Rs. 10.49 *lakhs* in 1922-23,
they had risen to Rs. 78.90 *lakhs* in 1926-27. In 1927 the Government
of India therefore reimposed the Viramgam Line allowing the Jam
Sahib to retain only Rs. 2 *lakhs* of duty on goods passing into British
India in any one year. The Jam Sahib protested on the grounds that in
1917 he had received an assurance that nothing would be done to
hinder the capacity of his port at Bedi Bander. The Government of
India, however, considered that this assurance had been given on
condition that the position would be reconsidered should any one of
the Kathiawar states develop a port capable of attracting a greater
quantity of sea-borne traffic than British Indian ports.[63] It was
because of this dispute that Nawanagar became the keenest exponent
of a paramountcy settlement involving arbitration to decide upon
justiciable disputes between the Government of India and the states
in which the former acted as both judge and party.

At the end of 1931 the Government of India acted upon Hoare's
advice and appointed a Court of Arbitration under Lord Dunedin to
determine the Nawanagar customs dispute. This gesture, however,

did not prevent the Jam Sahib using the dispute to create yet further difficulties over federation. In February 1932 he denounced federation as being dangerous to the states and advocated instead a return to the Statutory Commission's idea of a Council of Greater India. His views were endorsed by a conference of some fifty Kathiawar princes who assembled at Rajkot in the same month. According to Rushbrook Williams, who was now acting as Nawanagar's legal adviser, the reason for the conference decision was that many of the smaller states had only just begun to realize that princes like Bikaner and Bhopal were committing them to accepting arrangements over their heads. Moreover, the smaller states were becoming convinced that federation would lead to their extinction and therefore they were recoiling from an 'embrace which they feared might be octopus like in its effect on them'.[64]

This second *volte face* meant that Bikaner and Bhopal were forced to come to terms with the Chamber dissidents. In March 1932 the princes agreed that their ministers should meet in committee with the object of reconciling the different schemes for associating the states with the proposals for All-India constitutional reforms. On the personal level, Bikaner and Patiala agreed that neither they, nor Bhopal and Dholpur, their respective understudies, should contest the Chancellorship of the Chamber of Princes for the coming year. The result of this particular arrangement was to leave the way open for Nawanagar, by now the most dedicated opponent of federation, to assume the office of Chancellor for the period March 1932 to March 1933.

This series of princely defections from the federal ideal was also highly disturbing to Hoare. In October 1931 the National Government had emerged triumphant from a general election with an overwhelming majority of Conservative MPs who were not prepared to contemplate any changes in the central government of India unless by federation with a strong princely content. Moreover, since the first round table conference there had been no further commitment by any of the princes to federation. With another Chamber session due at the end of March 1932, Hoare impressed the gravity of the situation upon Lord Lothian who had been sent to India as Chairman of the Franchise Committee:

> On no account must the Princes be allowed to give a negative to All-India Federation. If they are in a negative mood at the forthcoming meeting of the Chamber of Princes they must almost at any price be induced to adjourn and not definitely to say 'No'. If they say 'No' all the fat in the world will be in the fire here. Nine out of ten members of the House of Commons will then go straight back to the unadulterated Simon Report.[65]

Hoare also wrote in a similar vein to Willingdon and to members of the Indian States (Financial) Enquiry Committee which had accompanied Lothian's Committee to India. In fact it was the chairman of the Financial Committee, Sir John Davidson, together with his colleague, Lord Hastings, who intervened in the matter

suggested by Hoare. In the evening of 30 March Davidson wrote
letters to Nawanagar and Bikaner, arranging for them to be delivered
during the afternoon of the following day when the Standing
Committee was discussing what its resolution on federation would
say. Bikaner was informed that 'nothing could be more disastrous
than that the Princes should, however innocently, convey to their
friends in England the impression that on the one hand they were
dilatory or on the other that agreement between themselves is never
likely to be reached'.[66]

As a result of this warning the Chamber passed a resolution on 1
April 1932 to the effect that the states would join an All-India
Federation on condition that the Crown would give them the
following guarantees:

(a) that the necessary safeguards will be embodied in the
constitution;

(b) that under the constitution the rights arising from Treaties, or
Sanads or Engagements, remain inviolate and inviolable;

(c) that the sovereignty and internal independence of the States
remain intact and are preserved and fully respected and that the
obligations of the Crown to the States remain unaltered.[67]

On 2 April Hastings confided to Hoare: 'What the official view
may be of the really rather dreadful intrusion of J.C.D. and self at
this critical moment is perhaps best not enquired into.'[68] Davidson in
fact never told Willingdon about his letters to Bikaner and
Nawanagar. He believed the Viceroy's attitude to be primarily
responsible for the difficulties encountered with the states. He
described Willingdon as 'perfectly charming from the ceremonial
point of view', but 'he has been out of touch with British politics for
so long that he really knows very little about the situation at home'.
Davidson's overall impression was that the Government of India was
totally opposed to federation: 'The fact is that there is not a
politically minded individual in India among the British officials, and
of course Willingdon is hopeless.'[69] Lord Lothian had a different
view. He considered that while the Government of India had never
been 'friendly' towards federation because the idea had been 'the
child of the Round Table Conference, and not of its own initiative',
opinion was now coming round to accept that federation was
inevitable.[70] When challenged by Hoare on the point in March
1932,[71] Willingdon replied that although officials in India, himself
included, had originally thought it unwise for the princes to 'tumble
into federation', they had always considered that once the princes had
committed themselves it would be impossible for them to keep out.[72]
However, like Irwin before him, Willingdon would have preferred, and
indeed had been preparing, to proceed first with reform at the British
Indian centre. In November 1931 he had informed Hoare that to
insist upon federation as a condition of central responsibility was
both 'unnecessary and dangerous, particularly as it leaves the fate of
India at the discretion of the states'.[73] Yet in his response to Hoare's
challenge, the Viceroy now expressed his full commitment to
federation because he realized that political opinion in Britain would
not tolerate central responsibility without federation and moreover

that without this responsibility 'probably the whole of British India would go over to the Congress side'.[74]

It would indeed appear therefore that it was not until 1932 that the Government of India appreciated the extent to which any meaningful reform was dependent upon the accession of the princes to a federation. Consequently, while it was legitimate to argue, as Willingdon had done, that the future of India should not be left to the discretion of the princes, the conclusion to be drawn is that it was also not until 1932 that the Government of India began considering the actual framework of a federal constitution in earnest.

Defeat for the Standing Committee on Paramountcy

Despite his belated appreciation of political realities in Britain, the Viceroy was optimistic about the princes in view of the recent Chamber resolution: '... the Princes as a whole now feel that Federation in some form is inevitable, and that if a reasonable scheme emerges, it must be accepted, even if they are not altogether satisfied with the details'.[75] Hoare's advisers in the India Office did not share this optimism. They were concerned at the implications of the second guarantee which had been included in the princes' resolution, particularly in view of the long-awaited paramountcy discussions which had taken place between Willingdon and the Standing Committee just before the formal Chamber session. During the discussions Bhopal had put forward a formula intended to reassure the princes as to the inviolability of their treaties. It stated that if, in any matter affecting the interests of both the states and British India, the former claimed that a proposed policy infringed their treaty rights, the Viceroy, after attempting to secure agreement by negotiation, would appoint an *ad hoc* impartial tribunal whose decision would be final.[76] When Hoare's advisers compared this formula with the second guarantee in the Chamber resolution they reached the conclusion that what the Standing Committee really wanted was 'provision whereby the protection of the Crown secured to them by their treaties and engagements, would remain operative even within the field of Federal subjects. In other words, potential protection against the action of the federal administration itself'.[77] Bhopal's formula, however, represented the price which he and Bikaner had been obliged to pay in order to effect a reconciliation with the Standing Committee. These two princes were really more interested in securing protection against infringements of their sovereignty by the paramount power than protection against the actions of a federal administration.[78] Yet for Nawanagar, who was motivated primarily by experience of his customs dispute, both these types of protection were to be treated as essential preconditions if he was ever to contemplate accession to a federation.

Hoare subsequently instructed Willingdon to hold a further and more representative conference with the princes. Clearly a stand had now to be taken against the pretensions of the Standing Committee. The princes were to be informed that under no circumstances would the protection of the paramount power be available to them in the field of federal subjects. Cases of dispute between the states and British India would, once the federation had become operative, be referred to a Federal Court from which there would be a right of appeal to the Privy Council.[79]

The more representative conference with the princes took place in September 1932. In the two months preceding it Nawanagar attempted to prevent any further discussion of federation until he had gained acceptance of his paramountcy views. In July he addressed a letter to the other members of the Standing Committee in which he stated that 'the authorities in England' should be told that the princes would not be able to federate until their views 'regarding the false doctrine of paramountcy' were effectively met. In August he wrote to Hoare requesting that the paramountcy discussions be transferred to London where he believed he would receive a more sympathetic hearing. Nawanagar also told the Secretary of State that the Standing Committee now regarded a satisfactory settlement of the paramountcy question not only as a condition of their accession to federation but also of their willingness to continue negotiations regarding the federal scheme in the interval. Hoare's India Committee construed Nawanagar's letter to be 'nothing short of a concerted attempt to blackmail (the government) into making concessions, hitherto regarded as outside practical politics, in order to secure an undertaking from the princes to federate'.[80] However, Nawanagar was unable to carry his colleagues on the Standing Committee with him. He had written to Hoare without consulting either Bikaner, Bhopal or Patiala. These three subsequently issued a statement declaring that: 'It is not our position that we decline to discuss further the federation scheme, although it is our position that we shall not enter Federation unless Government settles the Paramountcy question to our satisfaction.'[81] Nawanagar had therefore failed in his attempt to use the paramountcy issue to delay negotiations over federation. He was a conspicuous absentee when Willingdon met representatives from twenty-five states in conference at Simla from 20 to 22 September.[82] Discussion at the conference focused upon the relationship between the paramount power and the states in the federal and non-federal fields. As regards the former, Nawanagar's absence meant that the conference unanimously accepted the position which Hoare had described to Willingdon: disputes between the states and British India would be subject to interpretation by a Federal Court. Discussion on the latter was much more controversial and protracted. Bikaner and Bhopal argued strongly for a formula whereby alleged infractions of treaty rights by the paramount power would be submitted for arbitration to an *ad hoc* tribunal whose decision would be final. However, this attempt to restrict the discretionary authority of the paramount power was equally strongly opposed by Gulab Singh of Rewa and Sir Akbar Hydari. They argued that it would be suicidal for the princes themselves to weaken the protective function of the paramount power at a time when 'autocratic systems of government are being openly challenged in British Indian circles'. To this Willingdon added that it was improbable that the British government would ever 'consent to the subordination of the Crown's representative and the Crown itself to the ruling of an outside authority'. In the face of this oppostion Bikaner and Bhopal were forced to submit to revision of their formula. In future it would be obligatory to submit disputes of a justiciable nature to a tribunal but the decision reached would only be of an advisory character and not binding upon the paramount power.[83]

The Simla conference of September 1932 was not only a defeat for the Standing Committee but also a turning point in princely politics. After the conference the princes of the Committee began to lose that monopoly of influence which they had maintained unchallenged for the past decade. Willingdon observed:

> It seems to me that there is a great deal of feeling among the greater number of Princes owing to the fact that the Standing Committee of the Chamber of Princes has for long years been a very close corporation, largely controlled by Bikaner, Bhopal and Patiala.[84]

The reluctance of Hyderabad in particular to impose restrictions upon the exercise of paramountcy had come as an unwelcome surprise to members of the Committee. They had always assumed that the Nizam would be the first to want to impose restrictions. Evidently it was only now that they realized that the Nizam's sole concern was to prevent his state 'from being swallowed up ... by the monster of British India'.[85] This did not, however, indicate a smooth passage for the government with the Nizam. On the contrary, it was precisely because of this concern to gain protection from British India that the Nizam was beginning to raise the price for his accession to a federation. In addition to requesting a written guarantee that Britain would protect Hyderabad in accordance with the terms of his treaties, the Nizam now wanted to see Berar, a potential spring-board 'for attacks on Hyderabad from the Central Provinces, separated from that province and constituted as a federal unit in its own right.[86]

Federal Representation and Federal Finance

On 17 November 1932 the third and final round table conference opened in London. The only prince present was the Raja of Sarila on behalf of the smaller states. The reason for this was that Patiala, who had not attended the second conference because his own extravagance had brought his state to the verge of financial collapse, was again obliged to remain in India. For the sake of his reputation, Patiala requested Bikaner and Bhopal to do the same. When they agreed the Government of India decided that the princes would be represented by their ministers at the conference.[87] Hoare's first impression of these ministers was that they had 'explicit instructions not to commit their rulers too far'.[88]

Discussion relating to the states centred on the complex problems of their representation in the federal legislatures and their contributions towards federal finance. It proved impossible to make any substantial headway on either issue. On the first, representatives of the larger states advocated an upper chamber of less than 200 members with the states being represented in accordance with their importance and population. Hydari was particularly anxious to reduce as far as possible the number of British Indian politicians in both legislatures. The medium-sized states, however, wanted an upper chamber with something in excess of 250 members in order that each of the 108 Chamber princes could be individually represented. Without agreement on the size of the chambers, nothing could be done to decide the allocation of seats between the states themselves and between the states and British India. The problem of federal finance involved those states which paid tributes and those which enjoyed certain immunities. Contributions in the form of tributes amounted to Rs. 74 *lakhs* in 1932. Mysore, with its tribute of Rs. 24½ *lakhs*, contributed one-third of this total. The states concerned claimed immediate relief from these payments but were disappointed by the gloomy predictions being made about the prospective stability of federal finance. In order to maintain adequate reserves in the federal exchequer the government in London considered that it would be possible to remit the tributes only at the same time as the British Indian provinces were allowed to keep the proceeds of their income tax.[89] The Indian States (Financial) Enquiry Committee, which reported in July 1932, had calculated that upon this basis it would take twenty years before the tributes could be remitted in full. The only concession that the Committee had felt able to make was that immediate relief should be given by the remission of the amount of any contribution which was in excess of five per cent of the total revenues of the state.[90] This would reduce Mysore's tribute to Rs. 17½ *lakhs*, but it was by no means certain that this would prove acceptable. In February 1932 Willingdon had reported that Ismail had virtually 'put a pistol at our heads' by saying that Mysore would refuse to federate unless relieved of its tribute payment in full.[91]

Immunities constituted financial advantages which individual states enjoyed, by Treaty or Agreement, in respect of certain sources of revenue which under federation would normally lie at the disposal of the federal administration. The largest immunity was in respect of customs receipts. In 1932 the amount of customs receipts retained by the states totalled just over Rs. 182 *lakhs*. Bhavnagar, Nawanagar, Kashmir, Travancore and Cochin were the major beneficiaries of this arrangement and were therefore loath to yield such a large part of their income.[92] In its report, the Indian States (Financial) Enquiry Committee recognized that such immunities were important to the states, not only because of their financial value, but also because they represented the outward symbol of their cherished sovereignty. However, the Committee also considered that the retention of customs receipts by any federal unit would be 'hard to reconcile with the ideal of a true Federation'.[93] Hoare's India Committee agreed and thought that it might be necessary to exclude these states from the federation rather than admit them on such highly privileged terms.[94]

The third round table conference closed in December 1932. Such conclusions as the government in London had been able to reach were embodied in a White Paper which was published in March 1933. Here it was explained that when the new Government of India Act had been passed, each individual prince would be asked to sign an Instrument of Accession specifying those subjects which could be transferred from his own sovereignty to that of the federal administration. The princes would also be allowed to make certain limitations upon the extent to which they agreed to any particular subject's becoming federal, and it would fall to the British government to decide whether or not these limitations were compatible with the federal principle.[95] In the cases of the major tribute and customs states, it was already evident that the period after the Act had been passed would be one of prolonged bargaining and negotiation.

The Political Department and Federation

If therefore federation was to become a reality, time was of the essence. However, a further two years elapsed before the Government of India Act was passed. During this period the attitude of the princes hardly ensured a smooth passage for the government bill containing details of the federal proposals. A week before the appearance of the White Paper, Willingdon attempted to explain its contents to a gathering of some fifty princes and ministers at Delhi. The Viceroy subsequently regretted that he had bothered for he found the princes hopelessly divided by personal rivalries and jealousies.[96] The formal Chamber session at the end of March fared no better. Animosity between the princes resulted in Bhopal, Kashmir, Kolhapur and Travancore serving notice of their intention to quit the Chamber. The absence of Bhopal and Kashmir, and the death in April 1933 of the Jam Sahib, meant that when Patiala was elected Chancellor for the coming year he was given a Standing Committee which, with the exception of Bikaner, consisted largely of princely nonentities. Willingdon consoled himself with the thought that the defections indicated that the Chamber 'as an organized and representative body of princely opinion, is moribund for the time being at any rate'.[97] Hoare was not satisfied with this sentiment. Princely intransigence provided the diehard faction within the Conservative party with ample justification for condemning federation. The Secretary of State persistently badgered Willingdon to give him some assurance that the princes would federate. It was cold comfort for him to learn from the Viceroy that it was impossible to 'get any assurance from any of them until the Bill is an Act, and they see exactly what their position is going to be. This really is reasonable, and I don't see any other way out of it'.[98]

In these circumstances it was inevitable that nothing would come of a suggestion made by Hoare that political officers should be instructed to commend the federal scheme to the princes. Moreover, the Political Department was not the most reliable agency to use for the task. During his investigation in India, Sir John Davidson had been as critical of the Political Department as he had of Willingdon. In this respect he had written to Hoare in February 1932: 'Something is wrong, so wrong that it is almost incomprehensible to me that such a state of affairs should have been allowed to continue.'[99] Davidson reached the conclusion that although political officers in general were of a very poor calibre, the main problem was that the department had failed to give them any lead. Thus when the Jam Sahib and his adviser, Rushbrook Williams, had been hatching their 'absurd' scheme at Rajkot, E.H. Kealy, the AGG in Western India, who had formerly served in the same capacity in Central India, received no word from Delhi as to whether or not he was to intervene.[100]

Throughout the period of the round table conferences, the Political Department in fact remained committed to the position it had adopted in 1930. There could be no open encouragement for federation while the paramountcy issue remained unsettled. Federation, with federal agents operating in the states, would result not only in a loss of sovereignty for the princes, but also in a diminution of the authority of political officers. This was accepted by the department. However, if the Standing Committee had gained acceptance of their paramountcy views, then the role of the individual political officer would have been reduced to that of a mere dignitary. This line of argument had of course an essential weakness. Most political officers were already mere dignitaries because of the non-interference policy. For the Political Department, however, it was a matter of principle: the principle that political officers should not be made completely redundant.

The recent defeat of the Standing Committee made the Political Department more amenable than it might otherwise have been to Hoare's suggestion. A conference of political officers was held in March 1933. Willingdon briefed the officers and emphasized that the princes should be made fully aware of the consequences if they did not federate. The Viceroy would be unable to act independently of his Council on matters concerning the states. Moreover, it was inevitable that the Viceroy's Council would become more responsive to the views of the British India legislature in which the states had no say. In sum, if the princes did not federate, they would be 'exposed in many ways to the pressure of ideas against which defence may be difficult'.[101]

In one instance, however, action taken upon the basis of this brief had an unfortunate consequence. Colonel Wilberforce-Bell, the AGG for the Deccan states, chose to place his own interpretation on the consequences for the princes if they did not federate. He told the princes in his charge: 'If the Federal scheme breaks down because of the refusal of the States to adhere to it, it will inevitably be said that they are reactionary and not in tune with modern ideas of constitutional progress.' The Colonel was subsequently reprimanded not only because he had been over-zealous but also because his remarks came to the attention of two Conservative MPs who were visiting India. When news of this reached England it was used by the diehards as evidence that the Government of India was applying undue pressure on the princes to federate.[102]

It was largely because of diehard opposition, led by Winston Churchill in the House of Commons and Lord Salisbury in the House of Lords, that a further two years elapsed before Parliament approved the India Bill. In April 1934, in order to delay the report of the Joint Select Committee which had been examining the India Bill for a year, Churchill accused Hoare of having pressed the Manchester Chamber of Commerce into changing the evidence which it had submitted to the Committee. The Committee had to adjourn for two months while the Commons Privileges Committee examined the charge and eventually found it to be without substance.[103] Patiala gave every encouragement to the diehards. In February 1935 a meeting of princes and ministers at Bombay declared that the bill and a draft Instrument of Accession which had been prepared were unacceptable without fundamental modification. Through the offices of Madhava Rao, the editor of the *Morning Post*, Patiala was able to inform Churchill of the princes' decision before official confirmation reached the India Office.[104] The result was highly embarrassing for Hoare. On 26 February, Churchill informed an astonished House of Commons that the decision represented an outright rejection of federation by the princes.[105] Hoare was furious. In order to satisfy Parliament that the princes had not vetoed federation, he had to produce an additional White Paper explaining the basis of the princes' objections and detailing the extent to which the government was prepared to modify the bill and draft Instrument of Accession.[106]

Willingdon had long suspected that Patiala's intrigue with the diehards was based upon the belief that he would 'receive all the honours he was inclined to ask for so long as he came out against the reforms'.[107] Patiala was certainly vain enough to be persuaded in this manner but his action at the time of the Bombay meeting was much more politically motivated. In the formal Chamber session of January 1935, Patiala had delivered a vehement assault on democracy. With an obvious reference to recent political developments in Germany he declared:

> While the princes of India have always been willing to do what was best for their people and ready to accommodate themselves and their constitutions to the spirit of the times, we must frankly say, that if British India is hoping to compel us to wear on our healthy body politic the Nessus shirt of a discredited political theory, they are living in a world of unreality.[108]

This outburst had been inspired be certain remarks made by Rajendra Prasad, the President of the Indian National Congress, on the attitude of the Congress towards federation and the role that the states would play in it. Throughout the period of the round table conferences the Congress had shown a marked reluctance to become involved with the problems of the states. This did not mean that the

Congress was oblivious to these problems but rather that it intended to deal with them at a later and more convenient juncture. This is clearly illustrated by the brief prepared by the Congress Working Committee for Gandhi's use at the second round table conference. Here it was explained that the accession of the states to a federation should be made conditional, first upon a guarantee of the fundamental rights of their subjects, safeguarded by a Supreme Court, and secondly upon representation of the states in the federal legislatures on an elective basis. However, if the princes did not accept these terms:

> ... we suggest that the consideration of the question of the States be postponed for the moment and the future of what is known as British India may be discussed with the British Government ... In case a settlement is reached as between British India and the British Government the question of the States can be taken up afresh.[109]

When therefore at the second round table conference the princes refused to contemplate either of the aforesaid conditions, Gandhi did not attempt to make an issue of them. This apparent indifference to the problems of the states disturbed the leaders of the All-India States' People's Conference, as N.C. Kelkar indicated to Gandhi in June 1934:

> ... it will be well to refer to the apprehensions that have arisen in the minds of the Indian States people by passages in your speeches at the Round Table Conference. You pleaded earnestly in this Conference with the rulers of the Indian States for allowing the States' representatives in the federal legislature to be chosen by election and for allowing the fundamental rights of the States' people to be written into the federal constitution and placed under the protection of the federal court. But your pleadings on this occasion have given rise to an impression that if the Princes did not agree, as they did not and do not agree, you would accept a constitution in which provisions of the kind that you suggested did not find a place. If this impression is well founded, we cannot help saying, and saying it straight out, that you have done a grave wrong to the States' people.[110]

Kelkar asked for a categorical assurance that the Congress would not accept a federal constitution which did not include provision for the election of state representatives and a guarantee of fundamental rights. He also appealed for a clear statement of policy to the effect that the Congress supported 'all legitimate movements for the establishment of popular government in the Indian States under the aegis of their rulers'.[111] It was because of these attempts to commit the Congress that Prasad included a reference to the states in his presidential address to the Congress at Bombay in December 1934. Prasad was severely critical of the role assigned to the states in the government's White Paper. On the one hand the federal representatives of the states were to be nominated, while on the other, the princes would be able to continue their autocratic rule without any guarantee of fundamental rights 'which are, or rather ought to be, the basis and foundation of any allegiance which the people may be required to bear to the state'.[112]

It was this address which occasioned Patiala's outburst in the Chamber. Willingdon thought the Maharaja's remarks indiscreet but agreed with the opinion of his Political Secretary, Sir Bertrand Glancy, who had succeeded Watson in July 1933, that they were 'not of any serious account' as Patiala 'feels himself peculiarly exposed to attack and is more vulnerable than most'. With a view to the prospects for federation Glancy further believed that 'unless considerably more serious developments occur in this respect in British India, it is unlikely that the Princes will make any actual use of these attacks as a breaking-point'.[113] Opinion in the India Office was more cautious. Glancy's namesake, Sir Reginald, a member of the Secretary of State's India Council who had had a distinguished career as a political officer in Hyderabad, Baroda and Jaipur, believed that Patiala's remarks indicated that the 'ultimate decision of the princes will be largely influenced by the reactions of British India to the new bill'.[114]

The Prospects for Federation

Although the Government of India Act reached the statute book in August 1935, the prospect of its federal provisions becoming operative were extremely uncertain. Indeed the decisions which had finally been made about the size of the federal chambers and the representation of the states within them, made the task of actually negotiating with the princes extremely difficult. In November 1932, at the end of the third round table conference, it had been decided that the establishment of a federation would be dependent upon the accession of states with an aggregate of over half the total states' population, provided that these included not less than half of the states individually represented in the Upper Chamber.[115] A formula had then been devised and included in the White Paper which gave the states 104 out of 260 seats in the Upper Chamber and 125 out of 375 seats in the Lower Chamber but which made no detailed allocation of seats to individual states. Upon later reflection, however, Hoare expressed a preference for much smaller chambers on the grounds that they would offer greater prospects of political stability and make the task of negotiating with the princes more manageable. In December 1933 he therefore proposed that there should be an Upper Chamber of 100 seats, in which the states would have 40, and a Lower Chamber of 300 seats, with 100 for the states. The twenty largest states would be entitled to continuous individual representation in the Upper Chamber. This revised formula met with opposition from Willingdon. He argued that the size of the chambers outlined in the White Paper held out the prospect of some form of representation to a large number of states which would either lose out altogether or obtain less representation if Hoare's formula was accepted. In all probability the states concerned would demonstrate their annoyance by refusing to federate. Moreover, as most of the states were interwoven with various parts of British India, the Viceroy was convinced that from an administrative point of view, their abstentions 'would render practical federation more unworkable than if large self-contained areas like Hyderabad elected to hold aloof'.[116]

By reverting to the White Paper formula, the final Government of India Act incorporated Willingdon's preference for larger chambers. It was this decision that made the task of negotiating with the princes much more difficult. Although the consent of only 52 states represented in the Upper Chamber with the necessary population requirement was required to inaugurate the federation, negotiations would now have to be opened with the 144 states individually represented, whether on a continuous or rotational basis, in the Upper Chamber.[117] If Hoare's plan for smaller chambers had been adopted, it would have been possible to concentrate on the twenty states with continuous individual representation in the Upper Chamber, particularly as the first eight of these accounted for half the total states' population. As for Willingdon's objection to Hoare's formula, a recent authoritative study of the 1935 constitution has pointed out that the Viceroy had completely failed to recognize the validity of the argument that non-acceding states would find it difficult to resist the pressure of a federation in operation.[118]

Amongst the princes themselves, it had long since become apparent that the original sponsors of the federal idea had all failed to realize the ambitions which had prompted them to act. The remaining princes seemed to have very little conception of what federation actually involved. Sir Walter Monckton, who became the Nizam's legal adviser, commented in October 1935 on how few princes recognized even the most basic principle that federation involved a loss of sovereignty. According to Monckton the princes would therefore attempt to preserve as much as possible of their sovereignty intact when it came to negotiating their Instruments of Accession.[119] When to all this is added the unpredictability of the Congress attitude to both the states and federation, the enormity of the task confronting Willingdon's successor, Lord Linlithgow, can readily be appreciated.

NOTES TO CHAPTER V

[1] In this respect Irwin was also attempting to atone for his own error of judgement. That India had been brought to the verge of civil disobedience was largely due to the Viceroy's insistence that the review of the constitution in British India should be undertaken by a Statutory Commission consisting solely of representatives from the British parliamentary parties. The appointment of the Commission had been brought forward from 1929 to 1927 by the Conservative government in an attempt to prevent a Labour government supervising its proceedings.

[2] Hailey to Goschen (acting Viceroy), 8 August 1929, Hailey Collection, No. 156. Irwin discussed his strategy at length with Hailey shortly before his departure for England.

[3] For a full discussion of the background to this declaration, see R.J. Moore, *The Crisis of Indian Unity, 1917-1940*, Oxford, 1974, pp. 51-94.

[4] S.R. Mehrotra, *India and the Commonwealth, 1885-1929*, London, 1965, p.142.

[5] *Chamber of Princes*, February 1930.

[6] Viceroy to S/S, telg., 15 March 1930, PIC, 1931-50, Coll. 11, File 12, No. 1848/1930.

[7] Holland's note, 20 March 1930, ibid. Holland had been knighted in 1925 upon the expiry of his term of office as AGG in Rajputana and his appointment to the Secretary of State's India Council.

[8] S/S to Viceroy, telg., 26 March 1930, ibid.

[9] *Report of the Indian Statutory Commission*, Cmd. 3569, 1930, Vol. 2, paras. 228 and 368.

[10] Minutes of the proceedings of an informal conference held at Simla, 14 and 15 July 1930, PIC, 1931-50, Coll. 11, File 12, No. 1848/1930.

[11] ibid.

[12] Viceroy to S/S, telg., 17 July 1930, No. 4592A/1930, ibid. The Political Department of the India Office in London was unpleasantly surprised by the proceedings of the July Conference. It was felt that Irwin had gone too far in committing the government, particular disquiet being expressed that he had not informed the princes that paragraph 58 of the Butler report was still *sub judice*. A departmental minute commented: 'The general impression left by the proceedings is that the princes have on the whole scored.' Minute dated 19 August 1930, No. P5189/1930, ibid. Nor was the India Office as confident as the Viceroy that paramountcy would not be raised at the round table conference. The Political Secretary, Paul. J. Patrick, believed that it would be raised, if not by the princes, then by the British Indian delegates when discussing the future relationship between the states and the central government. Patrick's note, 24 July 1930, No. 4592A/1930, ibid.

[13] *Government of India Despatch on Proposals for Constitutional Reform*, 20 September 1930, Cmd. 3700, 1930, para. 16.

[14] Irwin to Fisher, 1 October 1930, Halifax Collection, No. 19.

[15] Sapru to Ranjit, 14 November 1930, Sapru Collection, IOL Microfilm, 1st series, R.66.

[16] Keyes to Nizam, 30 June 1930, Keyes Collection, No. 28.

[17] Keyes to Watson, 15 April 1930, ibid.

[18] Keyes wrote to Irwin of the Nizam: '. . . the queer little creature - he's so pathetically anxious to be liked; he never seems to bear malice; takes every setback with good humour and, within his limitations, I believe, really means to do well'. Keyes to Irwin, 4 May 1930, ibid.

[19] Keyes to Cunningham, 5 July 1930, ibid.

[20] Nizam to Hyderabad delegation at Simla, 9 July 1930, ibid.

[21] Keyes to Bray, 21 July 1930, ibid.

[22] 'Note on the Round Table Conference', Appendix to Hyderabad Administration Report, 6 October 1932 - 5 October 1933, PIC, 1931-50, Coll. 11, File 57(2), No. PY564/1936.

[23] Patrick's note, 9 April 1936, ibid.

[24] Findlater Stewart's note, 20 April 1936, ibid.

[25] Butler's note, 19 April 1936, ibid.

[26] *Government of India Reforms Despatch*, para. 116.

[27] Watson's memo., 28 March 1930, cited in R.J. Moore, op. cit., p.129.

[28] Willingdon to Hoare, 19 March 1934, Templewood Collection, No. 7. (Samuel Hoare, Secretary of State for India between 1931 and 1935 was created Viscount Templewood in 1944.)

[29] K.N. Haksar and K.M. Panikkar, *Federal India*, London, 1930.

[30] *Madras Mail*, 22 August 1930.

[31] ibid. See also departmental note on impression gained in conversation with representatives of Indian States at the approaching round table conference, 31 October 1930, PIC, 1931-50, Coll. 11, File 5, No.7639/1930.

[32] Mysore paid the largest tribute of all the states, Rs. 24½ *lakhs.*

[33] Hydari's note, 2 October 1930, Reading Collection, No. 56e.

[34] Schuster to Irwin, 9 October 1930, Halifax Collection, No. 19.

[35] Hydari's undated later supplement, Reading Collection, No. 56e.

[36] The Indian States delegation included all members of the Standing Committee - the Rulers of Alwar, Bhopal, Bikaner, Kashmir, Patiala and the Jam Sahib of Nawanagar; Manubhai Mehta and Kailas Haksar from the Chamber's Special Organization, plus seven other members chosen by Irwin. Four of the premier states were represented - Hyderabad by Sir Akbar Hydari; Mysore by Sir Mirza Ismail; Gwalior by Sahibzada Ahmed Khan; and Baroda by the Gaekwar. Prabhashankar Pattani represented those states under minority adminstrations; Gulab Singh, the Maharaja of Rewa, represented the so-called conservative states; and the Chief of Sangli was chosen to represent the smaller states.

[37] Barbara N. Ramusack, *The Princes of India in the Twilight of Empire*, p.200.

[38] Hailey to Irwin, 14 November 1930, Halifax Collection, No. 19.
(Lord Simon chaired the Statutory Commission).

[39] Minutes of Liberal Delegation meeting, 19 November 1930,
Reading Collection, No. 56g.

[40] Hoare's memorandum, 'Conservative Policy at the Round Table
Conference', 12 December 1930, Templewood Collection, No.
52(1).

[41] Hailey to Irwin, 14 November 1930, Halifax Collection, No. 19.

[42] Sapru to Setalvad, 29 November 1930, Sapru Collection, IOL
Microfilm, 1st series, S. 131.

[43] Irwin to Viscount Halifax, 23 November 1930, Halifax Collection,
No. 27.

[44] Nizam's instructions to the Hyderabad delegation before the
Second Round Table Conference, 9 August 1931, PIC, 1931-50,
Coll. 11, File 6, No. PY706/1931.

[45] Irwin to Lawrence, 17 November 1930, Halifax Collection, No.
19.

[46] Hailey to Irwin, 20 November 1930, ibid.

[47] Note on Proceedings at a meeting in the Prime Minister's room,
3 December 1930, PIC, 1931-50, Coll. 11, File 3, No. 6590/1930.

[48] Note on Proceedings at a meeting in the Prime Minister's room,
9 January 1931, PIC, 1931-50, Coll. 11, File 7, part 1, No.
6590/1930.

[49] Watson's note, 5 January 1931, GOI, FPD, No. 3 - Special
(Secret), 1931.

[50] Viceroy to S/S, telg., 8 December 1930, PIC, 1931-50, Coll. 11,
File 3, No. 8576/1930.

[51] For details of the rivalry between Bikaner and Patiala, see
Barbara N. Ramusack, op. cit., pp. 33 and 210-211.

[52] Patiala's 'Note on Federation and the Indian States' released to
the press 15 June 1931, PIC, 1931-50, Coll. 11, File 44, No.
1053/1931.

[53] The Dholpur–Patialia scheme for a Confederation of States, No.
1657/1931, ibid.

[54] Sir P. Pattani, 'The Indian States : A Letter on their relations
with British India', September 1930, Templewood Collection, No.
53a (2A).

[55] Bikaner's circular letter to princes, 11 July 1931, GOI, FPD, No.
5(3), Special, 1931, Nos. 1-3.

[56] 'Attitude of the Indian States Delegation towards Federation',
memorandum by Sir Reginald Glancy, member of the Secretary
of State's India Council, 1 September 1930, Templewood
Collection, No. 53A.

[57] Gulab Singh to Watson, 15 July 1930, GOI, FPD, No. 148 -
Political (Secret), 1930.

[58] Gulab Singh had expressed these opinions to Irwin when the
Viceroy initiated his first informal discussions with the princes in
1927. Rewa to Irwin, 2 February 1927, GOI, FPD, No. 654 -
Political, 1927, Nos. 1-3. He also dissociated himself from the
views of the Standing Committee at the meeting with
MacDonald in December 1930. S/S to Viceroy, telg., 4 December

1930, PIC, 1931-50, Coll. 11, File 3, No. 8576/1930.

[59] Hoare to Willingdon, 2 October 1931, Templewood Collection, No. 1.

[60] Willingdon to Hoare, 12 October 1931, Templewood Collection, No. 5.

[61] Bhopal to Willingdon, 6 August 1931, PIC, 1931-50, Coll. 11, File 7, part 1, No. 1653/1931.

[62] Hoare to Willingdon, 2 October 1931, Templewood Collection, No. 1.

[63] For a history of this dispute, see memorandum by J.C.C. Davidson, 27 July 1932, PIC, 1931-50, Coll. 13, File 45, No. 1305/1932.

[64] Rushbrook Williams to Hoare, 3 March and 1 April 1932, Private Office Papers, L/PO/58.

[65] Hoare to Lothian, 3 March 1932, Templewood Collection, No. 14.

[66] Davidson to Bikaner, 30 March 1932, enclosed with Davidson to Hoare, 31 March 1932, Templewood Collection, No. 14.

[67] *Chamber of Princes*, April 1932.

[68] Hastings to Hoare, 2 April 1932, Templewood Collection, No. 14.

[69] Davidson to Hoare, 31 March and 1 April 1932, ibid.

[70] Lothian to Hoare, 27 March 1932, ibid.

[71] Hoare to Willingdon, 18 March 1932, Templewood Collection, No. 1.

[72] Willingdon to Hoare, 27 March 1932, Templewood Collection, No. 5.

[73] Viceroy to S/S, telg., 29 November 1931, Templewood Collection, No. 11.

[74] Willingdon to Hoare, 27 March 1932, Templewood Collection, No. 5.

[75] Viceroy to S/S, telg., 29 November 1932, Templewood Collection, No. 11.

[76] Minutes of the proceedings of an informal conference, 10 March 1932, GOI, FPD, No. 125 - Reforms, 1932, Nos. 1-8.

[77] Committee on India, No. 14: Relations with the Indian States after Federation outside the Federal field, October 1932, PIC, 1931-50, Coll. 11, File 7, part 2, No. 1740/1932.

[78] Bikaner and Bhopal cherished ambitions of holding high office in a future federal ministry. Bikaner was said to covet the defence portfolio and, at a later stage, even the Viceroyalty itself. 'Attitude of the Indian States Delegation towards Federation', memorandum by Sir Reginald Glancy, 1 September 1931, Templewood Collection, No. 53A.

[79] Committee on India, No. 14, PIC, 1931-50, Coll. 11, File 7, part 2, No. 1740/1932.

[80] ibid.

[81] Haksar to Sapru, 4 September 1932, Sapru Collection, IOL Microfilm, 1st series, H. 95.

[82] The following states were represented: Dholpur, Panna, Bikaner, Bhopal, Sangli, Alwar, Dungarpur, Rewa, Bahawalapur, Cutch, Rampur, Malerkotla, Sarila, Hyderabad, Udaipur, Mysore, Kolhapur, Jhalawar, Travancore, Kashmir, Indore, Baroda,

Jodhpur, Jaipur and Cochin.

83 Committee on India, No. 14: PIC, 1931-50, Coll. 11, File 7, part 2, No. 1740/1932.

84 Willingdon to Hoare, 26 September 1932, Templewood Collection, No. 6.

85 Haksar to Sapru, 5 October 1932, Sapru Collection, IOL Microfilm, 1st series, H. 99.

86 Question of the future Administration of the Berars: Representations made by the Nizam's Government on the subject, GOI, FPD, No. 27 - Special, 1931, Nos. 1-17.

87 Ramusack, op. cit., pp. 219-220.

88 Hoare to Willingdon, 18 November 1932, Templewood Collection, No. 5.

89 Committee on India, No. 17: Federal Finance, November 1932, Templewood Collection, No. 56(s).

90 *Report of the Indian States (Financial) Enquiry Committee, July 1932*, Cmd. 4103, 1932, paras. 88-90.

91 Willingdon to Hoare, 5 February 1932, Templewood Collection, No. 5.

92 Of the total Rs. 182 *lakhs*, Bhavnagar accounted for Rs. 50 *lakhs*, Nawanagar Rs. 44 *lakhs*, Kashmir Rs. 25 *lakhs*, Travancore and Cochin, Rs. 12 *lakhs* each.

93 *Report of the Indian States (Financial) Enquiry Committee*, para. 380.

94 Committee on India, No. 17: Federal Finance.

95 *Proposals for Indian Constitutional Reform*, Cmd. 4268, 1933 (March), part 1, No. 2.

96 Wilingdon to Hoare, 26 March 1933, Templewood Collection, No. 6.

97 Viceroy to S/S, telg., 26 March 1933, Templewood Collection, No. 11. Whatever may be said of its organization, the Chamber had never been 'a representative body of princely opinion'. The inaugural session in 1921 had been attended by 70 out of 120 members but thereafter the average attendance had only been between 30 and 45. For a discussion of the weaknesses of the Chamber, see Barbara N. Ramusack, op. cit., pp. 133-136.

98 Willingdon to Hoare, 26 March 1933, Templewood Collection, No. 6.

99 Davidson to Hoare, 20 February 1932, Templewood Collection, No. 14.

100 Davidson to Hoare, 6 March 1932, ibid.

101 Memorandum prepared for the use of Political Officers at the Informal Conference, 7 March 1933, PIC, 1931-50, Coll. 11, File 58, part 1, No. PY 816/1933.

102 Allegations of pressure being placed upon the States to join the Federation, Private Office Papers, L/PO/88.

103 J.K. Middlemas and A.J.L. Barnes, *Baldwin, A Biography*, London, 1969, p.711.

104 Brabourne to Butler, 4 March 1935, Brabourne Collection, No. 20A.

105 Viscount Templewood, *Nine Troubled Years*, London, 1954, pp.

86-87.
[106] *The Government of India Bill : Views of Indian States*, Cmd. 4843, 1935 (March).
[107] Willingdon to Hoare, 30 April 1934, Templewood Collection, No. 7.
[108] *Chamber of Princes*, January 1935.
[109] Working Committee instructions to Gandhi, 11 September 1931, sent by J. Nehru to Gandhi in London, Gandhi Collection; by courtesy of Dr. B.N. Pandey.
[110] N.C. Kelkar to Gandhi, 22 June 1934, Gandhi Collection; by courtesy of Dr. B.N. Pandey.
[111] ibid.
[112] *Indian Annual Register, July-December 1934*, Vol. 2, pp. 237-250.
[113] B.J. Glancy's note on the Chamber session of Janaury 1935, Private Office Papers, L/PO/88. Patiala's financial extravagance and dubious personal conduct had been the subject of severe condemnation in a document entitled 'Indictment of Patiala', published by the All-India States' People's Conference in February 1930. After this date, special arrangements had to be made for Patiala to avoid hostile demonstrations whenever he left his state. Ramusack, op. cit., pp. 194 and 200.
[114] Sir Reginald Glancy's note, 27 July 1935, PIC, 1931-50, Coll. 3, File 1, No. 126/1935.
[115] S/S to Viceroy, telg., 21 November 1932, Templewood Collection, No. 11.
[116] Viceroy to S/S, telg., 26 January 1934, Templewood Collection, No. 12(b).
[117] The 104 state seats in the Upper Federal Chamber had been divided into three classes: 67 were to be filled by 42 states upon the basis of continuous individual representation, 31 by 102 states in alternating groups of between 2 and 5 states and 6 by non-alternating groups embracing the very small states. Under this arrangement, 144 states were to enjoy individual representation, 42 of them continuously by one or more nominee (Hyderabad was entitled to 5 seats), the remainder in rotation. For details, see Memorandum by the Secretary of State for India on the Proposed Distribution of Seats among Indian States, 22 February 1934, PIC, 1931-50, Coll. 11, File 46, part 3, No. PY263/1934.
[118] R.J. Moore, op. cit., p.302.
[119] Monckton to Zetland, - October 1935, PIC, 1931-50, Coll. 11, File 86, No. PY1897/1935.

CHAPTER VI

THE FAILURE OF FEDERAL NEGOTIATIONS AND THE END OF THE NON-INTERFERENCE POLICY: 1935-1939

The Failure of Federal Negotiations

The outstanding feature of the scheme for an All-India Federation was that it was never implemented. Negotiations to establish a federation were suspended in September 1939 upon the outbreak of the Second World War. However, it was not the outbreak of war that had brought the negotiations to a standstill. Between 1935 and 1939 they had been conducted mainly with a view to secure the accession of the requiste number of princes. In this respect they did not succeed because in June 1939 the princes declared that the terms of the British government's federal offer were unacceptable. The government's immediate response was that an improved offer could not be made. Thus a stalemate had been reached even before the outbreak of war.

Contemporary explanations of this failure are well known. Broadly speaking, they fall into two categories. The first is represented by the views of Viscount Templewood, formerly Samuel Hoare, and the Earl of Halifax, formerly Lord Irwin. In retirement, both Templewood and Halifax recorded their opinion that the failure to secure the requisite number of princely accessions, and indeed thereby the collapse of the entire federal scheme, was attributable to two factors: the limited time available for negotiating with the princes and the failure of the Government of India to inject sufficient urgency into the negotiations in what limited time there was. In 1954, Templewood expressed his conviction that if the Government of India Act had reached the statute book in 1933 instead of 1935 then the federation could have been established before the outbreak of war. That it did not he attributed to the delaying and obstructionist tactics pursued by the diehard faction within the Conservative party.[1] However, for the fact that an insufficient number of princes had agreed to federate by 1939, Templewood held the Government of India to be responsible. He believed that 'if greater efforts had been made in Delhi to explain the advantages of Federation, we could have obtained the voluntary assent of a sufficient number (of princes) for starting the Federation before the war'.[2] Similar sentiments were expressed in 1957 by Halifax. He considered that the authorities in India could have done more to push the princes had they not been so overawed by the strong tradition of respect for their treaty rights. Halifax also saw fit to exonerate the India Office: 'It was no longer a case of the India Office acting in restraint of the Government of India, for the India Office was working night and day to get the scheme for Federation adopted with the least possible delay.'[3] In private correspondence with Templewood, Halifax laid the blame for the delay at the feet of Lord Willingdon and Lord Linlithgow who succeeded him as Viceroy in April 1936:

> I have often thought, though this was after my time and I may
> have been wrong about it, that a good part of the trouble and
> delay came from the fact that Freeman (Willingdon) liked the
> Princes and really disliked the British Indian leaders and Hopie
> (Linlithgow) had not much use for the Princes and did not really
> get on in human terms with anybody ... If they had really been
> willing to push the Federal idea and had not been inhibited by one
> cause or another, either in approach to Princes or Congress, you
> would have been able to get the Cabinet and Party to move more
> quickly.[4]

In that Linlithgow was specifically charged with inaugurating
federation during his viceroyalty, Halifax presumably thought that he
was the more culpable of the two. Indeed his opinion of Linlithgow
was the conventional one - a distant and aloof individual who was
dilatory in his approach to Indian problems, particularly federation.[5]

A different view was expressed in 1970 by Sir Francis Wylie, a
former political officer who toured some of the states as a viceregal
emissary in 1936. According to Wylie there was never the slightest
possibility of the required number of princes giving their voluntary
consent to join a federation. He was extremely critical of the 1935
Act for giving so many states individual representation in the federal
chambers whether in their own right or on a rotational basis. Wylie
in fact believed that there were only about six states with any serious
claim to qualify as federal units and that to have afforded
representation to a host of others made the task of negotiating with
the princes much more difficult. When to this was added the fact
that federation entailed a surrender of certain sources of revenue
usually earmarked by the princes for their privy purses, Wylie
reached the conclusion that the only way in which the government
could have inaugurated the federal scheme ' would have been to take
the princes by the neck and to compel them to come in'.[6]

The purpose of the first section of this chapter is to establish
precisely why the princes rejected federation in June 1939 and
whether there ever had been a serious possibility of the required
number agreeing to accede. It should be emphasized that the
intention is not to prove that the federation could have been
established had the princes agreed but rather to examine the
importance of the time-factor in deciding their attitude and also the
argument that the Government of India was primarily responsible for
the delay in negotiating with the princes.

In September 1935, Arthur C. Lothian, who had been appointed
additional Political Secretary to the Government of India, asked the
India Office to approve the following method of negotiating with the
princes. Political officers would be instructed to communicate a
draft Instrument of Accession to the princes upon receipt of a draft
from the India Office. Upon the basis of this one draft the princes
would be asked to federate. They would be told that there was a
minimum number of subjects for which they would be required to

federate. They would also be invited to specify any limitations they wished to impose on the extent to which particular subjects could be administered by the federal authority within their states. Once these limitations had been examined by the Secretary of State and the Government of India, a formal Instrument of Accession would be presented to each prince for his signature.[7] The intention of the Government of India was therefore to obtain an immediate commitment from the princes to federate and then to work out the details of what this would involve in the case of individual states.

In London, Sir Archibald Carter, the Assistant Under Secretary of State, considered these proposals to be 'a trifle crude',[8] and an alternative method of approach was devised by the India Office. Before a draft Instrument of Accession could be drawn up it would be necessary for the Secretary of State and Viceroy to reach an agreement on the extent to which limitations for the states would be acceptable. There would also have to be preliminary discussions in London with the legal advisers of the states on the technicalities of the draft Instrument. In the light of any observations made by these advisers the draft would be drawn up and sent to India for communication to the princes. The princes would have a fixed time in which to record their opinions of the draft, although it was envisaged that it might be necessary to allow some of them to send their ministers to London for further consultation with their advisers before they did so. By the spring of 1936 it would then be possible to produce a document embodying the standard limitations for various categories of states. This would be presented to the princes for further comment. Once these comments had been examined by the Secretary of State and the Government of India, political officers would go back to the princes with formal Instruments of Accession and for the first time ask them to federate on the terms offered. Exactly when this would be, the India Office declined to predict. What it did say was that: 'It is considered that no specific enquiry as to the willingness of individual States to accede on the terms offered should be addressed to any State until this very late stage in negotiations had been reached and the prospects of achieving the proportion of accessions fixed in the Act seemed assured.'[9]

In India, Lothian was shocked by this procedure which he considered to be a 'radical departure' from his own. He pointed out that it would serve no purpose and indeed would waste a great deal of time for the government to fix standard limitations before some idea had been gained of what limitations the states wanted. Lothian also emphasized the time factor. The longer the delay, the greater the possibility of the princes becoming more lukewarm and critical in their attitude to federation. He was of the opinion that even if some of the princes did not like federation, they all regarded it as inevitable: 'Psychologically therefore we consider that it is sound to take the federation as an inevitable development and to strike while the iron is hot, rather than to make tentative and doubtful approaches towards it.'[10] In view of Lothian's objections the India Office did modify its position slightly. There would still be discussion with states' counsel but ministers from the states would not be allowed to come to London for further consultation. Once the draft Instrument had been drawn up the princes would be given six months to specify the limitations they wanted, on condition 'that nothing which they might say at this stage would be held to prejudge the question of their decision to execute an Instrument of Accession'. Following the classification of these limitations by the government, formal Instruments of Accession would be drawn up and presented to the princes by political officers. Although the princes would at this stage be asked to federate, the India Office thought it inevitable that in many cases a further period of bargaining and negotiation would take place before the states actually committed themselves.[11] In February 1936 Lothian was obliged to accept these proposals which had taken over five months to formulate.

Two points emerge from this lengthy correspondence. First, Lothian, on behalf of the Government of India, had undoubtedly been optimistic in assuming that the princes would commit themselves to a federation before they knew the terms for so doing. Secondly, it is clear that at the outset it was the India Office and not the Government of India that applied the brake to federal negotiations with the princes. As early as September 1935 Patrick confessed to Lothian that the India Office wanted 'to postpone early action on the accession problem'. He explained that the view in London was that '... we need not lay ourselves open to any criticism of forcing Federation on the princes and, if we exhibit a little patience ... the Princes may swim into the net of their own accord'.[12] Zetland, Hoare's successor at the India Office, reiterated the argument to Willingdon when he said that the India Office wanted to 'avoid any risk of the Government being accused of having unduly hurried their decision about federating'.[13]

The comments of Patrick and Zetland indicate the two considerations which weighed most with the India Office throughout the period of federal negotiations with the princes. On the one hand it was anxious to avoid any charge of applying pressure on the princes to federate. On the other, and perhaps more important, it was convinced that a leisurely approach to the princes would have the desired effect. The princes would of their own accord agree to federate once they realized their disadvantageous position. With no voice in matters of all-India concern, and with the executive, though not responsible certainly more responsive to the views of the central legislature, the princes would have no alternative but to federate.

It is not surprising that in the post-war period Lothian made attempts to absolve the Government of India of the charge that it had delayed federal negotiations with the princes. In October 1957 he was able to convince Halifax who confessed that had he known of the correspondence between Delhi and London when he published his memoirs he would not have implied so complete an exoneration of the India Office.[14] What most concerned Lothian, however, were the observations made by Templewood in his book *Nine Troubled Years*. In a note written in 1962 Lothian explained how he had once spent an afternoon with Hailey in the House of Lords showing the former Secretary of State copies of the relevant correspondence. This part of the note is somewhat confusing in that it does not indicate whether the meeting took place before or after the publication of Templewood's book. Either way it would appear that Lothian did not gain from Templewood an admission similar to the one made by Halifax and this encouraged him to dig deeper. The subsequent evidence that he uncovered led him to accuse Templewood of being 'altogether dishonest' in *Nine Troubled Years*. Zetland, in writing a first draft of his own memoirs, *Essayez*, had included a reference to how Templewood, who was then Foreign Secretary, had been responsible for vetoing the Government of India suggestions for negotiating with the princes. Zetland was later persuaded by Sir Norman Brook, Secretary to the Cabinet between 1947 and 1962, to drop this reference as it was too controversial. From this Lothian concluded that in *Nine Troubled Years* Templewood was trying to blame others for a failure which had been of his own making.[15] It seems likely, therefore, that Templewood was himself the originator of the India Office hypothesis that more haste less speed would produce the necessary results with the princes. One can only assume that the former Secretary of State, having spent four exhausting and often frustrating years bringing the 1935 Act into existence, was now anxious to avoid further controversy within his own Conservative party which he feared would be the case if there was the slightest hint of the princes being subject to pressure to secure their accession to the federation.

When Lord Linlithgow assumed office in April 1936 the procedure for negotiating with the princes had already been established. From the start the new Viceroy sought ways to shorten it. In June 1936 he was appalled when he received a time-table from the Political Department which envisaged six-month intervals between each stage of the negotiations. He immediately issued revised instructions to the effect that the princes would only have six months to consider the final offer, all other stages of the negotiations being reduced to three months.[16] The Political Department subsequently informed the Viceroy that it would be difficult to meet his requirements when so much time was spent in consultation between London and Delhi and between various departments of the Government of India. Linlithgow was impressed by this latter argument and commented himself on the extent to which 'the energy and experience of even the highest officials is absorbed to the detriment of the handling and control of major issues of policy, in the disposal or the pursuit of relatively minor side-issues'.[17] Undoubtedly, however, the main cause of delay lay in London. Originally it had been intended to forward the draft Instrument of Accession to India in the spring of 1936. By the beginning of July it had still not arrived. Patrick admitted to Lothian that he was 'disturbed' by the delay for which the India Office had been responsible. Indeed he feared that because the India Office was so dependent for constitutional advice on the Parliamentary counsel's office and the princes' lawyers 'who are up to their eyes in court work and only deal with these knotty problems in their spare time', federation might be indefinitely delayed.[18] The draft eventually arrived at the beginning of August.

Linlithgow was able to make one major alteration in the procedure for negotiating with the princes. His first idea had been to convene a conference of as many princes as possible to explain federation to them. He changed his mind when he realized that this would involve a risk of 'one or two voluble individuals' creating a sense of 'apprehension out of all proportion to the real importance of the issues involved'.[19]   However, having opted for an individual approach, the Viceroy decided that it should be made, not by political officers, but by three emissaries - Courtenay Latimer, Agent to the Governor-General for the states of Western India, who was to tour Baroda, the Gujarat and the Deccan states; Francis Wylie, a political officer holding an ex-cadre appointment, who was to tour Kashmir and the states of Rajputana and the Punjab; and Lothian, who was to tour Hyderabad, Mysore, Cochin, Travancore and the states in Central India.

Linlithgow has been criticized for his decison to use emissaries instead of political officers to make the first approaches to the princes.   As the emissaries were only instructed to explain the federal provisions of the 1935 Act to the princes, not to inquire whether or not they would federate, it has been suggested that the first approaches should have been made by political officers who were resident in the states and thus knew the princes much better. Moreover, with in excess of 100 states to be consulted, it has been argued that the use of emissaries inevitably slowed down the negotiating procedure.[20]   These criticisms, however, are not justified.

The decision to use emissaries instead of political officers was made because Linlithgow had very rapidly come to the conclusion that despite the briefing of 1933, most officers were extremely ignorant about federation.   He wrote to Zetland: 'I am sending Agents to the Governor-General a little reading for the monsoon in the shape of the Act of 1935 with a guide thereto written from the point of view of the Indian States.'[21]   Nor can the Viceroy be blamed for the fact that the emissaries were instructed only to explain the federal provisions of the Act to the princes.   Before the trio embarked on their tours, Zetland had been disturbed by reports received from Delhi which indicated that they had been briefed to inform the princes, 'authoritatively and without the necessity of reference back to the Government of India', on the maximum limitations in respect of certain financial matters that the government would be prepared to accept.   The Secretary of State pointed out to Linlithgow that it had already been decided that the first approach to the princes would only be one of an 'explanatory and elucidatory' nature. He did not wish to 'act as a drag on the wheel of the coach which you are driving with so much skill' but felt that the princes were 'shy birds' who might easily take fright if they thought they were being pushed.[22]   In reply Linlithgow explained that he had hoped to reach agreement on the type of limitations which would be applicable to all the states before the emissaries departed.[23]   This never materialized; the emissaries were restricted to a mere fact-finding mission. Linlithgow's last word to them when they departed in October 1936 was that he hoped to see federation in operation by 1 April 1938.[24]

The tours by the emissaries lasted until January 1937. Their first reports reached Delhi in November 1936. Wylie observed that none of the princes he had visited 'had displayed any practical appreciation of the contents of the Government of India Act'. All appeared obsessed by the fear that they would be 'flooded' with federal officials over whom they would have no control.[25] Wylie encountered formidable opposition from some of the princes. During the discussions he held in Patiala, Bhupinder Singh left the room on more than one occasion leaving Wylie to deal with his legal adviser. When the Maharaja did decide to participate, Wylie observed that he 'allowed a bitterness to come into his tone which betrayed how much he hates the whole thing'.[26] Bikaner was even more obstructive. He not only suggested some 116 limitations, in contrast to Patiala's 40, but also greeted Wylie's every remark with 'scorn and derision'. Wylie, however, did not attach too much importance to Bikaner's opposition. He considered that most of the other Rajputana princes regarded Bikaner as 'an out-of-date windbag whose capacity for self-advertisement is very nearly exhausted'.[27] Despite the difficulties, therefore, Wylie felt generally optimistic about the prospects for federation. He recognized that there would have to be concessions to the princes but felt that the limitations they had suggested were 'not excessively serious or numerous and provide a fairly reasonable basis for negotiation of a genuine Instrument of Accession'.[28]

From Mysore, Lothian reported that Sir Mirza Ismail, the Maharaja's Chief Minister, was concerned more with the financial than with the political aspects of federation. Ismail was of the opinion that Mysore would have no difficulty in federating if its tribute was fully remitted. In fact while Lothian was in Mysore, J. Raisman, his assistant from the Finance Department of the Government of India, suggested to Ismail that it might be possible to remit the tribute if in return Mysore would agree to surrender its postal immunity and the revenue it derived from match and sugar excises.[29] The suggestion caused a stir in London because it obviously contravened the terms of reference for the emissaries. Zetland expressed concern to Linlithgow that the suggestion, however informal and non-committal, might be seized upon by the other states as an indication that the government was prepared to entertain similar bargaining arrangements with them.[30]

Of all the states Hyderabad presented the greatest difficulty. Not only were the Nizam's conditions for acceding extensive, some of them were of a blatantly anti-federal character. He objected to the idea of federal officials working within his state. He demanded that he should be allowed to retain his own currency and postal system and substantial control over Hyderabad's railway network. Above all, he repeated his demand for a written guarantee that Britain would protect the ruling Osmania dynasty in Hyderabad and that any forces used to implement this guarantee would always be composed of races not politically hostile to his government. In this respect he also demanded an assurance that he would still be able to employ Arabs and Africans in his military and police forces.[31] Lothian was left in some doubt as to whether Sir Akbar Hydari, the Nizam's chief negotiator who had represented Hyderabad at the round table conferences in London, would be able to 'deliver the goods' as far as federation was concerned.[32]

By the end of February 1937 the final reports of the emissaries had been received and the Government of India began the process of classifying the limitations required by the states. In August 1937 Linlithgow informed Zetland that the results of this classification had convinced him that concessions were needed to persuade the states to federate and that in order to make them the Government of India Act would have to be amended. He suggested that with regard to those states which derived revenue from corporation tax, salt duties, match and sugar excises and also the customs duties collected by the maritime states, the Act would have to be amended upon the basis of the *status quo* principle.[33] What this meant in practice was that even though the states concerned would agree to federate on these subjects, they would retain what revenue they derived from them.

With regard to customs duties, the report of the Joint Select Committee in 1934 had indicated that the maritime states should be allowed to retain only the duty on goods which were consumed within their own territories. However, in 1936, following negotiations with the states concerned, the Government of India concluded agreements by which the states would retain the duty on goods entering British India provided that it did not exceed specified annual totals. As part of the agreements the states undertook to offer no improper inducements to shippers with a view to stimulating trade at their ports at the expense of those in British India and also agreed that the Government of India had the right of inspection to satisfy itself that these conditions were being observed. Linlithgow appreciated that the agreements were contrary to the recommendations of the Joint Select Committee but felt that they would have to stand in order to secure the accession of the maritime states.[34]

The Viceroy was even more convinced of the necessity of adopting the *status quo* principle for match and sugar excises. Following the imposition of these excises in 1934, the Government of India had made agreements with states manufacturing matches and sugar in order to prevent them flooding British India with untaxed or lightly-taxed products in the absence of effective customs barriers. The agreement on matches provided for the states to impose excise duty at the rate applicable in British India. It also provided for all proceeds of the match excise in British India and the states to be paid into a common pool and divided between them on a consumption basis calculated by reference to population. The agreement on sugar provided for the states to impose excise duty at the British Indian rate but allowed them to retain the proceeds. As most states benefited from the agreements Linlithgow was emphatic that none of them would federate unless guaranteed as a maximum the amount which they had derived from match and sugar excises for the year 1936-1937.[35]

The Viceroy was fully aware of the dangers implicit in his

recommendations. He recognized that an amendment might revive the controversy in Parliament which had surrounded the 1935 Act. He also recognized that the British Indian reaction would be one of hostility and thus intensify the already strong feeling that the federal scheme was biased in favour of the princes. At the same time, however, he was certain that the alternatives to making the concessions would be much worse. The government would either have to drop federation altogether or postpone it. If the latter course were adopted the time would inevitably come when the government would again have to face the question of concessions to the states. In all probability these would be the same as the Viceroy was now contemplating, but the princes 'having seen the first scheme successfully rejected, would undoubtedly pitch their demands for amendments much higher than they would dare now'.[36] Finally, in support of his proposals Linlithgow revealed that he did not accept the India Office view that the government could afford to wait for the princes themselves to realize that it was in their interests to federate:

> If federation means an immediate sacrifice of revenue, it will have no attraction whatever to the states. The only thing which could make them take a different view would be fear of the consequences if they did not federate. It may be that if the Rulers were as enlightened as they should be, that fear would be widespread among them. There is however no indication of its existence in fact, and I know of no reason for anticipating that it will emerge in the near future.[37]

In view of his reaction to the suggestion regarding Mysore's tribute it is not surprising that Zetland took strong exception to Linlithgow's proposals. In October 1937 he informed the Viceroy that the Prime Minister, Neville Chamberlain, would be very unwilling to contemplate a bill which would be likely to revive former divisions within the Conservative Party.[38]   He was emphatic that no concessions could be allowed for salt and customs duties or for corporation tax. However, he could not ignore Linlithgow's opinion that the states in general would refuse to federate unless ensured of some major concession over the match and sugar excises. Accordingly in November 1937 he suggested a compromise upon the basis of a 'sliding-scale' principle. The amount of match and sugar excises retained by the states would diminish over a fixed period of time until eventually they would be entirely at the disposal of the federal administration. Zetland justified this compromise on the grounds that it would be more acceptable to Parliament as it did not alter the principle or substance of the 1935 Act.[39] Linlithgow, however, did not feel that this would be acceptable to the princes and continued to press for the *status quo* principle.[40] There followed a prolonged controversy between London and Delhi over the nature of the concessions which could be accorded to the princes. The controversy was not finally resolved until the summer of 1938, some two months after the Viceroy had anticipated that federation would be in operation.

In June 1938, Zetland relented and agreed to the *status quo* principle for the match and sugar excises. This was the only concession he was prepared to make. He considered that it would be improper for the maritime states to federate on such privileged terms. Instead the 1936 agreements would remain in force in the hope that eventually the states concerned would agree to federate on the terms laid down by the Joint Select Committee.[41] A similar position was adopted with regard to salt duties and corporation tax. Zetland's agreement to the *status quo* principle for the match and sugar excises was made on the condition that 'the offer (to the princes) will be final and that there should be no concessions afterwards on any major issues'.[42] In the event the concession to be made did not require an amendment to the 1935 Act. Linlithgow suggested and Zetland agreed that the *status quo* principle for the match and sugar excises could be incorporated as a limitation for federal excises in the individual Instruments of Accession.[43]

What emerges from this controversy over the terms on which the states would be required to federate is that Linlithgow, in his anxiety to inaugurate federation, was moving steadily away from the principles of the 1935 Act. Yet it is equally clear that it was not simply a question of whether or not the princes should be allowed to retain the proceeds of their match and sugar excises but also one of how best to approach the princes to secure their accession. From the time when Linlithgow became Viceroy in April 1936 until the summer of 1938, when the terms of the federal offer to the princes were agreed upon, Zetland and his advisers in the India Office firmly believed that the princes would recognize the need to federate of their own accord and that it was therefore unnecessary and indeed dangerous to press them. Linlithgow could never reconcile himself to this view and constantly sought authority to apply more pressure on the princes. In January 1937, upon receipt of the first reports from his emissaries, the Viceroy had asked Zetland to allow him 'to take a few risks provided that I avoid saying anything which might fairly be interpreted as amounting to a threat to Their Highnesses or to the exercise of unfair pressure upon them'.[44] Beyond saying that he wanted to 'push hard and very directly',[45] Linlithgow never indicated what these risks would entail. Zetland, however, advised caution. Churchill was 'on the look out' for indications of pressure on the princes while influential pressure groups such as the Lancashire cotton merchants and the Chamber of Shipping were becoming increasingly opposed to federation for fear that it would lead to the rapid disintegration of their trade with India.[46] It is in the light of these considerations that the subject of concessions to the princes must be seen. Linlithgow was convinced that there would have to be some inducement to the princes to federate yet the suggestions he made in this respect irritated the India Office because they represented a marked departure from the principles of the 1935 Act. In reality, however, it is clear that the India Office had left Linlithgow very little room for manoeuvre.

Once the details of the offer to the princes had been finalized,

Linlithgow wanted to leave them alone to consider it in an atmosphere conducive to calm and thoughtful deliberation. For this reason he persuaded Zetland to withhold a White Paper which the Secretary of State had contemplated publishing at the same time as the offer was made to the princes. Zetland had frankly admitted that the White Paper would have the advantage of 'placing on princes publicly the onus of rejecting our proposals and of removing grounds for charge that progressive concessions were being made to them at the expense of British India'.[47] Thus it was intended as a safeguard to ensure that if the princes did reject the offer they and not the government would be blamed. Linlithgow objected on the grounds that if the White Paper did result in hostile criticism of the princes they would have a ready-made excuse to decline the federal offer before they had even considered the details.[48] It was therefore decided to indicate the terms of the offer informally to a few of the leading princes and then to present it to them all to consider in seclusion for a period of six months.[49] Unfortunately the conducive atmosphere sought by Linlithgow never materialized. The princes found themselves subject to external pressure conducted in the name of the Indian National Congress.

The Congress agitation began in Mysore in October 1937 and culminated in 1939 with two civil disobedience campaigns conducted by Gandhi and Jamnalal Bajaj in Rajkot and Jaipur respectively. Most British observers, and the princes themselves, were convinced that the agitation was part of a deliberate campaign to force democracy on the states in order that elected state representatives could be used by Congress to secure a majority in the federal legislature and thus power in the federal ministry.[50] This was a mistaken analysis of Congress policy towards the states, the principles of which had been declared by the Congress Working Committee when it met at Wardha in August 1935. While supporting the establishment of responsible government in the states the Working Committee had emphasized that:

> ... the responsibility and the burden of carrying on that struggle must necessarily fall on the States people themselves. The Congress can exercise moral and friendly influence upon the States and this it is bound to do wherever possible. The Congress has no other power under existing circumstances ... In the heat of the controversy the limitation of the Congress is often forgotten. Indeed any other policy will defeat the common purpose.[51]

Implicit in this statement was the recognition that Congress was not strong enough to wage a dual struggle against the British in British India and the British and the princes in the Indian States. In this respect the Working Committee's statement confirmed the tenor of Gandhi's instructions at the second round table conference: Congress would deal with the states from a position of strength once it had won the struggle in British India. This attitude continued to irritate leaders of the All-India States' People's Conference (AISPC) and also dissident Congressmen and women who resented the controlling influence exercised by right-wingers such as Rajendra Prasad and Vallabhbhai Patel in the formulation of Congress policy. One such dissident from the Karnatak, Shrimati Kamaladevi, sarcastically described the Working Committee's statement as an 'appeal to nobody' and an 'expression of helplessness' which had been 'colouring their imagination far too much and far too long'.[52]

After April 1936, when Jawaharlal Nehru had been elected Congress President, dissident Congressmen attempted to exploit the discontent of AISPC leaders and also to strengthen their own position *vis à vis* the Congress establishment by organizing Congress committees and civil disobedience campaigns in the states. N.S. Hardiker, the Bombay Karnataka Congress leader, was anxious to boost the voice of the Karnataka Provincial Congress Committee in All-India Congress circles by recruiting members from Congress sympathisers in Mysore. He met with considerable success when, in September 1936, he persuaded Nehru to write a letter of endorsement for his efforts.[53]   Hardiker's success was followed by a civil disobedience campaign in Mysore in the autumn of 1937 which attracted support from other dissidents such as K.F. Nariman and Yusuf Meherally, who were likewise anxious to strengthen their own power bases in Bombay. In late October Nariman was arrested in Bangalore City, the capital of Mysore, for a speech he had made which violated a government ban. The arrest sparked off rioting in the city as a result of which six people lost their lives.[54] Leaders of the Congress Socialist Party, with Nehru's assistance, responded by persuading the All-India Congress Committee, which met at Calcutta during the last week of October, to pass a resolution to the effect that Congressmen should give moral and material support to civil disobedience campaigns in the states.[55] These activities alarmed the right-wing Congress leaders and also Gandhi who feared that the resolution would lead to demands for civil disobedience campaigns in the states in support of the Mysore agitation. It was against this background that the Congress assembled at Haripura in February 1938 and after heated debate, approved the following resolution:

> The Congress ... directs that, for the present, Congress Committees in the states shall function under the direction and control of the Congress Working Committee and shall not engage in parliamentary activity nor launch on direct action in the name and under the auspices of the Congress. Internal struggles of the people of the States must not be undertaken in the name of the Congress. For this purpose, independent organisations should be started and continued where they exist already within the States.[56]

It is clear, therefore, that Congress agitation in the states was not part of a campaign to promote democracy in them, but a by-product of political infighting between Congress dissidents and the Congress establishment. Nevertheless, in the aftermath of Haripura, agitation in the states continued unabated. Independent organizations, known as *Praja Mandals* or People's Parties, proliferated throughout princely India. Although agitation was conducted in large states such as Hyderabad, Kashmir and Travancore, the most vulnerable were the smaller Deccan and Orissa states which were embedded in neighbouring British Indian provinces. In one of the Orissa states, Ranpur, the agitation was accompanied by violence which culminated in January 1939 with the murder of Major Bazalgette, the political agent.[57] Consequently during the first half of 1939, Congress leaders found that they could defuse a potentially explosive situation only by assuming direct personal control over activities in the states. Gandhi and Bajaj conducted agitations in their respective native states of Rajkot and Jaipur while Nehru became President of the AISPC.[58]

According to India Office calculations, the onset of Congress-inspired agitation was just the situation in which the princes would realize that they could best protect themselves by agreeing to federate. In fact it had precisely the opposite effect.

In September and October 1938, ministers from the states of Hyderabad, Mysore, Baroda, Gwalior, Travancore, Cochin, Patiala and Kolhapur were informed of the federal offer, the contents of which had been agreed by Linlithgow and Zetland in the preceding summer. Only D.A. Surve, the Prime Minister of Kolhapur, claimed to be fully satisfied;[59] the others all voiced dissatisfaction with specific points of detail. Ismail for instance agreed to Mysore's tribute arrangement but wanted it translated into practice before federation became operative.[60] Hydari explained that it would come as a 'profound shock' to the Nizam to find that federal subjects were to be administered by federal officers within his state rather than by Hyderabad officials.[61] However, with the exception of Surve, one fundamental objection was voiced by all the ministers: the terms offered contained inadequate protection for those treaty rights of the states which would remain outside federal jurisdiction. Hydari in particular was dismayed that the necessary defence guarantees for Hyderabad had not been included in the Instrument.[62]

Under the terms of the 1935 Act all treaty rights not affected by federation were to be protected by the Governor-General through the use of his reserve powers. Consequently it had been considered unnecessary to include in each individual Instrument of Accession a comprehensive schedule or list of such rights. Only federal subjects would be included in the Instrument. There would be a list of such subjects and under each heading the ruler would specify one of the following: non-accession; federation without limitations, which meant that the federal government would have unrestricted authority to make laws for a particular subject within the state; federation with limitations, which meant that the federal government would have authority to make laws for a particular subject upon certain conditions. Hence, as far as the match and sugar excises were concerned, the states would become subject to federal administration on condition that they were allowed to retain the proceeds at the rate for the year 1936-37. If the federal government infringed these arrangements, the states would have the right of appeal to the

Federal Court. However, for protection on subjects from which the federal administration was to be excluded, for example the customs rights of the maritime states and Hyderabad's defence guarantees, the states concerned would have to rely on the reserve powers of the Governor-General.

Recent experience had taught the princes that this was inadequate protection. They noted how reluctant provincial governors had been to invoke the special powers accorded to them under the 1935 Act to prevent incursions into the states from the provinces on the grounds that this would precipitate the resignations of the Congress ministries.[63] From this the princes deduced that the Governor-General might likewise be reluctant to invoke his reserve powers to protect their treaty rights should the occasion demand it. The princes therefore demanded the inclusion of a comprehensive schedule of these rights in their Instruments of Accession. These rights would thus become part of the federal constitution. If subsequently the federal administration infringed them, the states would not have to rely on the reserve powers of the Governor-General but could appeal to the Federal Court, the decision of which the paramount power would be bound to enforce.

Although the fallacy of India Office thinking had now been exposed, there was no modification of the terms of the federal offer before it was communicated to the general body of princes in January 1939. They were informed that they had six months in which to reach a decision.   The Chamber of Princes appointed a Committee of Ministers, chaired by Sir Akbar Hydari, to examine a standard Instrument of Accession. In April the Committee reported that in the absence of adequate protection for non-federal treaty rights, the standard Instrument was unacceptable.[64] In June 1939 a larger and more representative gathering of princes met at Bombay and passed a resolution endorsing the verdict of the Hydari Committee. The resolution concluded: '. . . At the same time the conference records its belief that it could not be the intention of His Majesty's Government to close the door on an All-India Federation.'[65] Although the princes had rejected the offer they clearly now expected the government to make it more acceptable.

In view of the comments of those ministers consulted on the terms of the federal offer in the autumn of 1938, the Bombay decision did not come as a surprise to either Zetland or Linlithgow. The former was now anxious to publish a White Paper in order to prove how favourable the offer was and how unreasonable the princes had been in rejecting it. The Secretary of State had already been informed that it would be impossible to safeguard the non-federal treaty rights of the princes in the manner they desired. In March 1939, Sir Findlater Stewart, the Permanent Under Secretary of State, recorded the view that Britain was not in a position to give Hyderabad the necessary defence guarantees.   It could only be guaranteed that Britain would fulfil its treaty obligations 'if it could', the implication being that the time would come when the paramount power would be unable to maintain the treaties it had concluded with the states. Findlater Stewart was of the opinion that because it would be regarded as a 'confession of weakness' to make such a declaration and also because the Nizam would in any case regard it as an 'empty promise', it would be better to say nothing about non-federal treaty rights.[66] In this respect the British had been less than honest with the princes, as Zetland admitted to Linlithgow in July 1939:

> It must be admitted that we share their doubts, even if we do not say so in so many words; yet we tell them that their only possible safeguard is to be found in the exercise by the Governor-General of the special responsibility vested in him and we say that they must rely upon the good faith and the ability of Great Britain to honour the treaties and engagements into which in the past she entered with them.[67]

Such observations foreshadowed what happened to the princes at the end of the second world war when the British did depart from India leaving the princes to negotiate their fate with British Indian politicians. They also shed new light upon Britain's obligations towards the states: paramountcy might have been paramount but it was also impermanent.

The Bombay decision in April 1939 represented the end of serious federal negotiations with the princes. In July 1939 Linlithgow did attempt to break the deadlock by suggesting that the customs rights of the maritime states should be safeguarded in the desired manner. He felt that this might persuade the maritime states to change their minds and thus 'turn the tide strongly in favour of federation'.[68] However, he could not guarantee that this would be the case and consequently Zetland rejected the idea.[69] On 11 September 1939 the Viceroy announced the suspension of federal negotiations for the duration of the war. He was at pains to point out that suspension was the operative word and that his announcement did not mean the abandonment of federation: 'We shall have to keep the threads in our hands, and if the situation admits of our doing so, be prepared to move without the least hesitation in the direction of Federation under the Act if that is still practicable at the end of the war.'[70] However, in March 1940 the Muslim League, meeting at Lahore, passed the famous 'Pakistan' resolution which declared that the north-western and north-eastern zones of India, where Muslims predominated, 'should be grouped to constitute "independent states" in which the constituent units should be autonomous and sovereign'.[71] For all practical purposes, federation was now a dead letter.

The princes had rejected the federal scheme in June 1939 on the grounds that it afforded inadequate protection for their non-federal treaty rights. The Congress campaign had made them aware of this deficiency in the 1935 Act. One is left to ponder how they would have reacted had they been asked to federate before the onset of the Congress campaign. It is evident that Hyderabad would never have agreed. The Nizam's anxiety to secure protection against the nationalist movement in British India had prompted him to support federation in 1930. Yet this in itself was insufficient and the government's refusal to give Hyderabad the sought-after defence guarantee, particularly when agitation had been launched against the state between 1938 and 1939, killed all prospect of the Nizam's agreeing to federate. Indeed he was already working on the idea that if he could secure an outlet to the sea at the port of Masulipatam in the Madras Presidency then he would be able to claim a viable existence for his state as an independent unit.[72]   A federation without the premier-ranking Indian State seems unthinkable but nevertheless it is not inconceivable that the requirements of the accession formula could still have been met had the offer been made before the Congress campaign.   Whereas the protection of non-federal treaty rights had always been the principal consideration for Hyderabad, the other important states had been mainly interested in the financial implications of federation.   Treaty rights for them only became significant as the Congress campaign gathered momentum. Before he announced the suspension of negotiations Linlithgow estimated that two-fifths of the required number of states had agreed to federate, in other words twenty of the fifty-two states represented in the Upper Chamber whose aggregate population was 11 million.[73]   These included Jaipur and Jodhpur, two of the first eight states in order of population.   The other five, now that Hyderabad was a non-starter, were Mysore, Travancore, Kashmir, Gwalior and Baroda. Although each had outstanding financial claims, these were capable of settlement.   They were now holding back because of the question of treaty rights. In view of the fact that the population requirement was 40 million, the agreement of these five would have pushed the total population of acceding states up to 32 million and this, as Linlithgow remarked to Zetland, would have been 'within measurable distance' of the target.[74]

Where then does the responsibility lie for the fact that the princes were asked to federate in 1939 instead of 1937 or even some earlier date before the Congress campaign?   Obviously the princes themselves must share some of the responsibility. Although they originated the idea at the first round table conference they were never particularly enthusiastic about federation, an attitude which they never concealed throughout the negotiating period. Undoubtedly, however, the responsibility for the delay in presenting the federal offer to the princes rests with the British authorities. Willingdon had made the task confronting Linlithgow's government more difficult than it need have been. Negotiations with a smaller number of states would not only have been more manageable but also less time-consuming.   This aspect of the problem was never considered by Halifax and Templewood but nevertheless account must now be taken of their view of the consequences of diehard opposition between 1933 and 1935.   Yet it is equally clear that after 1935 it was not the Government of India but the India Office that delayed negotiations. Indeed Templewood himself must shoulder some of the responsibility because he appears to have originated the idea of approaching the princes in a leisurely fashion.

During the first two years of the negotiations it was not force, as Wylie suggested, that was required to persuade the princes to federate but financial inducement. Linlithgow was prepared to make financial concessions to the states because he realized that the longer the negotiating process lasted the less chance there would be of establishing a federation. Admittedly some of the India Office objections to his proposals in this respect were quite justified. They militated against the principle of an equitable distribution of federal revenues between the states and British India. Opponents of the federal scheme could accuse the government of bribery. Moreover, if the government too readily agreed to make concessions the princes would press for still more. Yet none of these represent the main reason why the India Office objected to making financial concessions to the states. Unlike Linlithgow, Zetland was never convinced of the need for urgency in negotiating with the princes. He often confided to the Viceroy that although time was not on the side of the princes they themselves would eventually realize this and agree to federate. In one respect he was right. Time was not on the side of the princes, it was soon to catch up with them and bring their existence as rulers of semi-independent states to an end. Yet what the Secretary of State and his advisers failed to realize was that if federation was ever to be established then time was not on the side of the government either. Linlithgow appreciated this more than most, but all his warnings fell on deaf ears in the India Office.

The End of the Non-Interference Policy

The Congresss agitation also served to highlight the second major aspect of the states problem - the nature of their internal administrations. It had not taken Linlithgow long to realize that all was not well in this respect. In June 1936 he wrote to Zetland:

> I cannot help feeling very definitely that for whatever reason, certain of the Princes have been allowed to have too much of their own head in the recent past, and that whether because of uncertainty as to the degree to which they would find support from higher authority, or for some other reason, our local representatives have not always taken as firm a line with them as was desirable.[75]

However, it was not until the onset of Congress agitation that the authorities both in Delhi and London began to reappraise the policy of non-interference. They were prompted to do so by a memorandum written by the Chief of Sangli in the summer of 1938. Sangli was of the opinion that the smaller states were incapable of coping with the 'sweeping character' of demands being made for constitutional, revenue and financial changes within their states. He considered that the policy of transferring the states to direct relations with the Government of India had been a mistake, particularly for the smaller ones like his own which were enmeshed in neighbouring British Indian provinces. Previously the governors of the provinces could ensure that the interests of the states were safeguarded but with the inauguration of provincial autonomy in 1937 the transfers now meant

176. British Policy towards the Indian States

that legislation was frequently passed in the provinces without due consideration for these interests. The reluctance of the governors to exercise their special powers to protect the states only made the problem worse. As a possible solution Sangli suggested that groups of small states should pool their resources in matters such as public health, education and justice in order to raise administrative standards and thus 'anticipate criticism and disarm attack'.[76] Sangli's views are exceptional in that they represent the only recognition by an Indian prince that at least one aspect of the policy of non-interference had been misguided in its conception. In 1918 Sangli had petitioned for his state to be taken into direct relations with the Government of India; now his arguments served to vindicate the opinions of the Bombay and Punjab governments when they had opposed such a policy.

The problems confronting the smaller states were indeed serious. Their resources were totally inadequate to maintain reasonable administrative standards. Most of what little they did have was used to support the ruling family. They were an obvious target for external attack and criticism and it is not surprising that most of the Congress activities were directed against the petty states of the Western India, Deccan and Eastern state agencies. In 1938, the ruler of Aundh, a small state in the Deccan agency, agreed to grant his subjects a constitution in order to stave off external pressure. The constitution, which was introduced in January 1939, provided for a Legislative Assembly with the power to dismiss a ministry chosen from its members by the ruler on a vote of confidence and also with the power to enforce any measure which the ruler had previously rejected on three separate occasions.[77] Linlithgow was horrified, not only because of what had happened but also because of how it had happened: the ruler had been left to his own devices to deal with his critics and had received no advice or assistance from the Political Department.[78] The Viceroy now feared that unless the government took some action what had happened in Aundh might act as a catalyst with the smaller states scampering to come to terms with Congress.[79] Linlithgow was made fully aware that the initiative rested with the government as a result of an interview he held with the Maharaja of Bhavnagar in March 1939. The Maharaja wanted to introduce reforms within his state but he was at a loss as to where to start and what to do.[80] The interview was an awkward experience for Linlithgow as he was equally at a loss as to what advice he could give to the Maharaja. He confessed to Zetland: 'As you will see, he put me a somewhat embarrassing question and one which we will have to face up to without delay and which, I suspect, we shall get, in one form or another from a great many of the other Princes.'[81]

Thus at the beginning of 1939, Linlithgow and Zetland began devising a new policy to be adopted with regard to conditions within the states. The evolution of this policy continued well into the second world war but the main outlines had been established by the summer of 1939. Its most important principle was the renunciation of the non-interference policy. The Viceroy wrote to Zetland in April 1939: '. . . the policy of abstention from interference pursued for so many years can no longer be defended and must be abandoned'.[82]   It should be noted, however, that the new policy was never made official.   Neither Linlithgow nor Zetland, nor any other senior government official, ever made a formal and public pronouncement to the effect that the principles outlined in Minto's Udaipur speech no longer applied.   To make such a pronouncement would not only be a confession of failure but would also run the considerable risk of stampeding the princes into the arms of the Congress.   It was also significant that the new policy was designed primarily for the medium-sized and smaller states.   The larger ones, by virtue of their greater resources which enabled them to maintain adequate security forces, were more capable of looking after themselves and there was thus less risk of their surrendering to external pressure.

In revising previous policy towards the states, Linlithgow confessed that the dilemma in which the British now found themselves was one of their own making:

> The great mistake, I am now disposed to think, lay in the change of policy after Curzon's retirement which led us to relax our control over individual princes and over happenings inside their States to the extent which we have (a tendency inevitably encouraged by the transfer of control from provinces to the Centre); and we and the States have now, and will I suspect continue, to pay for thirty years of *laissez-faire*.[83]

Zetland fully agreed:

> When Minto succeeded George Curzon he undoubtedly went to extremes in relaxing the control which Curzon had exercised over the Princes. No doubt Curzon's intervention was bitterly resented by the Princes themselves, but as you of course know well enough, tact in matters of this kind was not George Curzon's strong suit, and while there was, I think, great justification for his policy, it was unfortunate that he pursued it in so dictatorial a manner.[84]

The new policy fell into three distinct parts: the question of constitutional advance in the states, suitable measures to raise administrative standards in the states, and the problem of how to secure an adequate and competent political staff to implement the new policy.

With regard to the question of constitutional advance in the states, a written reply to a parliamentary question put down in December 1938 had stated that while the paramount power would not obstruct constitutional changes in the states it would not encourage them either.   The initiative in this respect was to be left to individual princes.   However, the experience in Aundh and his interview with the Maharaja of Bhavnagar had convinced Linlithgow that something more than this was required.   It would be embarrassing if a prince approached the government for advice on constitutional reform and the government was not in a position to reply.   Linlithgow therefore suggested that a distinction should be drawn between the larger states and the medium-sized and smaller ones. For the former he advocated the creation of a small expert committee (he did not give details of its composition) which would devise constitutional schemes for communication to those princes who wanted advice in this respect. For the latter he advocated an *ad hoc* committee which would meet in Delhi and be chaired by the Political Adviser,[85] with the Reforms Commissioner of the Government of India as one of the other members. The committee would devise suitable constitutions for different categories of medium and small states on the understanding that the princes would not be bound to accept such advice as was offered.[86]

Zetland and Sir Bertrand Glancy, who became Linlithgow's first Political Adviser, were opposed to these suggestions. The Secretary of State appreciated that there were risks in leaving the princes to their own devices, but felt that there were still graver dangers in Linlithgow's proposals. Constitutional advance could not be regulated in the same manner as administrative reform. It was not inconceivable that constitutional advance could eventually result in full responsible government thus absolving the ruler of his obligations towards the paramount power.[87] Zetland and Glancy proposed that princes contemplating reforms should approach the Chamber of Princes for advice 'even though its advice is unlikely to be on progressive lines'. They were also of the opinion that any advice offered by political officers should be confined to such matters as reserve powers during emergency periods and how not to breach paramountcy obligations.[88] In that the views of Zetland and Glancy ultimately prevailed it is not surprising that none of the states made significant constitutional advances during the war. In fairness, however, this was not because of the nature of advice given by the Chamber or political officers but more the result of the cessation of Congress activities against the states when war broke out which meant that they were rarely consulted. With the pressure off most princes felt no need to consider constitutional reforms.

In considering measures to raise administrative standards in the medium and smaller states, Linlithgow and Zetland agreed on the following proposals. Groups of smaller states were to pool their resources in order to establish joint administrative services for police, justice, public health, education, rural development and transport. This would apply to all states whose revenue was less than Rs. 10 *lakhs* per annum. Zetland urged that compulsion should be used for states refusing to co-operate: 'If, however, their own financial and other resources cannot provide what is essential for good administration, we cannot be expected to defend them from the consequences of their shortcomings or to supplement their individual resources at the expense of the Indian tax-payer, when the desired result could be achieved by co-operation with neighbouring States.'[89] The privy purses of the rulers of the medium and smaller states were to be fixed at ten per cent. Irwin had only suggested this figure in his note on administration in 1927; now an attempt would be made to enforce it. Each of the states would be required to publish an annual budget statement and also, within six months of the end of each financial year, an Administration Report containing details of all revenue expenditure, administrative improvements and constitutional changes. It was appreciated that these requirements would be beyond the competence of most of the princes. Zetland therefore suggested that more advice should be given to them when they appointed ministers and subordinate officials to ensure a minimum degree of competence.[90] Linlithgow also recognized the need for a revision of government policy during minority periods. He was appalled to learn that many of the small Orissa states had been under minority rule for at least fifty years yet their administrative standards still left much to be desired.[91] Finally, Viceroy and Secretary of State came to the conclusion that the host of petty estates and *jagirs* could no longer survive as individual entities and would therefore have to be merged into larger neighbouring states.[92]

Linlithgow was aware that the change in policy might antagonize many of the princes but he was convinced that it was in their own interests to co-operate. As he told Zetland in April 1939, it was not simply a question of ensuring that the states did not yield to Congress agitation but also one of their own survival:

> But there, too, I feel that the risk is one that must be taken; and if in fact, as I believe to be the case unless the States are to disappear, administrative improvements (and, too, constitutional change) are bound to come, I would rather they came as a result of pressure from us than as a result of pressure from the Congress acquiesced in by the Ruler and by the Paramount Power.[93]

The final aspect of the new policy, how to secure an adequate and competent political staff, was a constant nightmare for Linlithgow. Ever since his appointment as Viceroy he had had serious misgivings about the calibre of the Political Department; hence his use of personal emissaries instead of political officers to make the first approaches to the princes over federation. In fact he had been loath to delegate any major responsibility to political officers throughout the period of federal negotiations. However, they could not be kept in the background when a deliberate attempt was to be made to reform the states. It was essential, to ensure success for the new policy, that residents and political agents should make it their business to keep in far closer touch with the states within their charges. Their tours would have to be more regular and more frequent, they would have to advise on constitutional changes, administrative reforms and on the selection of ministers and officials. They would have to intervene to remedy delays in dealing with grievances and ensure that accurate budget accounts and administration reports were published. For years political officers had been under the impression that, in the words of the Political Department Manual, they 'should leave well alone: the best work of a Political Officer is very often what he has left undone'. Would they now be able to cope with their new responsibilities?

Linlithgow had serious doubts. He considered that the Political Department contained a 'large proportion of somewhat second-rate men' and even contemplated abolishing it altogether and transferring its responsibilities to ordinary Indian Civil Service (ICS) cadres: 'I feel sometimes that nothing short of a shake-up of this kind will purge the Political Service of their mediaevalism, the consequence of generations of experience in the Indian States.'[94] Such sentiments were the result of Linlithgow's experience of the handling of Gandhi's civil disobedience campaign in Rajkot. An ICS official, Reginald Maxwell, Home Member of the Viceroy's Executive Council, had intervened to assist Glancy and Courtenay Latimer, his assistant as additional secretary to the Political Department, in settling the dispute. For the Viceroy the contrast in approach between Maxwell on the one hand and Glancy and Latimer on the other was poignant:

> It is the contrast of approach of the civil servant of ability who has for the last 20 years been in British Indian politics, dealing with various ups and downs of our relations with Congress and with the development of institutions of a representative character in the Provinces, with the civil servant of equal ability who has lived in an entirely different atmosphere and inherited a different tradition, and who now for the first time hears the sound of the mob outside his own house.[95]

There were two inter-related problems to be confronted in overhauling the Political Department. The first was a problem of manpower; there were simply not enough officers to cope with the projected increase in the workload. This was a direct result of the amalgamation and retrenchment programme of the 1920s. That programme had been designed not only to save money but also to conform to the principles of the non-interference policy. Ironically the grave consequences of implementing such a programme which had been illustrated so graphically by men like Blakeway, Holland and Kealy, had now materialized. The second problem concerned the qualifications of political officers. They had no experience of financial and revenue administration, the two subjects which were at the heart of the new policy. Zetland suggested that all political officers above the rank of political agent should take a course in these subjects,[96] but Glancy pointed out that it would be extremely difficult to fill the temporary vacancies which would arise from the deputation of officers to such courses.[97] As a result it was decided that political officers should merely familiarize themselves with revenue manuals provided by neighbouring provinces.[98]

Linlithgow did attempt to ease the burden by adding to the numbers in the Political Department. Recruiting more army officers to assist with purely administrative matters was one of his ideas, but it was cut short by the outbreak of war in 1939. The Viceroy was therefore forced to fall back on the conventional stand-by of seconding ICS officers for service in the states. Even here there were grave difficulties as the case of the United Provinces illustrates. In October 1938, H.G. Haig, governor of the United Provinces, pointed out that although officially the province was supposed to maintain a staffing ratio of forty-five to thirty between

Europeans and Indians, from 1931 to 1936 the number of Indian recruits had been thirty compared with only fourteen Europeans.[99] This was largely due to an overall reduction in European levels of recruitment but the position in the United Provinces was not helped by the secondment of European officers for service in the states. Haig explained that his civil service was under a severe strain because the Congress ministry was encouraging the people of the province to press for redress of every kind of grievance or injustice, however petty.[100] He considered that it would be impossible for him to spare any more men and indeed he was even contemplating requesting the return of a European finance officer who had been lent to the state of Rampur.[101] Linlithgow's efforts to strengthen the Political Department therefore met with little success. To implement the new policy he was forced to rely largely on the existing cadre which was both under-manned and lacking in essential qualifications.

Given the circumstances and the magnitude of the task, it is hardly surprising that the new policy did not achieve a great deal. It was an attempt to reverse within two or three years the trends of the previous thirty. To stand even the remotest chance of success an air of urgency had to surround the new policy but this was lost upon the outbreak of war when the Congress agitation ceased and the Congress itself reverted to the priority of the struggle for power in British India. Relieved of the external pressure the attitude of the princes towards administrative reform was the same as their attitude towards constitutional change - they simply lost interest.

Admittedly there were some achievements. The publication of a report in November 1940 by J.S.H. Shattock provided the basis whereby the smaller states and estates of the Gujarat and Kathiawar agencies were to be absorbed by the larger states in their neighbourhood.[102] Some groups of smaller states did manage to devise joint services. By 1943 states in the Bundelkhand and Malwa agencies in Central India had established a Joint High Court and a Joint Police Adviser. In the Eastern agency the states of Orissa and Chattisgarh had created a Joint Armed Police Force. In the Punjab the tiny hill states had agreed to co-operate for police and judicial services. In the Deccan a Joint Police Force had been established but this was serviced by detachments from the largest of the Deccani states, Kolhapur, and could hardly therefore be regarded as a co-operative measure.[103] There was little disposition to extend the co-operative principle to spheres other than the police and judiciary. The princes who acted did so primarily from the point of view of defence in order to protect themselves should there be a repeat of the Congress campaign. Nothing was done to improve conditions for their subjects by devising joint schemes for public health, education and transport.

It is also significant that none of the princes submitted voluntarily to the establishment of joint police and judicial services. They each resented the loss of sovereignty and indeed it was only by inviting the participation of the Maharaja of Kolhapur that the Deccan scheme was introduced.[104] It was a similar story with the Punjab Hill states where the Nawab of Loharu was loath to co-operate with the Nawab of Pataudi because he was jealous of Pataudi's international reputation as a cricketer.[105] In southern Rajputana the proposal to establish a Joint High Court and a Joint Inspector General of Police for the smaller states met with persistent opposition from the Maharawal of Dungarpur. In February 1941 the Maharawal informed Arthur Lothian, who had been appointed as the AGG in Rajputana upon completion of his tour as one of Linlithgow's emissaries, that joint services would lead to the extinction of the states and leave their rulers as mere pensioners. He was very 'fond and proud' of his 'ancient state' and considered that any state with an area of 500 square miles and a population of 100,000 deserved to be retained as an individual entity.[106] That the Political Department did not share his opinions clearly annoyed the Maharawal and he complained to Lothian: 'Comparatively, Dungarpur is small and I know it. But it cannot serve any useful purpose reminding me of it.' Above all, however, the Maharawal felt deeply humiliated because Dungarpur, which covered an area of 1,447 square miles and had a population of nearly 230,000, had been grouped with the state of Shahpura, which was only 405 square miles in area with a population of just over 54,000.[107] No doubt officials within the Political Department of the India Office had rulers like the Maharawal of Dungarpur in mind when, in May 1941, they made the following summary of the efforts which had been made to encourage co-operative groupings of states:

> The present Viceroy ... has done his utmost to impress upon the Rulers the importance of 'collective security' through combining the appropriate administrative services of separate states. So far, however, this doctrine has yielded as little result in the states as it did in the field of defence in the Europe of recent years. No ruler will willingly sink a portion of his separate sovereignty in a joint stock concern. Rulers who are neighbours seem particularly prone to mutual jealousy and suspicion, often increased by communal divergence. Vested interests in the official class are banded against reduction of posts. Court flatterers warn petty monarchs of the risk of parting with one jot of their autonomy.[108]

It was not only the smaller states that created difficulties; very little could be achieved in the medium-sized states. It was often the rulers of these states who had campaigned vigorously for a policy of non-interference and they were determined that its principles should not be relinquished. Arthur Lothian wrote after visiting Ganga Singh of Bikaner in 1939:

> Although His Highness showed me anything which I asked to see, and allowed me to talk to his officials, he was always present, and I could get no opportunity of seeing them alone. I do not, however, think this is so much a result of design as of inability to conceive of the State functioning apart from himself. Far more than in any other Indian State that I have visited *l'état*

c'est moi'.[109]

The problems created by the mentality of the princes were compounded by the attitude of most political officers. When asked in January 1939 to consider joint services between groups of small states, only Kenneth Fitze in Central India replied immediately and with practical suggestions of his own.[110] Indeed it was Fitze's perseverence in the face of persistent oppositon from the rulers of Bundelkhand and Malwa that eventually led to the creation of the joint police and judicial services. Elsewhere political officers were leisurely and lukewarm in their response. Typical was Colonel Wilberforce-Bell for the Punjab states, whose first reaction was that it would be pointless to sound out the princes within his agency on joint services. He considered that as the Punjab states were so lacking in indigenous adminstrative talent there was no alternative but to continue the existing policy of relying on the neighbouring government of the Punjab either to train officials or to lend experts of their own to the states.[111] To this Glancy retorted:

> Col. Wilberforce-Bell like so many political officers has not had sufficient experience of modern Indian administration to appreciate when the shoe pinches. I still think there should be an expert inspection staff for minor states to reveal the skeletons in the cupboard. Once the actual trouble has been diagnosed - it is no doubt easy to borrow specialists from a province like the Punjab. To remain in ignorance of maladministration till the place blows up - is to court disaster and that is where Col. Wilberforce-Bell's attitude would leave us.[112]

No doubt what Glancy said was true. What he did not point out was that Wilberforce-Bell was a very experienced political officer having joined the service in 1909 and having served as Deputy Political Secretary and in the Deccan states before his appointment to the Punjab in 1934. Like so many of his counterparts, Wilberforce-Bell lacked administrative experience because he had been nurtured under a policy of non-interference. When Harcourt Butler established that policy during Minto's day he had been of the opinion that the 'leopard cannot change its spots' and that it would require a change of generation before political officers became fully reconciled to the principles of the policy. By 1939 Wilberforce-Bell was a product of the change and it was equally unrealistic now to assume that he had the ability or indeed the desire to change his spots. Unfortunately for the British and also for the princes, the damage done to the concept of empire by the second world war would not allow them the luxury of another change of generation.

By 1939 the princes had conspicuously failed in their role as imperial allies. Their refusal to embrace federation meant that the British had been denied the means of transplanting a conservative element into the Indian constitution which would support the maintenance of British rule in India. Future constitutional negotiations were soon to proceed upon the basis of a British withdrawal from India. Moreover, it was apparent that the princes were not only reluctant to give the support that the British required of them, but also actually incapable of so doing. In their review of the position of the states in 1918, the authors of the Joint Report on Constitutional Reforms had been of the opinion that democratic and nationalistic 'hopes and aspirations may overleap frontier lines like sparks across a street'. By the late 1930s the sparks had begun to fly and the princes were woefully unprepared to resist the challenge which appeared in the form of Congress agitation. Many were hard pressed to maintain internal security and some were in positive danger of losing the support of their subjects. This state of affairs was attributable to the non-interference policy which had stimulated a totally negative mentality in both princes and political officers. It enabled the princes to live a sheltered existence cut off from the mainstream of developments in British Indian politics. It also gave them a false sense of security as it encouraged their continued belief in what in fact was the fallacious theory that the paramount power was duty bound to preserve their precarious existence whatever the circumstances.   Similarly, as Linlithgow's comparison of Maxwell with Glancy and Latimer, and Glancy's own comment about Wilberforce-Bell indicate, the inability of most political officers to deal with novel situations, caused by the repercussions of British Indian politics within the states, was due to the fact that the non-interference policy had either allowed or obliged them to lead an equally sheltered existence.[113]   In an administrative sense, the shortcomings of the princes and the decline in the calibre of political officers, were also directly attributable to the policy of non-interference.   Having been released from constant checks and supervision, many princes allowed administrative standards in their states either to deteriorate or to stagnate. For their part, political officers, having been given specific instructions that they were to interfere in the domestic affairs of the states only in exceptional circumstances, received no relevant administrative training whatsoever. By confessing in 1939 that the British were being forced to pay for the thirty years of *laissez-faire* which had elapsed since the end of Lord Curzon's viceroyalty, Linlithgow was under no illusions as to where the responsibility lay for the difficulties he was encountering in his dealings with the states. In this respect it is appropriate, and indeed ironic, to recall the remark which had been made by his illustrious predecessor to the Queen-Empress at the turn of the century:

There is not a day in my life in which I do not say to myself, 'What is going to happen in this country 20 years, or 50 years hence?' And I say with the proudest conviction that any Viceroy, or any Government that adopted the attitude of letting all these Princes and Chiefs run to their own ruin, would be heaping up immeasurable disaster in the future.[114]

NOTES TO CHAPTER VI

1 Viscount Templewood, *Nine Troubled Years*, London, 1954, p.48.

2 ibid., p.103.

3 Earl of Halifax, *Fulness of Days*, London, 1957, p.125.

4 Halifax to Templewood, 13 July 1953, Templewood Collection, No. 76.

5 The views of Templewood and Halifax have by no means been accepted by historians. Professor R.J. Moore has disputed their belief that the federal scheme could have operated successfully. He is of the opinion that it was unworkable because the constitution of 1935 not only failed to satisfy the minimum demands of the political representatives of the two major communities in British India but even tended to exacerbate the differences between them. R.J. Moore, *The Crisis of Indian Unity, 1917-1940*, Oxford, 1974. In one of his contributions to the partition seminar papers, Moore also expressed reservations about the view that the Government of India was responsible for delaying negotiations with the princes. Of Lord Zetland, Secretary of State for India between 1935 and 1940, he wrote: 'towards the princes his leisureliness of approach was studied'. R.J. Moore, 'British Policy and the Indian Problem, 1936-1940', in C.H. Philips and M.D. Wainwright (eds.), *The Partition of India : Policies and Perspectives 1935-1947*, London, 1970, p.81. Professor C.H. Philips agreed with this view when he wrote in respect of federation that Linlithgow was 'rather more enterprising than his opposite number, Zetland, in the India Office'. ibid., p.17. Nevertheless Philips and Moore have expressed general reservations about Linlithgow as a Viceroy. On the whole Philips considered him to have been too 'cautious' and as such he could 'never have provided an adequate answer to the political question of the Indian States'. For Moore, Linlithgow would have been 'admirable at operating a federal constitution but he did not possess the imagination required to bring it to life'. ibid., pp. 17 and 82.

6 Sir Francis Wylie, 'Federal Negotiations in India, 1935-39, and After', ibid., p.520.

7 Lothian to Patrick, 9 September 1935, PIC, 1931-50, Coll. 11, File 45(6), No. PY1711/1935.

8 Carter's note, 30 September 1935, ibid.

9 Rumbold to Lothian, 18 October 1935, ibid.

10 Lothian to Patrick, 2 December 1935, No. PY2081/1935, ibid.

11 Patrick to Lothian, 10 January 1936, ibid.

12 Patrick to Lothian, 12 September 1935, Lothian Collection, No. 3.

13 Zetland to Willingdon, 18 January 1936, Zetland Collection, No. 6.

14 Halifax to Lothian, 4 October 1957, Lothian Collection, No. 12.

15 Lothian's 'Note on the Foreign and Political Department of the

Government of India', 1962, Lothian Collection, No. 15. Although the evidence produced is second-hand, the most recent account of Linlithgow's viceroyalty confirms this view; see Gowher Rizvi, *Linlithgow and India: A Study of British Policy and the Political Impasse in India, 1936-1943*, London, 1978, p.87. In his third chapter on the Indian States (pp. 55-88), Rizvi absolves Linlithgow of the blame for the failure over federation, but misses the important point that the procedure for negotiating with the princes had been decided before the Viceroy took office.

[16]   Linlithgow to Zetland, 29 June 1936, Linlithgow Collection, No. 3.

[17]   Linlithgow to Zetland, 4 July 1936, ibid.

[18]   Patrick to Lothian, 1 July 1936, Lothian Collection, No. 3.

[19]   Linlithgow to Zetland, 1 June 1936, Linlithgow Collection, No. 3.

[20]   Sir Conrad Corfield, Political Adviser to the Crown Representative 1945-1947, 'Some thoughts on British Policy and the Indian States, 1935-47', Philips and Wainwright, op. cit., pp. 527-528. Corfield has reiterated this view in his recent book, *The Princely India I Knew : From Reading to Mountbatten*, Madras, 1974, pp. 91-94. In his seminar paper, 'Federal Negotiations in India, 1935-39, and After', Wylie sought in general terms to refute the argument that Linlithgow had delayed the federal negotiations. However, he too was critical of the fact that the emissaries were not instructed to try to persuade the princes to join the federation. Philips and Wainwright, op. cit., p.520.

[21]   Linlithgow to Zetland, 22 June 1936, Linlithgow Collection, No. 3.

[22]   Zetland to Linlithgow, 25 September 1936, ibid.

[23]   Linlithgow to Zetland, 11 October 1936, ibid.

[24]   ibid.

[25]   Wylie to Glancy, 27 November 1936, enclosed with Linlithgow to Zetland, 4 December 1936, ibid.

[26]   Wylie to Glancy, 4 January 1937, enclosed with Linlithgow to Zetland, 17 January 1936, Linlithgow Collection, No. 4.

[27]   Wylie to Glancy, 9 January 1937, ibid.

[28]   Wylie to Glancy, 27 November 1936, enclosed with Linlithgow to Zetland, 28 January 1937, Linlithgow Collection, No. 3.

[29]   Lothian to Glancy, 26 November 1936, enclosed with Linlithgow to Zetland, 4 December 1936, ibid.

[30]   Zetland to Linlithgow, 15 March 1937, Linlithgow Collection, No. 4.

[31]   Memorandum showing Hyderabad's Requirements for Accession to Federation, 1937, PIC, 1931-50, Coll. 11, File 57(3), No. PY1906/1937.

[32]   Lothian to Glancy, 21 November 1936, No. PY 2095/1936, ibid.

[33]   Linlithgow to Zetland, 19 August 1937, Linlithgow Collection, No. 4.

[34]   Cabinet Memorandum: 'The Negotiations with the Indian States as to the Terms of their Accession', 21 July 1938, PIF, 1931-50,

[35] File 1135/1938, No. PY1135/1938.

[35] ibid.

[36] Linlithgow to Zetland, 19 August 1937, Linlithgow Collection, No. 4.

[37] ibid.

[38] Zetland to Linlithgow, 6 October 1937, ibid.

[39] Zetland to Linlithgow, telg., 1 November 1937, Linlithgow Collection, No. 26.

[40] Linlithgow to Zetland, 11 November 1937, Linlithgow Collection, No. 4.

[41] Cabinet Memorandum: 'Negotiations with the Indian States as to the Terms of their Accession', 21 July 1938.

[42] Zetland to Linlithgow, 12 June 1938, Linlithgow Collection, No. 5.

[43] Linlithgow to Zetland, telg., 9 February 1938, Linlithgow Collection, No. 26.

[44] Linlithgow to Zetland, 4 January 1937, Linlithgow Collection, No. 4.

[45] ibid.

[46] Linlithgow to Zetland, 25 January 1937, ibid.

[47] Zetland to Linlithgow, telg., 21 February 1938, Linlithgow Collection, No. 26.

[48] Linlithgow to Zetland, telg., 18 March 1938, ibid.

[49] Linlithgow to Zetland, telg., 3 March 1938, ibid.

[50] Cabinet Memorandum: 'Congress and the Indian States', 9 February 1938, Private Office Papers, L/PO/89.

[51] *Indian Annual Register, July-December 1935*, Vol. 2, p.224.

[52] ibid., p.279.

[53] B.R. Tomlinson, *The Indian National Congress and the Raj, 1929-1942 : The Penultimate Phase*, London, 1976, p.119.

[54] James Manor, *Political Change in an Indian State: Mysore 1917-1955*, New Delhi, 1977, p.105.

[55] Rajendra Prasad to Nehru, 24 December 1937, Rajendra Prasad Collection; by courtesy of Dr. B.N. Pandey.

[56] *Indian Annual Register, January-June 1938*, Vol. 1, pp. 299-300.

[57] Cabinet Memorandum: 'Congress and the Indian States', 9 February 1938.

[58] For further details on Congress policy towards the states during this period, see Tomlinson, op. cit., pp. 118-122, and Manor, op. cit., pp. 105-111. For an analysis of the civil disobedience campaign in Rajkot, see John R. Wood, 'Rajkot: Indian Nationalism in the Princely Context: the Rajkot Satyagraha of 1938-9', in Robin Jeffrey (ed.), *People, Princes and Paramount Power: Society and Politics in the Indian Princely States*, New Delhi, 1978, pp. 240-274.

[59] Informal discussions with D.A. Surve, 21 and 22 October 1938, PIC, 1931-50, Coll. 11, File 45/10(5), No. PY1590/1938.

[60] Informal discussions with Sir Mirza Ismail, 20 September 1938, No. PY1410/1938, ibid. It had been agreed that Mysore would abandon its salt and customs immunities in return for the remission of its tribute.

[61]   Informal discussions with Sir Akbar Hydari and Mirza Ali Yar Jang, 12 and 13 September 1938, PIC, 1931-50, Coll. 11, File 57(3), No. PY1371/1938.

[62]   ibid.

[63]   In the provincial elections of 1937 the Congress secured a clear majority in six out of the eleven British Indian provinces. The governors of five of these provinces were convinced that if they used their special powers to protect the states, the Congress ministries would resign. Haig (United Provinces) to Linlithgow, 21 October 1938, Linlithgow Collection, No. 101;   Lumley (Bombay) to Linlithgow, 16 February 1938, No. 51;   Erskine (Madras) to Linlithgow, 15 November 1938, No. 66;   Wylie (Central Provinces and Berar) to Brabourne, acting Viceroy, 11 October 1938, No. 59;   Boag (Orissa) to Brabourne, 19 October 1938, No. 80.

[64]   Cabinet Memorandum: 'The Indian Federation - Negotiations with the Indian States as to the terms of their Accession', 27 July 1939, Zetland Collection, No. 25B.

[65]   ibid.

[66]   Sir Findlater Stewart's minute for the S/S, 10 March 1939, PIC, 1931-50, Coll. 11, File 57(3), No. PY311/1939.

[67]   Zetland to Linlithgow, 17 July 1939, Linlithgow Collection, No. 8.

[68]   The maritime states had not been asked to accede for entry no. 44 (customs duties) in the Federal Legislative List. Linlithgow was therefore proposing that they should be allowed to accede for this entry upon the basis of the 1936 Agreements and thus gain the right of appeal to the Federal Court for the retention of their customs receipts. Viceroy to S/S, telg., 18 July 1939, PIC, 1931-50, Coll. 11, File 45/10(8), No. PY1871/1939.

[69]   S/S to Viceroy, telg., 22 July 1939, ibid.

[70]   Linlithgow to Zetland, 18 September 1939, Linlithgow Collection, No. 8.

[71]   For the full text of the resolution, see C.H. Philips, (ed.), *The Evolution of India and Pakistan, 1858-1947 : Select Documents*, London 1962, pp. 354-355.

[72]   'Desire of Hyderabad for an outlet to the sea', GOI, Political Branch, No. 241 - Political (Secret), 1945, Nos. 1-15.

[73]   Linlithgow to Zetland, 7 September 1939, Linlithgow Collection, No. 8.

[74]   ibid.

[75]   Linlithgow to Zetland, 22 June 1936, Linlithgow Collection, No. 3.

[76]   Memorandum by the Chief of Sangli, 1938, enclosed with Zetland to Brabourne, 15 September 1938, Linlithgow Collection, No. 6.

[77]   Political Department note, 'Recent Constitutional Developments in Indian States', July 1940, PIC, 1931-50, Coll. 13, File 105, No. PY1351/1940.

[78]   Linlithgow to Zetland, 13 December 1938, Linlithgow Collection, No. 6.

[79]   ibid.

[80] Note of an interview with the Maharaja of Bhavnagar, 24 March 1939, enclosed with Linlithgow to Zetland, 28 March 1939, Linlithgow Collection, No. 7.

[81] ibid.

[82] Linlithgow to Zetland, 5 April 1939, Linlithgow Collection, No. 13.

[83] Linlithgow to Zetland, 21 February 1939, Linlithgow Collection, No. 7.

[84] Zetland to Linlithgow, 5 March 1939, ibid.

[85] Under the terms of the Government of India Act of 1935, the relations of the princes were still with the Crown, not with the central government, and this position would continue until the federation came into being and the princes joined it. In order to make this clear the Viceroy was, in 1937, given a new title, that of Crown Representative. To assist the Crown Representative in his relations with the states a new post of Political Adviser was created. The Political Adviser became the head of the Political Department, above the Political Secretary, and was given the status of a member of the Governor-General's Council. In this capacity he attended Council meetings to help the Crown Representative watch over the interests of the states.

[86] Linlithgow to Zetland, 5 April 1939, Linlithgow Collection, No. 13.

[87] In this respect the ruler of Aundh was subsequently informed that the government interpreted his constitution as leaving him free to discharge his obligations towards the paramount power. Political Department note, 'Recent Constitutional Developments in Indian States', July 1940, op. cit.

[88] Zetland to Linlithgow, 3 May 1939, Linlithgow Collection, No. 13, and Glancy's memorandum, 'The attitude of the Paramount Power to Constitutional Reforms in the States', enclosed with Linlithgow to Zetland, 12 April 1939, ibid.

[89] Zetland to Linlithgow, 3 May 1939, ibid.

[90] ibid.

[91] Linlithgow to Zetland, 5 April 1939, ibid.

[92] ibid. In 1929 the Indian States Committee reported that there were some 327 estates and *jagirs*, covering an area of 6,406 square miles with a population of 801,674. *Report of the Indian States Committee, 1928-1929*, Cmd. 3302, 1929, para. 11. Most of them were located in Kathiawar in Western India, and as such they were a legacy of the political settlement which the British had imposed at the beginning of the nineteenth century in order to defend the region against Maratha invasions. In July 1939 the situation in Kathiawar was described by the *Tribune* in the following terms: 'As many as 46 States in this Agency have an area of two, or less than two square miles. Eight of them, namely Bodanoness, Gandhol, Morchopra, Panchabda, Samidhiala, Chabbadia, Sanala, Satanoness and Vangadhra are just over half a mile each in area. Yet none of these is the smallest State in Kathiawar! That distinction goes to Vejanoness which has an area of 0.29 square mile, a population of 206 souls and an income

of Rs. 500/- a year ... This is not all. Even these tiny principalities do not seem to be indivisible units. Some of them are claimed by more than one "sovereign" officially described as a shareholder. Thus Dahida, with an area of two square miles, has six shareholders and Godhula and Khijadia Dosaji, being one square mile in extent, have two shareholders each; while Sanala, 0.51 in area, is put up against two shareholders. Such instances can be easily multiplied up to thirty to forty.' Cited in V.P. Menon, *Towards the Integration of the Indian States*, Calcutta, 1956, p.177.

[93] Linlithgow to Zetland, 5 April 1939, Linlithgow Collection, No. 13.

[94] Linlithgow to Zetland, 7 February 1939, Linlithgow Collection, No. 7.

[95] Linlithgow to Zetland, 28 February 1939, ibid.

[96] Zetland to Linlithgow, 27 December 1938, Linlithgow Collection, No. 6.

[97] Linlithgow to Zetland, 28 July 1939, Linlithgow Collection, No. 13.

[98] ibid.

[99] Haig to Brabourne, 3 October 1938, Linlithgow Collection, No. 100.

[100] Haig to Linlithgow, 23 April 1938, ibid.

[101] ibid. For an assessment of the problem of European recruitment to the Indian Civil Service, see David C. Potter, 'Manpower Shortage and the End of Colonialism: The Case of the Indian Civil Service', *Modern Asian Studies*, 7 (February 1973), pp. 47-73. For a detailed analysis of the defects of the Political Service in terms of its recruitment, training and political outlook, see Ian Copland, 'The Other Guardians: Ideology and Performance in the Indian Political Service', in Robin Jeffrey (ed.), *People, Princes and Paramount Power*, op. cit., pp. 275-305.

[102] 'A Report on the future of the Smaller States and Estates of Gujarat and Kathiawar', by J.H.S. Shattock, 1 November 1940, PIC, 1931-50, Coll. 11, File 94B, No. POL 1288/1942. In April 1943, a few months before his departure from India, Linlithgow announced an attachment scheme to implement Shattock's proposals. The *thakurs* of the areas concerned refused to comply. They argued that their states were sovereign and that the British government had no right to transfer them. When they appealed, their case was upheld by both the Judicial Commissioner in Kathiawar and the High Court on the grounds that the implementation of the scheme was *ultra vires* in respect of the powers of the Crown Representative. The Government of India therefore had to obtain parliamentary sanction for the scheme which eventually came into force as a result of an Attachment Act in 1944. The Standing Committee of the Chamber of Princes was strongly critical of this action. As a result of princely opposition, the government had to abandon any further attachment schemes and concentrate its efforts on

establishing joint administrative services for groups of smaller states. For a discussion of the attachment scheme, see Urmila Phadnis, *Towards the Integration of the Indian States, 1919-1947*, London, 1968, pp. 140-144.

[103] For details of these schemes, see circular letter from the Political Secretary, Sir Kenneth Fitze, to Residents, 20 May 1943, PIC, 1931-50, Coll. 11, File 7, part 4, No. POL.1053/1943, Annex 10(2).

[104] Creation of a Joint Police Force for the Deccan States, GOI, FPD, No. 14(24) - I.A. (Secret), 1940, Nos. 1-7.

[105] Pataudi, Loharu and Dujana joint administrative scheme, PIC, 1931-50, Coll. 13, File 94, No. PY732/1940.

[106] Maharawal of Dungarpur to Lothian, 5 February 1941, Lothian Collection, No. 1. The rulers of Dungarpur claimed descent from the Sisodia clan of Udaipur at the end of the twelfth century.

[107] ibid.

[108] The future of the Indian States in relation to Constitutional Developments, Memorandum sent to the Viceroy under cover of the Secretary of State's letter dated 16 May 1941, PIC, 1931-50, Coll. 11, File 7, part 4, No. POL.1053/1943, Annexure VIII.

[109] Lothian to Glancy, 1 December 1939, GOI, FPD, Political Branch, No. 40(17) - Political (Secret), part 2.

[110] Fitze to Glancy, 19 January 1939, PIC, 1931-50, Coll. 13, File 94, No. PY406/1939.

[111] Wilberforce-Bell to Glancy, 18 February 1939, No. PY636/1939, ibid.

[112] Glancy's note, 8 March 1939, ibid.

[113] From the evidence available in autobiographies and memoirs it is clear that certain individuals deliberately chose careers in the political service as a means to escape the hostility and rancour they sometimes encountered in the provinces of British India. Sir Conrad Corfield who joined the political service in 1925 from the Punjab, has recently explained why he was initiallly attracted to the states. His first encounter with princely India occurred when the Lieutentant-Governor of the Punjab invited the Punjab princes to a farewell Durbar on the eve of the transfer of relations with their states to the Political Department of the Government of India. Corfield recalls the occasion thus: 'I was the only junior officer available on the spot and was put in charge of the arrangements. This gave me a chance to see the only Indians who at that time had real power. I was struck by their individuality. Dressed for the Durbar they represented the ancient history and culture of India. Their independent attitude was a pleasant contrast to the subservience of many who served the Raj. Was I right in thinking that the real India existed in their territories rather than in the Provinces of British India? My instinct said that I was.' Sir Conrad Corfield, *The Princely India I Knew : From Reading to Mountbatten*, Madras, 1975, pp. 15-16. Corfield also recalls another occasion when, as private secretary to Lord Reading, he witnessed the proceedings of the Chamber of Princes: 'It seemed to me that

the proceedings compared favourably with those of the British Indian Legislative Assembly. The atmosphere was perhaps more like that of the House of Lords than the House of Commons, but the speeches were often of a higher standard and certainly more dignified. I was further attracted to this one-third element of India which they ruled.' ibid., p.26. Sir Edward Wakefield also joined the political service from the Punjab. In a career which spanned seventeen years from 1930 he served in Western India, Baluchistan, Ajmer in Rajputana, the Punjab, and Rewa in Central India. The last twenty months of his career were spent at Delhi as an assistant in the Political Department. He too has recalled the reasons which led him to apply for a transfer from the Punjab: 'The Punjab was certainly a magnificent Province. But members of the services in British India were the target of incessant vilification, abuse and insult by nationalist politicians. The prospect of being endlessly humiliated was not alluring. The Foreign and Political Department, on the other hand, opened up a pleasing vista of possibilities and uncertainties. I might be sent to an Indian State anywhere from Travancore to Kashmir. I might be sent to Persia or Afghanistan, to Nepal or Sikkim or even Aden; or I might be given an administrative post in the North-West Frontier Province, Baluchistan or Ajmer-Merwara. In any case, I reflected, I would be out of range of irresponsible criticism from a hostile Legislative Assembly'. Sir Edward Wakefield, *Past Imperative : My Life in India 1927-1947*, London, 1966, p.81.

[114] Curzon to Hamilton, 29 August 1900, Curzon Collection, No. 159.

CHAPTER VII

CONCLUSION AND EPILOGUE

The Legacy of Non-Interference

It would not be possible to attribute the disappearance of the Indian States system after the transfer of power in 1947 to the policy pursued by the British towards the states between 1905 and 1939. Irrespective of British policy this had become an inevitable development. Recent research on individual states, particularly that of James Manor on Mysore, has demonstrated that even the introduction of progressive reform was not sufficient to warrant the retention of political power by the princes in an independent India. Mysore had long since enjoyed a reputation as being one of the best-administered states yet its princely government had still been one of the first to be challenged by a state congress in the thirties and was also one of the first to capitulate to the demands for democratization in the aftermath of the British withdrawal.[1] Moreover, with the consummation of Indian independence it was inconceivable, unless the country was to become balkanised into five or six separate regions, that the autocratic tradition of the states could co-exist with the democratic structure of the new dominion. That the politicians of the dominion would not countenance such fragmentation had been made perfectly clear by Jawaharlal Nehru just a few months before the transfer of power when he warned the princes that any state refusing to participate in a constituent assembly which had been summoned to devise a new constitution would be regarded as 'hostile' and would have to 'bear the consequences of being so regarded'.[2] Being dependent for their very existence upon the protection of the paramount power, the vast majority of states could not resist such a challenge. They were so small and their financial resources so limited that they could not possibly survive on their own once this protection had been withdrawn. Armed resistance by the great states was, as Hyderabad found to its cost in 1948, a futile gesture. However, if British policy between 1905 and 1939 was not responsible for the ultimate downfall of the princes it was certainly responsible for the abrogation of the unwritten alliance which the British had entered into with the princes at the beginning of the twentieth century in order to defend their position in India. In effect the British had invalidated their own justifications for maintaining the states and thus had no alternative in 1947 but to leave the princes to fend for themselves and eventually to submit to the insistent demands of the new Indian government.

The introduction of a policy of non-interference during the viceroyalty of Lord Minto was a landmark in the development of Britain's relationship with the Indian States. The principles underlying this policy stood in marked contrast to the principles underlying the policies pursued during the nineteenth century.

Although the British had never contemplated adopting the Mughal strategy whereby the princes could become equal partners in the administration of the empire, they had nevertheless been aware, in the period both before and after the mutiny, that the Indian States system they had created contained an essential flaw. Many of the states were British creations but those that existed before the British arrived in India were ruled by princes who derived their position and power from their ability to protect their charges and cater for the needs of their subjects. However, by guaranteeing them protection against either internal revolt or external attack in return for the surrender of their right to conduct external relations with foreign powers or each other, the British had made it possible for the princes to neglect their responsibilities towards their states. Many in fact lapsed into a life of frivolity and luxury content in the knowledge that the British were duty bound to safeguard them against the consequences of their follies. The attempts made in the first half of the nineteenth century to eliminate this flaw within the system threatened the existence of the system itself. The mutiny revealed that annexation was not the answer to the problem. Moreover, the mutiny demonstrated that the princes might, after all, be able to serve some useful purposes. They had potential as political allies and their military support could prove invaluable in times of crisis. At a time when the British realized that it was dangerous to interfere with indigenous religious and social practices, the princes could also assist in the administration of the country because their legitimacy enabled them to retain the loyalty of their subjects in a way that the British as aliens could not. Hence Canning's adoption *sanads* which guaranteed the princely dynasties. There were thus two aspects to the Indian States system: the system itself was far from perfect but there were advantages to be derived from it. In the years after the mutiny, however, the British could afford to view these advantages separately. Although they belatedly utilized the military potential of the states, they retained their traditional distrust of the princely order. Furthermore they were never under any pressure to develop a political partnership with the princes. Thus the basic advantage of the system was that the states were an administrative convenience. In order to ensure that this advantage would not be rendered meaningless by the essential flaw within the system the British increasingly pursued an interventionist policy. Miscreant rulers were deposed and minority periods deliberately used to raise administrative standards in the states. The interventionist policy reached its height at the turn of the century when Curzon was Viceroy. Characteristically, however, Curzon went too far. His belief that the advantages of the system could not be maintained unless the princes were reduced to the level of a governing aristocracy did not meet with the approval of the government in London. In India, his dictatorial policies and methods caused a widespread and hostile reaction. Yet with his departure in 1905 the framework of a new policy was devised which was ultimately to exaggerate the flaw within the system at the complete expense of its advantages.

The authors of the non-interference policy were Lord Minto, Viceroy between 1905 and 1910, and Harcourt Butler, Foreign Secretary to the Government of India between 1908 and 1910. Both were convinced that during the first decade of the twentieth century British rule in India was under greater threat than at any time since the mutiny. Confronted with the rise of extreme nationalism following Curzon's partition of Bengal in 1905, Minto and Butler reached the conclusion that the princes were Britain's only dependable political allies in India. Their policy towards the states was based therefore upon the contention that the princes should be both capable and willing alliance partners. At the beginning of the reform discussions which led to the Indian Councils Act of 1909, Minto suggested that a Council of Princes might serve as a possible counterpoise to the Indian National Congress, the vehicle for the nationalist movement. John Morley, the Secretary of State, doubted the wisdom of the suggestion on the grounds that if the princes were allowed to combine and confer they might conceivably use the opportunity to unite against the government. However, although Minto failed to secure constitutional recognition for the princes, he was determined that his viceroyalty would not leave them empty-handed. In a speech at Udaipur in November 1909 he unveiled the principles of a new non-interference policy, the precise details of which had been formulated by Butler in the Political Department Manual. In sharp contrast to the policy of Curzon, political officers were now given specific instructions that they were not to interfere in the domestic affairs of the princes unless misrule reached a pitch which violated the 'elementary laws of civilization'. A relaxation of British control over the conduct of their internal affairs was the bait that Minto and Butler dangled before the princes in order to persuade them to become willing alliance partners. Butler's faith in the durability of the Indian aristocracy led him to assume that the princes would also be capable alliance partners if they were in receipt of the necessary British support.

Minto and his Foreign Secretary were aware that the new policy could not become immediately applicable. They realized that the then generation of political officers could never reconcile themselves to these new guidelines and that the political service itself would only become amenable when it was staffed by a new generation of officers who had no ties with the old interventionist practices. However, a development of immediate significance was the emergence of princes who were ready to take advantage of the new spirit which was slowly being introduced within the government hierarchy. Although never representative of the princely order as a whole, these princes were educated men who were acutely aware of the arbitrary manner in which they had been treated while the British pursued interventionist policies. Although they welcomed the announcement of a change in policy they were disappointed that the government had not seen fit to grant them constitutional recognition by agreeing to the establishment of a Council of Princes. During the viceroyalties of Lord Hardinge and Lord Chelmsford, their leading spokesman, Ganga Singh of Bikaner, constantly reminded the

Government of India that the princes would become effective allies only if they were allowed to meet to discuss important political issues and also matters of common concern to themselves. The First World War and the support of Edwin Montagu when Secretary of State between 1917 and 1922 eventually enabled the princes to achieve constitutional recognition. The contribution that the princes made to the war effort seemed to confirm their alliance value. Montagu was anxious to consolidate this position. Resenting the bureaucratic obdurance which he encountered within the political cadres of the Government of India, the Secretary of State was prepared to embark upon a policy of wholesale concessions to a select group of princes of medium-sized states. As a result of such preferential treatment these princes began to assume that they could claim to represent the princely order as a whole. The establishment of a Chamber of Princes in February 1921 was, however, more than simply a triumph for princes such as Bikaner, Alwar, Patiala and the Jam Sahib of Nawanagar. It marked the end of an old isolationist tradition which for a century had precluded contact between the princes. It also coincided with the first determined effort to translate the principles of a non-interference policy into practice. In 1921 the princes were firmly acknowledged as imperial allies. Between 1921 and 1939 their willingness and capacity to act as such were put to the test.

The conflict over paramountcy which was such a major feature of princely politics between 1921 and 1939 soon raised doubts about the willingness of the princes to serve as allies. In that the government was pursuing a policy of non-interference it appears at first sight somewhat illogical that there should have been a conflict of this nature. For the princes who dominated the Chamber, however, the paramountcy issue was central to their relationship with both the British Government and the growing democratic movement in British India. Seeking complete independence in the conduct of their domestic affairs these princes could never be satisfied while paramountcy remained vague and undefined and the paramount power retained a discretionary element of interference. Moreover, they needed a strict interpretation of paramountcy to safeguard themselves against the possibility of paramountcy rights being transferred to a successor government in British India. These princes were dismayed in 1926 by Reading's definition of paramountcy in his letter to the Nizam and positively shocked in 1929 when the Indian States Committee recommended a further dimension to the discretionary element of paramountcy by suggesting that the princes could be required to implement changes in their systems of government should popular disturbances within their states be prompted by demands for such. They sought refuge in the proposal for an All-India Federation which emerged from Hyderabad in 1930. They would only contemplate accession to a federation if paramountcy was defined to their satisfaction, an attitude which initially placed the paramount power in a dilemma. The British could stem the tide of nationalist advance in British India only by conceding a degree of responsibility within the Government of India but the political situation in Britain itself dictated that central reform could not be contemplated unless by federation with a strong princely content. However, the British were fully aware that if they surrendered over paramountcy they would be placing the princes in a position of complete internal independence. Moreover, if the princes were internally independent they would have no need to federate as they would also have secured for themselves an unassailable position in regard to their relationship with their neighbours in British India. Although in 1932 the Government of India managed to defeat the views on paramountcy as represented by the Chamber princes there were other difficulties with which it had to contend. The larger states, whose support was essential if federation was to become a reality, entered the negotiations in a similar bargaining frame of mind. Mysore required remission of its tribute, the maritime states demanded the retention in full of their customs receipts, while the Nizam of Hyderabad would not even contemplate federal officials operating within his state. In considering constitutional developments between 1921 and 1939 one can only conclude therefore that the princes were not willing but were wholly unreliable allies. However, the ultimate failure of the federal idea cannot be attributed entirely to princely intransigence. The attitude of the princes towards federation eventually turned on the crucial question of timing. They rejected federation in 1939 because the Congress campaign of the previous two years had convinced them that the scheme contained inadequate protection for their treaty rights. It is not inconceivable that sufficient numbers of them would have agreed to federate had they been asked to do so before the agitation, which began in Mysore in 1937, spread to other states. That they were not asked to federate earlier was due to the obstructionist tactics of the diehards in London, which delayed by two years the 1935 Government of India Act, and also to the influence of Sir Samuel Hoare's ideas which meant that in the period after 1935 the India Office constantly urged restraint upon those in India responsible for federal negotiations with the princes.

If the princes were never particularly willing alliance partners, their capacity to act as such was completely destroyed by the non-interference policy. The policy became effective during the decade which followed the Reform Act of 1919. For the sake of establishing direct relations with the Government of India many states were detached from the supervisory control of neighbouring provincial governments. Similarly, within the large agencies of Central India and Rajputana, some of the more important states were removed from the influence of local political agents and placed in a position whereby they communicated with the Government of India through the distant figure of an AGG. Subsequent retrenchment proposals requiring the abolition of many political posts resulted in the remaining states being amalgamated into vast subordinate charges under the control of a single political officer. These measures were officially justified on the grounds that the princes would more willingly serve as allies if the control that the paramount power exercised over them was relaxed. This was an erroneous assumption for it was the capacity, not the willingness, of the princes to serve as allies that was at stake. The princes could never be regarded as capable allies unless their authority was accepted by their own subjects. Yet in retrospect it can now be seen that the relaxation of control by the paramount power was followed by a rapid deterioration of administrative standards in the states which, together with the spread of democratic and nationalist ideas from British India, enabled the subjects of the states first to question and then openly to challenge the autocratic powers of their princes.

There had been frequent warnings about the possible consequences of a policy of non-interference. During the 1920s these warnings came principally from provincial governments protesting about the establishment of direct relations, and senior political officers complaining not only about the establishment of direct relations but also about the implications of amalgamation and retrenchment proposals. Admittedly these protests had been originally inspired by concern for the prestige and status of provincial governments and political officers, but nevertheless the arguments actually used by Lloyd in Bombay, Holland in Rajputana and Blakeway in Central India were irrefutable. As Lloyd had indicated, the establishment of direct relations with states which had previously been supervised by provincial governments militated against the administrative standards in the states concerned keeping pace with the progress in neighbouring provinces. In the large agencies of Central India and Rajputana the situation was more serious because here the establishment of direct relations and the amalgamation of subordinate charges meant that those political officers who survived the retrenchment measures were hard-pressed to perform even the perfunctory tasks required of them by the dictates of the non-interference policy.

The adoption of a policy of non-interference did not, of course, completely rule out the possibility of intervention within a state by the paramount power. The cases of Hyderabad, Udaipur and Alwar all bear testimony to this. However, as far as the intervention in Hyderabad was concerned, it soon became obvious that no successful reforms could be introduced while the Nizam remained in power. Fearful of the consequences if they deposed the premier Muslim prince of India, the British reconciled themselves to the abuses that existed in Hyderabad in the vain hope that natural causes would remove the Nizam for them. Nor do the interventions in Udaipur and Alwar reflect any credit upon British policy. In both states misgovernment had not only existed but had also been identified long before the paramount power decided to intervene. Moreover, the cases of Udaipur and Alwar revealed that the theoretical reference to intervention which appeared in the Political Department Manual was in practice a situation in which the subjects of the states were on the verge of open rebellion. Successive Viceroys were aware of this. In 1927 Lord Irwin summoned a conference of political officers after reading a note by a junior officer entitled 'British India is advancing along the lines of Evolution: The Indian States are on the road to Revolution'. Yet despite being impressed by the arguments outlined in the note and also by the opinions expressed at the conference, which in general were very critical of the non-interference policy, Irwin did nothing to stop the drift. The lack of compulsion behind his subsequent note on administration was indicative of a reluctance on the part of the British to commit themselves in favour of reform in the states for fear that they would lose princely support. Yet what British policy-makers never seemed to appreciate was that because of the policy of non-interference, princely support was not worth having.

The non-interference policy accentuated the basic flaw in the Indian States system. While it enabled the princes to become more despotic and irresponsible it also generated a stifling atmosphere of inertia within the Political Department. Above all it damaged beyond repair the British justifications for the very existence of the states. The Congress campaign of the late 1930s revealed that even in so-called progressive states like Mysore the much-vaunted notion of a benevolent Maharaja had been dealt a blow from which it would be difficult to recover. In fact the onset of Congress agitation proved conclusively that the princes could no longer be considered as capable or dependable allies for the British: on the contrary the non-interference policy had converted them into serious liabilities. If the Congress had no wish to embark upon a simultaneous war of attrition against the British in British India and the princes in the Indian States, the British for their part had no wish to embark upon a similar campaign against the Congress in both territories. Yet this was precisely the position in which the depleted administration of Lord Linlithgow found itself from 1937 until the outbreak of war in 1939. Lord Linlithgow was the only Viceroy between 1905 and 1939 who made a serious effort to repair the damage caused by the non-interference policy. By attempting in 1939 to effect a return to the interventionist policies of Curzon's day, Linlithgow had brought British policy towards the states full circle. Indeed in 1941 he even went so far as to authorize the communication of instructions to political officers concerning the preparation of Indian States administration reports which had been drawn up by the Curzon administration in 1904 and which had lain dormant in the Political Department archives since Curzon's resignation in the following year.[3] Yet, as Linlithgow himself appreciated, any attempt to turn back the clock in the hope of producing some tangible improvement could not possibly succeed. Princes and political officers alike were not only reluctant but also incapable of changing their ways.

In that there had been many warnings about the implications of a policy of non-interference perhaps the gravest indictment of British policy concerns an episode which occurred towards the end of the constitutional negotiations in London. In June 1933, Ronald Wingate was appointed Joint Political Secretary to the Government of India. In May of the following year he became Officiating Secretary. Having served in the foreign branch of the Foreign and Political Department Wingate had no previous experience of the states. He was appointed to relieve the Political Department Secretariat which at the time was permanently occupied examining details of the federal scheme. Nevertheless, Wingate was soon able to identify the essential flaw within the Indian States system. In August 1934 he produced a note in which he wrote: 'In the India of the future the conservatism and loyalty of the States is to be the makeweight against the democracy and disloyalty of British India. In fact the White Paper scheme is based by implication upon this assumption'.[4] Wingate described this statement as the 'theory of the balance of power in India'. The remainder of the note was devoted to a penetrating analysis of how the non-interference policy was destroying this balance of power. Writing in the aftermath of the tribal uprising and notorious revelations in Alwar and government intervention to supress an uprising by the Muslim subjects of the Hindu Maharaja of Kashmir, Wingate was of the opinion that the Government of India 'must now face the fact that their policy of the last 30 years has failed'. To reverse the trend he urged the restoration of interventionist policies: 'Advice must in future be given if it is not sought and it must be accepted, and if it is not we must compel acceptance.' In conclusion Wingate suggested that the Viceroy, Lord Willingdon, should immediately make a public pronouncement to this effect and that new instructions should be issued to political officers 'enlarging the scope of their responsibilities'.[5]   In London, Wingate's note met with varying responses. Patrick considered the problem to be one of political officers maintaining secrecy in communication when forwarding reports of maladministration to higher authority. Information sent through 'ordinary office channels' too often proved to be a 'timely indirect warning to the Ruler to prepare his defence'.[6] Sir Reginald Glancy considered that Wingate's note conveyed the impression that 'things are worse than they actually are'. He also reiterated the point which had been made at the conference of political officers in 1927 that the Commission of Enquiry procedure which had been established in 1920 made it extremely difficult to take action against princes considered guilty of either misconduct or maladministration. Nevertheless Glancy did admit that political officers were seldom experts in either financial or revenue administration. In view of the fact that the 'majority of cases where intervention has been too long delayed are cases of extravagance or financial folly leading to bankruptcy', he recommended that this defect in the training of political officers should be remedied without delay.[7]

At this juncture Bertrand Glancy, the Political Secretary in Delhi, intervened. Had he seen Wingate's note before it was sent to London, he would certainly have censored it. He was now faced with the awkward task of explaining the contents of the note. This he did by referring to the state of Wingate's health. In December 1934 he wrote to Patrick that Wingate had been 'suffering from strain lately due to overwork' and thus his views were not to be taken seriously.[8] He even reported that Wingate had changed his mind about the note just eleven days after it had been sent to London.[9]   There was obvious friction between Glancy and his deputy. As Wingate was due to take some leave as soon as his services could be spared, Patrick suggested that the work he had done within the Political Department should receive a commendation from the Secretary of State. This acknowledgement was never sent because in the words of J.P. Gibson, a Principal in the Political Department of the India Office, 'this will only make matters worse with Mr. Glancy'.[10]   Needless to say no action was taken upon the basis of Wingate's note. Admittedly it would not have been an auspicious moment to act upon his advice. The government was in the process of attempting to persuade the princes to accept the federal scheme embodied in the White Paper in the hope that their status as imperial allies could be further consolidated. Yet as Wingate had been at pains to point out, the alliance value of the princes had been virtually destroyed by the policy of non-interference.   A further five years elapsed before Wingate's views were officially endorsed and the non-interference policy abandoned. By then, however, it was far too late. The alliance value of the princes no longer existed.

The End of the Princely States

The disaster of which Curzon had warned at the beginning of the twentieth century was, by 1939, a mere eight years away for the princes. Many of the principal actors on the princely stage did not live to see the final demise of the states. The original stalwarts of the Standing Committee of the Chamber of Princes had passed on in the ten years between 1933 and 1943. The death in 1933 of Ranjit Sinhji, the Jam Sahib of Nawanagar, has already been mentioned. Jey Singh of Alwar, deposed in 1933, died four years later. Bhupinder Singh of Patiala died in 1938, and Ganga Singh of Bikaner died in 1943. Of the princes that have been frequently mentioned in this study, only Hamidullah, the Nawab of Bhopal, and Mir Osman Ali Khan, the Nizam of Hyderabad, remained to witness the transfer of British power to the new dominions in India and Pakistan. During these final eight years, however, the essential anarchy of the princely order still persisted. To the very last they remained hopelessly divided amongst themselves and as such they possessed neither the moral nor political fibre to enable them to survive the withdrawal of British protection.

In the years leading up to 1947, the future of the states seemed to depend upon three possibilities. First, they could be merged with British India to become part of either one or two dominions, in which case their paramountcy relationship with the British Crown would cease. Secondly, they could remain apart from British India, either individually or collectively, and thus retain the protection of British paramountcy. Finally, they could become separate units with full sovereign status and thus become completely independent of the Crown and British India.

These possibilities were first discussed at length during the Cripps mission to India in the spring of 1942. Sir Stafford Cripps, then Lord Privy Seal, had been sent by the British Cabinet to propose that a constituent assembly should be elected at the end of the war with the task of framing a constitution for an Indian Union with dominion status. The proposal included provision for any province or group of provinces to secede from the Union should they so desire. As far as the states were concerned, arrangements would be made for them to participate in the constitutent assembly and, irrespective of whether or not they decided to join the Union, it would be necessary to negotiate a revision of treaty arrangements in order to meet the requirements of the new situation. In April 1942, in order to clarify these points, Cripps met a delegation consisting of the Chancellor of the Chamber of Princes, Digvijay Sinhji, Ranjit's successor as the Jam Sahib of Nawanagar; Sadul Singh, son and heir to Ganga Singh of Bikaner; Yadavindra Singh, Bhupinder's successor as the Maharaja of Patiala and the Nawab of Chhatari who represented the Nizam of Hyderabad. In discussion the Jam Sahib maintained that any state or group of states that decided not to accede to the Union should be accorded the right to form a union of their own with full sovereign powers. Cripps could not give an undertaking in this respect but promised that he would raise the subject on behalf of the princes upon his return to London. He did, however, make it clear that whereas the Crown would retain its obligations towards states which did not accede, for those that did paramountcy would be automatically dissolved. In subsequent correspondence, the Nawab of Chhatari sought to challenge the assertion that the Crown would retain its obligations towards non-acceding states. The Nizam's objective was evidently complete independence but Cripps replied to the effect that paramountcy would remain in force for those states that did not join the Union.[11]

The Cripps mission did not succeed because the proposals were rejected by the two major parties in British India. The Congress had objected, not only to the provincial option of secession, but also to the idea of the states being represented in the constituent assembly by princely nominees. However, the Cripps proposals had eliminated, at least for the time being, the third possibility of the states becoming separate units with full sovereign powers. Of the two that remained, Leo Amery, who had succeeded Zetland at the India Office in April 1940, expressed a clear preference for the second. As he explained to Linlithgow, he wanted to encourage the idea of a federation or dominion of states 'from the point of view of teaching Congress what it may have to face if it is not prepared to work for a constitution acceptable to Muslims and Princes, or is going to insist on separation from the Empire'.[12] Linlithgow, however, had serious doubts and informed Amery that a federation or dominion of states was not practical politics and that it was not worth considering.[13] The Viceroy's views in this respect were explained to the Nizam of Hyderabad when, in December 1942, he expressed a desire for his state to become a separate unit having no organic connection with an Indian Union but maintaining direct treaty relations with the British government. The Political Department informed the Nizam that his idea was not practicable because Hyderabad would be isolated in the midst of a fully self-governing dominion. Although British troops might remain in India to protect the states, on all matters of common concern with the dominion, the treaty relations between the states and the paramount power would have to be replaced by new agreements between the dominion and non-acceding states. In these circumstances, Hyderabad could hardly expect to receive favourable treatment.[14] This was an argument which was reminiscent of the one used by the government to recommend federation to the princes in the thirties. However, it had as little effect on the Nizam in 1942 as it had then. He resolved to pursue his ambition of complete independence.

Despite Amery's preference and the promise made by Cripps at the April meeting with the princes, the Political Department's correspondence with the Nizam served to invalidate the second possibility for the future of the states. Whatever the personal ambitions of the Nizam might have been, the British were left only with the first possibility of the states joining a successor dominion or dominions. However, they had persistently guaranteed that they would never transfer their paramountcy rights in relation to the states to a successor government in British India. They could not therefore force the princes into a merger; they could only advise them in this respect. And if they could only advise them, they also had to leave them with an alternative. Hence, however unrealistic it might seem, the British had to resurrect the third possibility of the states becoming completely independent.

This became clear when a three-man Cabinet Mission visited India in March 1946 in a yet further attempt to solve the constitutional impasse in British India. In May 1946 it was announced that paramountcy could neither be retained by the British Crown nor be transferred to a new government. The situation thus confronting the states was explained in a memorandum presented by the Cabinet Mission to the Nawab of Bhopal, who had become Chancellor of the Chamber of Princes at the end of 1944:

When a new fully self-governing or independent Government or Governments come into being in British India, His Majesty's Government's influence with these Governments will not be such as to enable them to carry out the obligations of paramountcy. Moreover, they cannot contemplate that British troops would be retained in India for this purpose. Thus, as a logical sequence and in view of the desires expressed to them on behalf of the Indian States, His Majesty's Government will cease to exercise the powers of paramountcy. This means that the rights of the States which flow from their relationship to the Crown will no longer exist and that all rights surrendered by the States to the paramount power will return to the States. Political arrangements between the States on the one side and the British Crown and British India on the other will thus be brought to an end. The void will have to be filled either by the States entering into a federal relationship with the successor Government or Governments in British India, or failing this, entering into particular political arrangements with it or them.[15]

The references to the return of rights previously surrendered and to particular political arrangements, theoretically opened up the prospect of independence for the states. As we shall see, the Political Department wanted to maintain an illusion of theoretical independence right up until the transfer of power to a successor government or governments in British India in order to leave the princes in a strong bargaining position. For the present the princes were urged to take the ninety-three seats they had been allocated in a constituent assembly which, although boycotted by the Muslim League, assembled for the first time in December 1946 to devise a new constitution. It was now, however, that the differences amongst the princes began to surface. For the Nizam, the prospect of independence was neither theoretical nor illusory. His government opened negotiations with the Portuguese for the use of Goa and requested the British for an easement to guarantee their rail-link across British territory to that port.[16] An open rift appeared in the Chamber of Princes. Encouraged by the Muslim League's boycott, the Nawab of Bhopal orchestrated a campaign to persuade the princes against taking their seats in the constituent assembly. Bhopal argued that the princes should first obtain definite guarantees that a new dominion would recognize successions in their states and refrain from interference in their internal affairs. He was opposed by Bikaner and Patiala. They criticized the Chancellor's 'wait and see' attitude and urged that it was in the interests of the princes to negotiate immediately within the constituent assembly. It was the defiance of princes like the Nizam and the procrastination of those like Bhopal that occasioned Nehru's outburst in mid-April 1947 that the new dominion would regard non-acceding states as hostile. At the end of the month the representatives of Baroda, Bikaner, Cochin, Jaipur, Jodhpur, Patiala and Rewa took their seats in the constituent assembly. As others began to follow suit Bhopal was left to resign as Chancellor of the Chamber.[17]

In March 1947 Lord Mountbatten became the last Viceroy of India charged initially with the task of relinquishing British power in India by a date not later than June 1948. On 3 June 1947 he issued a statement to the effect that power would be transferred to the new dominions of India and Pakistan at a much earlier date. The subsequent choice was 15 August 1947. Mountbatten had been briefed to negotiate with the states upon the basis of the memorandum presented by the Cabinet Mission to the Nawab of Bhopal. In this respect a serious difference of opinion arose between the new Viceroy and his Political Adviser, Sir Conrad Corfield. Fearing the fragmentation of India, Mountbatten wanted to ensure that the lapse of paramountcy coincided with the inauguration of a mutually agreed relationship between the states and the new dominion governments.[18] Corfield, however, wanted to leave the states in a position of theoretical independence and argued that Mountbatten's objective ran contrary to the spirit of the promises made in the Cabinet Mission memorandum. According to H.V. Hodson, a former Reforms Commissioner of the Government of India, Corfield and the Political Department believed that if the threat of independence had been sustained up to and beyond the transfer of power it would have 'given the rulers a great bargaining advantage in relation to Congress; for such independence was what its leaders most feared'.[19] Corfield himself has since revealed that he never believed in 'actual independence' for the states. Instead he thought that 'permanent arrangements negotiated at leisure would be more satisfactory and preserve more good will'.[20] In reality, as Hodson recalls, Corfield and the Political Department anticipated that a prolonged process of bargaining after the transfer of power would enable 'more of the values of indigenous personal rule in India' to be preserved.[21]

Corfield's difference of opinion with Mountbatten led to his resignation at the end of July 1947. With the Political Department devising its own liquidation, the fate of the princes became the responsibility of a new States Department which had been created in June 1947 with Sardar Patel as its head and V.P. Menon as its Secretary. Patel and Menon proceeded to devise a scheme whereby the princes would be asked to accede to India for three subjects only - defence, external affairs and communications. All other matters of common concern were to be covered by Standstill Agreements. Mountbatten endorsed the scheme and commended it to the princes when he addressed the final session of the Chamber on 25 July. When the day for the transfer of power arrived, apart from the few destined to accede to Pakistan, the rulers of all the states except Junagadh, two small states of Kathiawar, Kashmir and Hyderabad, had signed Instruments of Accession. Many did so with obvious reluctance. The Nawab of Bhopal first refused and then proposed to abdicate in favour of his daughter. He changed his mind when Mountbatten told him that this would be a 'cowardly act'. The Nawab's pride led him to stipulate that his accession should not be disclosed until ten days after the transfer of power. The Maharaja of Indore yielded only in the face of combined pressure from his fellow Maratha princes and the Viceroy. Similar difficulty was experienced with the Maharajas of Jodhpur and Travancore. In the case of Jodhpur, the Maharaja had been sorely tempted to accede to Pakistan. Jinnah had offered him the use of Karachi as a free port, free imports of arms and jurisdiction over the railway between Jodhpur and Hyderabad in Sind on condition that he would declare his independence on 15 August and subsequently accede to Pakistan. Menon had to counter this by conceding free imports of arms and jurisdiction over a railway to be built between Jodhpur and a port in Cutch in order to secure the Maharaja's accession to India.[22]

The problem of the non-acceding states was eventually solved by force. The Nizam's ambitions were finally crushed in September 1948 when units of the Indian army invaded Hyderabad. Similar action had been required in June of the preceding year to thwart the plans of the Muslim Nawab of Junagadh who had announced his intention to accede to Pakistan against the wishes of the majority of his subjects of whom approximately eighty per cent were Hindus. The bulk of the state of Kashmir has also been united with India *de facto*. In October 1947 Muslim tribesmen from Pakistan's North West Frontier Province invaded Kashmir. The Hindu Maharaja of this predominantly Muslim state appealed to the Indian government for armed support but had to agree to accede to India before this was forthcoming. It was not until January 1949, under the auspices of the United Nations, that a truce was established which left India in possession of three-fifths of Kashmir and Pakistan the rest. The Kashmir problem has remained a persistent source of conflict and tension between India and Pakistan.[23]

Elsewhere following the transfer of power, the States Department began the task of integrating the states. It was a process which extended over many years and which involved the surrender of much more than powers relating to defence, external affairs and communications. Some of the states were eventually merged with the neighbouring provinces such as Pudokkottai with Madras and Baroda with Bombay. Most of the princes suffered a fate not dissimilar to that of the German imperial princes at the hands of Napoleon when the latter abolished the defunct Holy Roman Empire and established the Confederation of the Rhine. While they retained their princely rank (it was not until the Princely Derecognition Act of 1971 that their formal existence was finally brought to an end), their authority was mediatized and their states merged to form larger unions over which one of their number presided with the largely honorific title of Rajpramukh. Thus the Maharaja of Jaipur became the Rajpramukh of the state of Rajasthan, the Maharaja of Patiala the Rajpramukh of the Patiala and East Punjab States Union and the Jam Sahib of Nawanagar the Rajpramukh of the Union of Kathiawar, more commonly known as Saurashtra. In some instances, most notably Hyderabad and Mysore, the princes were sworn in as Rajpramukhs of their former states. During the initial stages of the integration process generous privy-purse allowances were used to persuade the princes to accept the proposals. In most cases a ceiling of Rs. 10 *lakhs* was fixed although exceptions were made for the eleven most important princes.[24] However, with the introduction of a uniform system of democracy, enshrined in the republican constitution of 1950, the ruling powers of the princes were effectively liquidated. Indian India was now a single entity.

It was only to be expected that the new political situation would produce a variety of responses from the princes. Some readily adjusted in anticipation of new opportunities that would become available to them. In this respect a recent study of the princes has demonstrated how many forms of princely activity overlapped into the era of independence. Having served as Rajpramukhs, Digvijay Sinhji of Nawanagar and Yadavindra Singh of Patiala embarked upon careers within the diplomatic service. Both served at the United Nations and Yadavindra also served as ambassador to Italy and the Netherlands. These two princes were essentially following in the footsteps of their respective fathers, Ranjit and Bhupinder, both of whom had attended the League of Nations in the 1920s.[25] The princes were obviously well-suited to the ceremony and protocol of the world of diplomacy, a fact which could not have been lost on the new Indian government which was prepared to utilize the pedigrees of the princes in much the same way as the British had utilized their legitimacy. However, for many princes the mergers and unions, together with the loss of sovereign powers, were obviously a painful and bitter experience. Typical in this respect was the Maharawal of Dungarpur who had hoped that after the creation of Pakistan, the states might have been allowed to form an independent union of their own - a Statistan. Describing the mergers and unions in a letter to Sir Arthur Lothian in January 1948, the Maharawal wrote: 'It utterly fails me why a third and separate entity was not created after Pakistan ... Most of us - not me - never dreamt that this would be our fate after being made to sign our Instruments of Accession ... The whole picture seems to me so dismal that if the present Central government continues for another year most of the States could be dead.'[26] The passage of time did little to ease the Maharawal's feelings. In February 1950, it was not only with bitterness, but also with a deliberate touch of sarcasm, that he commented upon the teething problems involved in establishing the new state of Rajasthan: 'I often wonder why the Political Officers in the past repeatedly drew so much attention of the princes towards the efficiency of their administrations. You ought to see the efficiency of the Rajasthan administration; so wonderful it is that it can only be believed when seen.'[27]

If, some thirty years on, the views of the Maharawal of Dungarpur still evoke a sympathetic response from former British officials who remember the princes as rulers of their states, two points should perhaps be borne in mind. First, apart from the innumerable practical difficulties that would have been involved, the creation of a Statistan would have required of the princes a unity of purpose and resolve that had never previously existed. It is difficult to imagine how even the instinct of self-preservation could have overcome their mutual jealousies and rivalries. Indeed it should not be forgotten in this respect that the Maharawal of Dungarpur had persistently shunned any form of co-operation with his fellow rulers for the sake of establishing joint administrative services. Secondly, although the British claimed that they could not transfer paramountcy, they could not deny that the Indian government that succeeded them had also become the new paramount power. Equally, they could not deny that the lapse of their own paramountcy had not in any way invalidated the fundamentals upon which the doctrine of paramountcy rested. If the British had persistently refused to define their paramountcy rights in relation to the states, the same could reasonably be expected of the new Indian government. In reality the Instruments of Accession of 1947 were the equivalent of the treaties concluded by the British with the states at the beginning of the nineteenth century. Both had been devised as the starting point for an evolutionary relationship between the paramount power and the states. Of course, after 1947 the Indian government modified the Instruments much sooner than the British had modified the treaties. But the British themselves had always argued that the pace and extent of such modifications should be dictated by changing needs and circumstances. In the twentieth century they had lost sight of this principle. Their belated attempts at reform could not overcome the problems that had accumulated as a result of their commitment to a policy of maintaining what had become an increasingly anachronistic system. After 1947 therefore, and despite the initial dislocation, the Indian government could at least claim relevance for its policy of dismantling the system as quickly as possible.

NOTES TO CHAPTER VII

1. James Manor, *Political Change in an Indian State: Mysore 1917-1955*, New Delhi, 1977.

2. Jawaharlal Nehru's speech at the Gwalior session of the All India States' People's Conference, April 1947, cited in U. Phadnis, *Towards the Integration of the Indian States, 1919-1947*, London, 1968, p.172.

3. 'Preparation and publication of administration reports of Indian States', circular letter from the Secretary to the Crown Representative to Residents, 16 June 1941, PIC, 1931-50, Coll. 10, File 7, No. POL. 3286/1941. The Residents were referred to GOI, Foreign Department, circular letter No. 4064-4067 - I.A., 2 November 1904.

4. Wingate's note, 18 August 1934, PIC, 1931-50, Coll. 11, File 7, part 2, No. PY 1506/1934.

5. ibid.

6. Patrick's note, 27 October 1934, ibid.

7. Sir Reginald Glancy's note, 29 October 1934, ibid.

8. B.J. Glancy to Patrick, 3 December 1934, PIC, 1931-50, Coll. 11, File 7, part 3, No. PY 1745/1934.

9. ibid.

10. J.P. Gibson's note, 18 December 1934, ibid.

11. For details of the Cripps proposals that concerned the states, see V.P. Menon, *The Story of the Integration of the Indian States*, Calcutta, 1956, pp. 48-52. For a more recent scholarly study of the Cripps mission, see R.J. Moore, *Churchill, Cripps, and India, 1939-45*, Oxford, 1979. One interesting point to emerge from Professor Moore's work is a reference he makes to a special Cabinet meeting held in November 1939. Summarizing the proceedings he writes: 'Hoare, too, was anxious. He was prepared to abandon the old waiting game and favoured an early attempt to bring federation into being: the princes, especially the Nizam, might be pressed, and perhaps they would now cooperate with the Muslims.' (pp. 22-23). Moore also reveals that Hoare was very critical of a statement made by Linlithgow on 18 October 1939 in which the Viceroy invited the Indian leaders to associate themselves in a consultative capacity with the central government for the duration of the war, and to participate in a reconsideration of the federal scheme when the war was over. Apparently Hoare suggested the need for Linlithgow to be 'more elastic and less negative' on the question of constitutional discussions. (p. 23, n.). Substantial evidence seems to be accumulating to demonstrate Hoare's hypocrisy.

12. Amery to Linlithgow, 24 April 1942, Linlithgow Collection, No. 11.

13. Linlithgow to Amery, 18 May 1942, ibid.

14. Urmila Phadnis, *Towards the Integration of the Indian States*, London, 1968, pp. 137-138.

[15]   'Memorandum on States' Treaties and Paramountcy', presented by the Cabinet Mission to His Highness the Chancellor of the Chamber of Princes, 12 May 1946. Transfer of Power 1942-7, London, 1970-, Vol. VII, No. 262.

[16]   Menon, op. cit., p.63.

[17]   ibid., pp. 74-78.

[18]   H.V. Hodson, *The Great Divide : Britain - India - Pakistan*, London 1969, pp. 359-360.

[19]   ibid., p.360.

[20]   Sir Conrad Corfield, *The Princely India I knew : From Reading to Mountbatten*, Madras, 1975, p.157.

[21]   Hodson, op. cit., p.360. The difference of opinion between Corfield and Mountbatten has, since 1947, been the subject of some controversy. Corfield and Sir Edward Wakefield, one of his former assistants in the Political Department Secretariat in 1947, have maintained that Mountbatten was solely interested in presiding over an orderly transfer of power in British India and that he was thus insensitive to the plight of the princes. They argue that once the date for the transfer had been fixed, Mountbatten was persuaded by Nehru and Patel to accept a formula, deliberately designed to ensnare the princes, which not only violated the principles laid down by the Cabinet Mission but also exceeded his own instructions from Attlee. Put crudely, Corfield and Wakefield believe that Mountbatten allowed himself to be persuaded by the Congress leaders to do their dirty work for them in relation to the states. In the late 1960s, Wakefield was particularly anxious that Corfield should relate his version of what happened. With Hodson's *Great Divide* due for publication, Wakefield was concerned that it should not become the last word on the circumstances preceding the demise of the princes. He felt that Hodson, having had access to the Mountbatten papers, would inevitably be biased in favour of the last Viceroy. See Wakefield's correspondence with Corfield in a file entitled, 'Partition of India' in the Corfield Collection, IOL, Mss. Eur. D580. (The Corfield Collection has yet to be listed by the IOL: the file in question consists of letters and notes concerning Corfield's contribution to the seminar on partition which was held in London at the School of Oriental and African Studies in 1968). For the most recent account of the controversy, which concedes that Mountbatten did exceed his brief in relation to the princes but which nevertheless decides in his favour, see James Manor, 'The Demise of the Princely Order: A Reassessment', in Robin Jeffrey, (ed.), *People, Princes and Paramount Power*, op. cit., pp. 306-328.

[22]   Hodson, op. cit., pp. 356-380.

[23]   For details see ibid., pp. 475-498, 441-474 and 427-440; and Menon, op. cit., pp. 314-389, 390-415, and 124-150.

[24]   ibid., p.478.

[25]   Barbara N. Ramusack, *The Princes of India in the Twilight of Empire: Dissolution of a Patron-Client System, 1914-1939*, Columbus, 1978, pp. 243-246. Many of the ex-princes have also

entered domestic politics.   Recent research by William L.
Richter has revealed that of the 284 princely families which
were granted privy-purse allowances at the time of the merger
of their states, more than one-third have put forward candidates
for legislative assembly or Lok Sabha seats.   Many of the
individuals concerned have been elected more than once and
several have held party and ministerial office at both state and
national level. Richter's research covers a wide area of princely
political behaviour and participation.   One interesting point to
emerge is that very few of the princes have entered politics
voluntarily.   They have usually been persuaded to stand as
candidates by individual political parties. The Congress Party in
particular has drawn heavily upon the prestige of the princes in
order to capture votes.   Richter reaches the conclusion that
princely participation will continue to be a factor in Indian
politics as a new generation of *Rajvanshis* (members of princely
families), uninhibited by the aloofness and resentment of many
of their predecessors who witnessed the eclipse of the princes in
1947, comes of age. William L. Richter, 'Traditional Rulers in
Post-Traditional Societies: The Princes of India and Pakistan', in
Robin Jeffrey, (ed.), *People, Princes and Paramount Power*, op.
cit., pp. 329-354.

26   Maharawal of Dungarpur to Lothian, 24 January 1948, Lothian
Collection, No. 1.

27   Maharawal of Dungarpur to Lothian, 1 February 1950, ibid.

APPENDIX

Statement Showing the First Six, the First Eight,
the First Twenty-One, and the First Twenty-Eight
States in Order of Population

	Population in Thousands	Revenue in *Lakhs*	Area in Square Miles
STATES WITH A POPULATION OF TWO MILLION AND OVER			
1. Hyderabad	14,395	657	82,698
2. Mysore	6,557	360	29,528
3. Travancore	5,090	248	7,625
4. Kashmir	3,645	246	85,885
5. Gwalior	3,520	214	26,382
6. Jaipur	2,630	132	16,682
Percentage of total	*44.7*	*43*	*41.5*
7. Baroda	2,442	262	8,135
8. Jodhpur	2,126	136	35,066
	40,405	2,255	292,001
Percentage of total	*50*	*50*	*50*
STATES WITH A POPULATION OF ONE MILLION BUT LESS THAN TWO MILLIONS			
9. Patiala	1,625	126	5,932
10. Rewa	1,587	60	13,000
11. Udaipur	1,563	51	12,691
12. Indore	1,315	124	9,519
13. Cochin	1,204	86	1,417

	Population in Thousands	Revenue in *Lakhs*	Area in Square Miles
STATES WITH A POPULATION OF HALF A MILLION BUT LESS THAN A MILLION			
14. Bahawalpur	984	45	15,000
15. Kolhapur	965	140	3,217
16. Bikaner	934	45	23,315
17. Mayurbhanj	886	28	4,243
18. Alwar	749	55	3,213
19. Bhopal	732	62	6,902
20. Kotah	685	53	5,684
21. Cooch-Behar	590	41	1,307
	54,215	3,220	397,441
Percentage of total	67	71	67.5
22. Patna	566	7	2,399
23. Junagadh	544	82	3,336
24. Bastar	522	8	13,062
25. Cutch	513	31	7,616
26. Kalahandi	513	6	3,745
27. Bhavnagar	500	110	2,860
28. Surgiya	500	6	6,055
	57,873	3,470	436,514
Percentage of total	71	75.5	73
TOTAL FOR ALL STATES	80,838	4,579	598,138

SOURCE:

Appendix B of documents issued by the Nawab of Bhopal, Chancellor of the Chamber of Princes, concerning questions relating to the Indian States which emerged from the First Round Table Conference. PIC, 1931-50, Coll. 11, File 5, No. 912/1931. The division of the twenty-eight states into three classes was superimposed by officials within the Political Department of the India Office.

GLOSSARY

Amir: In the thirteenth and fourteenth centuries a rank of nobility. In the fifteenth century also a provincial governor.

Arya Samaj: Hindu reform movement founded in the Punjab in the late nineteenth century.

Begum: A princess, a Muslim lady of rank. In the context of the Indian States, a Muslim woman ruler or wife of a Muslim ruler.

Brahmin: A member of the Hindu priestly caste and, in the orthodox view, of the highest of the four major subdivisions of Hindu society.

Chauri Chaura: A village in the Gorakhpur district of what used to be the United Provinces. Scene in February 1922 of the mob murder of twenty-one policemen. As a result of this incident Gandhi suspended his first non-cooperation movement.

Crore: One hundred *lakhs* or ten millions.

Darbar (Durbar): The court or levée of a ruler. It is also used to signify the executive government of an Indian State and various ceremonial occasions such as the coronation of a ruler or the birth of an heir.

Desmukh: Under native government, an hereditary official with police and revenue authority in a district; under the British a revenue official.

Dewan (Diwan): The Chief Minister of an Indian State.

Firman (Farman): A government mandate; a formal order issued by the ruler of an Indian State.

Gadi (Gaddi): The throne.

Izzat: Dignity, honour, reputation.

Jagir: A tenure common under Mughal rule, in which the collection of the revenues of a given tract of land was made over to a servant of the state. The assignment was either conditional or unconditional. In the former event, some public service such as the levy and maintenance of troops was engaged for.

Jagirdar: The holder of a *Jagir.*

Khalsa: Land reserved for the state, as opposed to land assigned or granted to individuals.

Khilafat: A movement organized by Indian Muslims after the First World War in defence of the office of Khalifa (Caliph), acknowledged by Sunnis to be the religious and temporal head of Islam.

Lakh: One hundred thousand.

Maharaja: The Hindu ruler of an Indian State. Other names include Maharana, Maharao and Maharawal.

Mahasabha: Great assembly. The All-India Hindu Mahasabha was a communalist party founded in 1915.

Mansabdar: The holder of a civil and/or military appointment, graded according to a decimal ranking system, within the Mughal Imperial service.

Mulkis: Natives; people from the country or rural area. In

Hyderabad the *Mulkis* were descendants of families who had migrated from north India upon the foundation of the Osmania dynasty. Although predominantly Hindu, they were isolated from the majority of Hyderabad's Hindu population by virtue of their Persian culture and use of Urdu. They made their presence felt by demanding the removal of foreign influences from Hyderabad, whether in the shape of British paramountcy or rival Muslim administrators from outside the state.

Nawab: A viceroy or governor of a province under Mughal government, whence it became a mere title of any man of high rank upon whom it was conferred, without office being attached to it. Many of the Muslim rulers of the Indian States assumed the title of Nawab.

Nazar: An offering or gift made to a ruler to signify the loyalty of the donor.

Nizam: An administrator: the viceroy of the Deccan, a title retained by the ruler of Hyderabad.

Paigahs: The most important *jagirs* in Hyderabad, created by Asaf Jah, the founder of the Osmania dynasty.

Peshwa: Originally the chief minister of the Maratha power; in the eighteenth century becoming prince of an independent Maratha State. The Peshwa's power ceased with the surrender of Baji Rao II, the last to hold the title, to the British in 1817.

Phulkian States: The three principal states of the Punjab: Patiala, Jind and Nabha. The ruling families of these states were descended from Phul, a Sikh official of the local Mughal governor during the first half of the seventeenth century.

Pindaris: Originally bodies of irregular horse allowed to attach themselves to Mughal armies, employed especially in collecting forage, and permitted, in lieu of pay, to plunder. During the early years of the nineteenth century Pindaris were organized associations of mounted marauders in Central India, finally suppressed by the British in 1817.

Raj: A rule, sovereignty. The 'Raj' denotes British rule.

Raja: Hindu ruler of a small Indian State. Other names include Chief, Rana and Rao. These terms were also used as titles by the nobility in certain states and by big landlords in British India.

Rajpramukh: First among rulers. A Governor of a former princely state or union of such states in India between 1947 and 1956.

Rani: Wife of a Hindu ruler of a small Indian State.

Sanad: A title deed or Charter.

Subahdar: Viceroy, governor of a province.

Swaraj: Self-government, political independence.

Taluq: A division of a province, an estate.

Taluqdar: The holder of a *taluq.*

Thakur: A minor Rajput Chief.

BIBLIOGRAPHY

PRIMARY SOURCES

A. *Unpublished Sources*

1. *Private Papers*

   India Office Library, London

Brabourne Collection.	Mss. Eur. F97.
Butler (Sir Harcourt) Collection.	Mss. Eur. F116.
Chelmsford Collection.	Mss. Eur. E264.
Corfield Collection.	Mss. Eur. D580.
Curzon Collection.	Mss. Eur. F111.
Hailey Collection.	Mss. Eur. E220.
Halifax Collection.	Mss. Eur. C152.
Hamilton Collection.	Mss. Eur. C126/D510.
Keyes Collection.	Mss. Eur. F131.
Lee-Warner Collection.	Mss. Eur. F92.
Linlithgow Collection.	Mss. Eur. F125.
Lothian (Sir Arthur) Collection.	Mss. Eur. F144.
Lytton Collection.	Mss. Eur. E218.
Montagu Collection.	Mss. Eur. D523.
Morley Collection.	Mss. Eur. D573.
Reading Collection.	Mss. Eur. E238.
Sapru Collection.	consulted on microfilm, first and second series.
Tasker Collection.	Mss. Eur. D798.
Temple Collection.	Mss. Eur. F86.
Templewood Collection.	Mss. Eur. E240.
Thompson Collection.	Mss. Eur. F137.
Zetland Collection.	Mss. Eur. D609.

   National Library of Scotland, Edinburgh

Minto Collection.	Mss. 12588-12803.

2. *Official Papers, India Office Library, London*

   India Office Records, Political and Secret Department
   (I.O.L. Ref. L/P & S)

Political Correspondence with India, 1792-1874.	L/P & S/6.
Political and Secret Correspondence with India, 1875-1911.	L/P & S/7.

Political and Secret Subject Files, 1902-1931.	L/P & S/10.
Political (Internal) Files and Collections, 1931-1950.	L/P & S/13.
Political and Secret Memoranda.	L/P & S/18.
Political and Secret Department Library.	L/P & S/20.

India Office Records, Private Office Papers,
(I.O.L. Ref. L/PO)

Federation, Miscellaneous Papers, 1930-1936.	L/PO/58.
Allegations of pressure being placed upon the states to join the Federation, 1934-1935.	L/PO/88.
Congress and the States, 1938-1939.	L/PO/89.
Attitude of the States towards Federation, 1930-1936.	L/PO/92.
The Princes and Paramountcy, 1930-1935.	L/PO/93.
The Indian States Committee, 1927-1929.	L/PO/401.

Crown Representative Records, Files of the Foreign and Political
Department of the Government of India, (I.O.L. Ref. R/1)

Deposit Internal (Deposit I), October 1910 - July 1922.	R/1/3.
Establishment Branch.	R/1/4.
Internal (I), 1922-1934.	R/1/18.
Secret (I), April 1884 - May 1922.	R/1/19.
Internal A (I.A.), 1885-1946.	R/1/20.
Confidential A, Internal Branch, Section A (Conf. A. Int.A), 1894-1915.	R/1/21.
Confidential B, Internal Branch, Section A (Conf. B. Int.A), 1892-1918.	R/1/22.
Internal B (I.B.), 1907-1944.	R/1/23.
Confidential A, Internal Branch, Section B (Conf. A. Int.B), 1891-1908.	R/1/24.
Confidential B, Internal Branch, Section B (Conf. B. Int.B), 1891-1912.	R/1/25.
Confidential B, Internal Branch, Section C (Conf. B. Int. C), 1905-1921.	R/1/26.
Political (P), 1922-1947.	R/1/29.
Reforms (R), February 1920-1947.	R/1/30.
Special (S), 1930-1931.	R/1/32.

Indian States: Residency Records, 1800-1947, Records complementary to those in R/1, being the letter books and files maintained by the Residents and Agents in the Indian Princely States (I.O.L. Ref. R/2)

Rajputana Residency Files, Box 182, No. 81, 1898-1907.

N.B.
The India Office Library is at present processing these records, as yet only those of the Mysore Residency have been given an R/2 classification. The remaining records are in boxes. Details are available on request.

B. *Published Sources*

1. *Official Publications*

> *Parliamentary Papers*, 1831-32, Vol.XIV, No.735(VI), Affairs of the East India Company.
>> 1849, Vol.XXXIX, No.83, Correspondence between the Court of Directors of the East India Company and the Government of India respecting the Disposal of the Sattara State, in consequence of the Death of the late Raja.
>> 1856, Vol.XLV, No.341, Papers Relating to Oude.
>> 1866, Vol.LII, No.122, Mysore: Claim of the Maharaja to be restored to the Government of the Territories ceded under the Partition Treaty of 1799, and to be allowed to adopt an heir.
> Tupper, Sir Charles Lewis. *Indian Political Practice: A Collection of the Decisions of the Government of India in Political Cases, Vol.1*, Calcutta: Office of the Superintendent of Government Printing, 1895.
> *The Imperial Gazetteer of India, Vol.IV, The Indian Empire*, Oxford: Clarendon Press, 1907.
> *Proceedings of the Conference of Ruling Princes and Chiefs held at Delhi on the 30th October 1916, 5th November 1917, 20th January 1919 and 3rd November 1919.* Delhi: Government of India Press.
> *Report on Indian Constitutional Reforms, 1918*, Cmd. 9109, 1918 (July).
> *Report of the Indian Retrenchment Committee, 1922-1923*, London, His Majesty's Stationery Office, 1923.
> *Proceedings of the Meetings of the Chamber of Princes (Narendra Mahal), 1921-1947*, Delhi : Government of India Press.
> *Report of the Indian States Committee, 1928-1929*, Cmd. 3302, 1929 (March).
> *Report of the Indian Statutory Commission*, Cmd. 3568-9, 1930 (May).
> *Government of India Despatch on Proposals for Constitutional Reforms, 20 September 1930*, Cmd. 3700, 1930 (November).

Indian Round Table Conference, Sub-Committee Reports, Conference Resolution and Prime Minister's Statement, Cmd. 3772, 1931.

Indian Round Table Conference, 12 November 1930 - 19 January 1931, Proceedings, Cmd. 3778, 1931.

Indian Round Table Conference, 7 September - 1 December 1931, Proceedings, Cmd. 3997, 1932.

Report of the Indian States (Financial) Enquiry Committee, Cmd. 4103, 1932 (July).

Indian Round Table Conference, 17 November - 24 December 1932, Reports and Secretary of State's Closing Speech, Cmd. 4238, 1933.

Proposals for Indian Constitutional Reform (White Paper), Cmd. 4268, 1933 (March).

The Government of India Bill : Views of Indian States (White Paper), Cmd. 4843, 1935 (March).

2. *Collected Documents*

Aitchison, Charles, *Collections of Treaties, Engagements and Sanads Relating to India,* 11 Vols. Calcutta: Office of the Superintendent of Government Printing, 1862-1892.

Mansergh, Nicholas and Penderel Moon (eds.). *The Transfer of Power 1942-7,* London: HMSO, 1970 - (nine of the twelve volumes have been published to date).

Philips, C.H. (ed.). *The Evolution of India and Pakistan, 1858 to 1947: Select Documents,* London: Oxford University Press, 1962.

3. *Speeches and Letters*

Jagadisan, T.N. (ed.). *Letters of the Right Honourable V.S. Srinivasa Sastri,* London: Asia Publishing House, 1963.

Nehru, J. *A Bunch of Old Letters,* 2nd edition, Bombay: Asia Publishing House, 1960.

4. *Newspapers and Periodicals*

The Madras Mail.

The Indian Annual Register, 1919-1947, N.N. Mitra (ed.), Calcutta. (Quarterly Register from 1924 to 1929).

The Times, London.

The Times of India, Bombay.

SECONDARY SOURCES

A. *Journal Articles*

Copland, I.F.S. 'The Baroda Crisis of 1873-77: A Study of Governmental Rivalry.' *Modern Asian Studies* 2 (April 1968): 97-123.

'The Maharaja of Kolhapur and the Non-Brahmin Movement, 1902-1910.' *Modern Asian Studies* 7 (April 1973) : 209-225.

Elliott, Carolyn M. 'Decline of a Patrimonial Regime: The Telengana Rebellion in India, 1946-51.' *Journal of Asian Studies* 34 (November 1974) : 27-47.

Holdsworth, W.S. 'The Indian States and India.' *Law Quarterly Review* 46 (1930): 407-446.

Manor, James. 'Princely Mysore before the Storm: The State-level Political System of India's Model State, 1920-1936.' *Modern Asian Studies* 9 (February 1975): 31-58.

Potter, David C. 'Manpower Shortage and the End of Colonialism: The Case of the Indian Civil Service.' *Modern Asian Studies* 7 (February 1973): 47-73.

Qanungo Bhupen. 'A Study of British Relations with the Native States of India, 1858-62.' *Journal of Asian Studies* 26 (February 1967): 251-265.

Ramusack, Barbara N. 'Incident at Nabha: Interaction between Indian States and British Indian Politics.' *Journal of Asian Studies* 28 (May 1969): 563-577.

Richter, William L. and Barbara N. Ramusack. 'The Chamber and the Consultation: Changing Forms of Princely Political Association in India.' *Journal of Asian Studies* 34 (May 1975): 755-776.

Rudolph, Lloyd I. and Susanna Hoeber Rudolph. 'Rajputana under British Paramountcy: The Failure of Indirect Rule.' *Journal of Modern History* 38 (June 1966): 138-160.

Spodek, Howard. 'On the Origins of Gandhi's Political Methodology: The Heritage of Kathiawad and Gujarat.' *Journal of Asian Studies* 30 (February 1971): 361-372.

'Urban Politics in the Local Kingdoms of India: A View from the Princely Capitals of Saurashtra (Kathiawar) under British Rule.' *Modern Asian Studies* 12 (April 1973): 253-275.

B. General Works

Abhyankar, G.A. *Problem of Indian States.* Poona: Aryabhushana Press, 1928.

Abhyankar, G.R. *Native States and Post-War Reforms.* Poona: Anant Vinayak Patwardhan, 1917.

Argov, D. *Moderates and Extremists in the Indian Nationalist Movement, 1883-1920.* London: Asia Publishing House, 1967.

Athar Ali, M. *The Mughal Nobility under Aurangzeb.* London: Asia Publishing House, 1966.

Balfour, Elizabeth. *The History of Lord Lytton's Indian Administration, 1876 to 1880.* London: Longmans, Green, 1899.

Bazaz, Prem Nath. *The History of the Struggle for Freedom in Kashmir: From the Earliest Times to the Present Day.* New Delhi: Kashmir Publishing Company, 1954.

Bennett, G. (ed.). *The Concept of Empire from Burke to Attlee, 1774-1947.* London: Adam and Charles Black, 1953.

Butler, Harcourt. *India Insistent.* London: William Heinemann, 1931.

Butt, I.A. 'Lord Curzon and the Indian States, 1899-1905.' Unpublished Ph.D. Thesis: University of London, 1963.

Chamber of Princes. *The British Crown and the Indian States.* An Outline Scheme drawn up on behalf of the Standing Committee of the Chamber of Princes by the Directorate of the Chamber's Special Organization. London: P.S. King and Son, 1929.

Chirol, Valentine. *Indian Unrest.* London: Macmillan, 1910.

Chudgar, P.L. *Indian Princes under British Protection.* London: Williams and Norgate, 1929.

Coatman, J. *Years of Destiny: India, 1926-1932.* London: Jonathan Cape, 1932.

Coen, Terence C. *The Indian Political Service: A Study in Indirect Rule.* London: Chatto and Windus, 1971.

Corfield, Sir Conrad. *The Princely India I Knew: From Reading to Mountbatten.* Madras: Indo-British Historical Society, 1975.

Coupland, Reginald. *The Indian Problem, 1833-1935.* 5th impression. Oxford: Clarendon Press, 1968.

Cumming, Sir John (ed.). *Political India, 1832-1932: A Co-operative Survey of a Century.* London: Oxford University Press, 1932.

Das, M.N. *India Under Morley and Minto.* London: George Allen and Unwin, 1964.

Demontmorency, G.F. *The Indian States and Indian Federation.* Cambridge: Cambridge University Press, 1942.

Dilks, D. *Curzon in India.* 2 vols. London: Hart-Davis, 1969 and 1970.

Fitze, Kenneth S. *Twilight of the Maharajas.* London: Murray, 1956.

Forbes, Rosita. *India of the Princes.* London: The Book Club, 1939.

Forster, E.M. *Hill of Devi: Letters and Journal While Secretary to the Maharaja of Devi.* Harmondsworth: Penguin Books, 1965.

Fraser, Lovat G. *India Under Curzon and After.* London: William Heinemann, 1911.

Gandhi, M.K. *The Indian States' Problem.* Ahmedabad: Navajivan Press, 1941.

Gangulee, N. *The Making of Federal India.* London: J. Nisbet, 1936.

Gilbert, M. *Servant of India: A Study of Imperial Rule from 1905 to 1910 as Told through the Correspondence and Diaries of Sir James Dunlop Smith.* London: Longmans, Green, 1966.

Glendevon, J. *The Viceroy at Bay: Lord Linlithgow in India, 1936-43.* London: Collins, 1971.

Gopal, S. *British Policy in India, 1885-1905.* Cambridge: Cambridge University Press, 1965.

The Viceroyalty of Lord Irwin, 1926-1931. Oxford: Clarendon Press, 1957.

Gundappa, D.V. *The Problem of Native States.* Madras: Home Rule League, 1917.

Haksar, K.N. and K.M. Panikkar. *Federal India.* London: M. Hopkinson, 1930.

Halifax, Earl of. *Fulness of Days.* London: Collins, 1957.

Handa, R.L. *History of Freedom Struggle in Indian States.* New Delhi: Central News Agency, 1968.

Hardinge, Charles, Baron. *My Indian Years, 1910-1916.* London: John Murray, 1948.

Hardy, P. *The Muslims of British India.* Cambridge: Cambridge University Press, 1972.

Heber, Bishop. *The Narratives of a Journey Through the Upper Provinces of India from Calcutta to Bombay 1824-1825 and of a Journey to Madras and the Southern Provinces.* Edited by Anthony X. Soares under the title *India A Hundred Years Ago.* 2nd edition. Calcutta: Longmans, Green, 1944.

Hodson, H.V. *The Great Divide: Britain-India-Pakistan.* London: Hutchinson, 1969.

Hunter, W.W. *A Life of the Earl of Mayo.* 2 vols. London: Smith, Elder and Co., 1876.

Ismail, Mirza. *My Public Life: Recollections and Reflections.* London: George Allen and Unwin, 1954.

Jeffrey, Robin (ed.). *People, Princes and Paramount Power: Society and Politics in the Indian Princely States.* New Delhi: Oxford University Press, 1978.

Kodanda Rao, P. *The Right Honourable V.S. Srinvasa Sastri: A Political Biography.* Bombay: Asia Publishing House, 1963.

Koss, S.E. *John Morley at the India Office, 1905-1910.* New Haven and London: Yale University Press, 1969.

Krishna Rao, M.V. and G.S. Halappa. *History of Freedom Movement in Karnataka.* 2 vols. Government of Mysore Publication, 1962-1964.

Lawrence, W.R. *The India We Served.* London: Cassell, 1929.

Lee-Warner, William. *The Native States of India.* Revised 2nd edition. London: Macmillan, 1910.

Lord, J. *The Maharajas.* London: Hutchinson, 1972.

Lothian, Arthur C. *Kingdoms of Yesterday.* London: Murray, 1962.

Low, D.A. (ed.). *Soundings in Modern South Asian History.* Berkeley: University of California Press, 1968.

Low, S.J. *The Indian States and Ruling Princes.* London: E. Benn, 1929.

Maclagan, E. *"Clemency" Canning.* London: Macmillan, 1962.

MacMunn, G.F. *The Indian States and Princes.* London: Jarrold, 1936.

Malcolm, J. *Political History of India, 1784-1823.* London: John Murray, 1826.

Malleson, G.B. *An Historical Sketch of the Native States of India in Subsidiary Alliance with the British Government.* London: Longmans, 1875.

Manor, James. *Political Change in an Indian State: Mysore 1917-1955.* New Delhi: Manohar, 1977.

Martin, Briton, Jr. *New India, 1885: British Official Policy and the Emergence of the Indian National Congress.* Berkeley: University of California Press, 1969.

Mehrotra, S.R. *India and the Commonwealth, 1885-1929.* London: George Allen and Unwin, 1965.

Mehta, M.S. *Lord Hastings and the Indian States, 1813-1823.* Bombay: D.B. Taraporevala, 1930.

Menon, V.P. *The Story of the Integration of the Indian States.*
Calcutta: Orient Longmans, 1956.
Metcalf, T.R. *The Aftermath of Revolt: India 1857-1870.* Princeton:
Princeton University Press, 1964.
Middlemass, J.K. and A.J.L. Barnes. *Baldwin: A Biography.* London:
Weidenfeld and Nicholson, 1969.
Minto, Mary C. *India, Minto and Morley, 1905-1910.* London:
Macmillan, 1934.
Montagu, E.S. *An Indian Diary.* London: William Heinemann, 1930.
R.J. Moore. *Churchill, Cripps and India, 1939-1945.* Oxford:
Clarendon Press, 1979.
The Crisis of Indian Unity, 1917-1940. Oxford: Clarendon Press,
1974.
Nehru, Jawaharlal. *An Autobiography.* London: John Lane, 1936.
Nicholson, A.P. *Scraps of Paper: India's Broken Treaties, Her Princes
and the Problem.* London: E. Benn, 1930.
O'Malley, L.S.S. *The Indian Civil Service, 1601-1930.* London: John
Murray, 1931.
Palmer, J. *Sovereignty and Paramountcy in India.* London: Stevens,
1930.
Panikkar, K.M. *His Highness the Maharaja of Bikaner: A Biography.*
London: Oxford University Press, 1937.
Indian States and the Government of India. London: M. Hopkinson,
1930.
*The Indian Princes in Council: A Record of the Chancellorship of
His Highness the Maharaja of Patiala, 1926-1931 and 1933-1936.*
London: Oxford University Press, 1936.
Pattani, P.D. *The Indian States: A Letter on Their Relations with
British India.* London: Published by the author, 1930.
Phadnis, U. *Towards the Integration of the Indian States, 1919-1947.*
London: Asia Publishing House, 1968.
Philips, C.H. and M.D. Wainwright (eds.). *The Partition of India:
Policies and Perspectives, 1935-1947.* London: Allen and Unwin,
1970.
Prasad, S.N. *Paramountcy under Dalhousie.* Delhi: Ranjit Printers
and Publishers, 1964.
Ramusack, Barbara N. *The Princes of India in the Twilight of Empire:
Dissolution of a Patron-Client System, 1914-1939.* Columbus:
Ohio State University Press, 1978.
Reading, Gerald Rufus Isaacs, Second Marquess of. *Rufus Isaacs:
First Marquess of Reading. Vol.2. 1914-1935.* London:
Hutchinson, 1945.
Rice, S. *Life of Sayaji Rao III, Maharaja of Baroda.* 2 vols. London:
Oxford University Press, 1931.
Rizvi, Gowher. *Linlithgow and India: A Study of British Policy and
the Political Impasse in India, 1936-1943.* London: Royal
Historical Society, 1978.
Robb, P.G. *The Government of India and Reform: Policies towards
Politics and the Constitution 1916-1921.* Oxford: Oxford
University Press, 1976.

Robb, P.G. and D. Taylor (eds.). *Rule, Protest and Identity: Aspects of Modern South Asia*. London: Curzon Press, 1978.

Ronaldshay, Earl of (later Marquess of Zetland). *The Life of Lord Curzon, Vol.2, Viceroy of India*. London: E. Benn, 1929.

Rose, K. *Superior Person: A Portrait of Curzon and His Circle in Late Victorian England*. London: Weidenfeld and Nicolson, 1969.

Seal, A. *The Emergence of Indian Nationalism: Competition and Collaboration in the Late Nineteenth Century*. Cambridge: Cambridge University Press, 1968.

Simon, J.A. *Retrospect: The Memoirs of Viscount Simon*. London: Hutchinson, 1952.

Sinh, Raghubir. *Indian States and the New Regime*. Bombay: D.B. Taraporevala, 1938.

Smith, F.W.F. Second Earl of Birkenhead. *Halifax: The Life of Lord Halifax*. London: Hamish Hamilton, 1965.

Walter Monckton: The Life of Viscount Monckton of Brenchley. London: Weidenfeld and Nicolson, 1969.

Srivastava, A.L. *A Short History of Akbar the Great*. Agra: Shiva Lal Agarwala and Co., 1957.

Templewood, Viscount. *Nine Troubled Years*. London: Collins, 1954.

Thompson, E.J. *The Making of the Indian Princes*. London: Oxford University Press, 1943.

Tomlinson, B.R. *The Indian National Congress and the Raj, 1929-1942: The Penultimate Phase*. London: Macmillan, 1976.

Tupper, Sir Charles Lewis. *Our Indian Protectorate*. London: Longmans, Green, 1893.

Varadachariar, N.D. *Indian States in the Federation*. Bombay: Oxford University Press, 1936.

Wakefield, E. *Past Imperative: My Life in India, 1927-1947*. London: Chatto and Windus, 1966.

Waley, S.D. *Edwin Montagu: A Memoir and an Account of His Visits to India*. New York: Asia Publishing House, 1964.

Wasti, S.R. *Lord Minto and the Indian Nationalist Movement, 1905 to 1910*. Oxford: Clarendon Press, 1964.

Wedderburn, D. *Protected Princes in India*. London: British Committee of the Indian National Congress, 1914.

Wolpert, S. *Morley and India, 1906-1910*. Berkeley: University of California Press, 1967.

Tilak and Gokhale: Revolution and Reform in the Making of Modern India. Berkeley: University of California Press, 1962.

Woodruff, Philip. *The Men Who Ruled India*. 2 vols. London: Jonathan Cape, 1953.

Wrench, John E. *Geoffrey Dawson and Our Times*. London, Hutchinson, 1955.

Yazdani, Zubaida. *Hyderabad during the Residency of Henry Rusell, 1811-1820: A Case Study of the Subsidiary Alliance System*. Oxford: The University Press, 1976.

Zetland, Marquess of. *'Essayez': The Memoirs of Lawrence, Second Marquess of Zetland*. London: John Murray, 1956.

INDEX